AFTE
MIRACLE

THE CODY PARMER STORY

AFTER THE

MIRACLE

THE CODY PARMER STORY

BRENDA & KREG PARMER

Aspen Grove Books

BOISE · SALT LAKE CITY

After the Miracle: The Cody Parmer Story
By Brenda Parmer & Kreg Parmer

Copyright 2016, Aspen Grove Books.
ISBN 10: 1539388727
ISBN 13: 978-1539388722

All photos courtesy of Brenda & Kreg Parmer

Printed in the United States of America.

Paperback
First Edition, November 2016

This publication is also available as an e-book on Kindle and other devices.

For permission requests, author appearance requests, or volume purchase discounts pertaining to this book, contact the publisher at:
AfterTheMiracle@aspengrovebooks.com

Note about names changed in this book:
In order to protect the personal and professional privacy of doctors, medical professionals, and unrelated parties, some names have been changed. The following is a true story concerning real individuals, however the depictions of individuals and events herein represent the author's own memories and personal opinion, and do not represent any legal or professional judgment.

"Whosoever shall put their trust in God shall be supported in their trials, and their troubles, and shall be lifted up at the last day."

- The Book of Mormon, Alma 36:3

PROLOGUE

IT WAS A BEAUTIFUL EVENING, THE KIND OF WARM SUMMER NIGHT THAT Rick really wished he could just kick back and enjoy, but he couldn't. Not since his friend Shayne had died.

It was July 22nd, just over a month since Shayne's accident. Shayne and a few other friends were driving back to Idaho Falls when their truck left the road, overcorrected, and rolled. Three of them had lived, but not Shayne. Instead, there was a small wooden cross with fresh white paint on the grassy hillside where the truck had veered off the road.

Rick couldn't get it off his mind. It was just so unfair to die so young, just 20 years old. Rick decided he had to do something to make peace with what had happened, so he grabbed his friend Joe and set off right before sunset to go out and see the place where Shayne had died. Maybe just being there would give him a sense of peace. Maybe paying his respects could help him lift this feeling that life wasn't fair, that our lives could be over in the blink of an eye.

The accident had been just a mile or two east of Idaho Falls on Sunnyside Road. They passed the Ammon Cemetery where Shane had been buried, then continued on as the houses got further and further apart. They passed the last house on the right and began to slow down. It was just a few minutes after 9:00 p.m. and the sun had just set, leaving the edges of the road difficult to make out in the shadows of the rolling hills. As they rounded the last corner Rick began looking for the cross on the south side of the road, but he couldn't see it.

"What in the world…" Rick wondered out loud. A cloud of dust was strung out across the road, blocking their view and drifting right toward them. As it began to settle and clear, they could make out a battered gray pickup truck off the side of the road, upside down, with the wheels still spinning slowly in the air, in nearly the exact spot where Shayne's truck had rolled. He was stunned for a moment, but quickly realized there was no one else around to help. He had to do something.

Rick pulled over into the loose gravel and put the car in park. The two young men jumped out of the car and rushed through the tall grass toward the truck. How could anyone survive a wreck like that? The whole cab was twisted and deformed with little headroom left. As they got closer and peered through the broken windows and torn metal, the last rays of sunlight revealed two empty seats. Where was the driver? Rick's eyes traced the path that the truck must have taken.

Marks in the gravel off the right side of the road and skid marks on the asphalt told the whole story. The right tires had gone off the pavement into the gravel as the road ended a long straightaway and began to curve to the left. The driver hit the gravel, over-corrected, and sent the truck across both lanes where it ran off the embankment on the left side and began flipping. One, two, three, four marks in the dirt where the truck had flipped again and again. It was a terrible scene of broken glass and plastic, and the air smelled of coolant and gasoline. If the driver wasn't in the vehicle, he had to be somewhere along that path.

Rick jumped up and started tracing the path backward. He was only a few steps from the truck when he saw the outline of a person lying in the tall brown grass. "Over here!" he yelled to Joe, and they both rushed to the spot, crushing pieces of broken glass in the weeds as they ran.

There, lying only a few yards from the overturned truck, was the outline of a teenage boy. As Rick got closer, his stomach sank. The boy was lying chest down in the grass, his body tossed like a rag doll. His shorts had been torn and his white shirt was covered with a muddy mix of dust and blood. His left arm was lying limp at his side but the other was a mangled mess, broken and twisted around more than once. The skin from the shoulder to the elbow looked like a washrag being wrung out. The broken arm was perched awkwardly in the air, and the hand looked like it was covering his mouth. He stepped closer. No, the hand was *in* his mouth, shoved into a fist inside his gaping jaws. Rick's stomach turned as he realized the boy's head was twisted almost 180 degrees, facing up to the sky, while the body lay chest down in the dirt.

Rick stepped back, he didn't notice any movement, surely the boy was dead. How could anyone survive something like that? His knees got weak and he shuddered at the thought of being the first to find a dead body. Then he heard gurgling, low and wet, coming from the boy's chest and mouth.

"He's choking!" Joe called out, "What do we do?"

Rick thought for a second and tried to evaluate the situation with a clear head. He had to get the boy breathing, he wouldn't make it very long with the fist shoved in his mouth. Rick bent down and reached for the boy's hand. He had to be gentle, moving the arm too sharply could damage it even further. He grabbed the wrist and placed one hand on the boy's head to stabilize it. He could feel broken bones in the boy's skull shifting as he pressed on it, but he knew he had to clear the airway. With a firm but slow movement he removed the fist from the mouth and set it at the boy's side. The injured victim labored to suck in air, but he was breathing, somehow.

"Jeff!" the boy groaned through his twisted windpipes. The bubbling of fluids in his throat and lungs made a terrible sound.

"It's going to be alright, we're going to get help!" Rick said.

"Where's Jeff?" the boy groaned again.

"Was he in the truck with you? Is there someone else?"

Again the boy moaned Jeff's name.

Rick looked up at Joe and without saying anything, Joe knew what to do. He immediately began running further down the path created by the rolling truck, checking for anyone else. In a moment he called out, "There's another one, over here!" With the first boy breathing, for now, Rick ran to look at the second victim. It was another teenage boy, about the same age as the first, but he had been tossed from the vehicle closer to the road as it had first begun to roll.

"He's alive, I can see his chest moving up and down, but he's hurt bad," Joe said. They inspected the boy without touching him, looking for anything that might pose an immediate threat. He was beaten up and only partially conscious, but who knew how long he could survive there. Rick knew the only thing to do was to get these kids to the hospital, but he couldn't just throw them in the back seat of his car, it was too dangerous to move them. Both boys would probably die if they didn't get help to the scene immediately.

"Come on man, we've got to go call 911, there's nothing else we can do," Rick decided, and ran back to the first victim, kneeling down beside him. "We found your friend Jeff, he's alright, we're going to get help but we'll be right back, I promise! Just hold on! We'll be right back!"

The two young men jumped in their car and raced a mile or so back to the first house they could find. They ran to the door and began pounding on it and ringing the doorbell. A middle-aged man opened the door cautiously.

"Can I help you?" he asked.

"There's an accident down the road just a mile! There are two boys, they're hurt bad, really, really bad! You need to call 911!"

"Where is it, at the bottom of the hill where the crash was a few weeks ago?"

"Yes, yes, exactly the same spot!" Rick answered. He was surprised the man knew about Shayne's accident, but he was right on.

"How many people?"

"Two, I think. Two teenage boys. You need to get people out there now. The guy's neck is…it's twisted…it's really bad. We've got to go back, just call 911!"

"Alright, go, I'll call them right now!"

Rick and his friend sped back down to the crash. Rick knelt by the first boy and kept talking to him, but the boy drifted in and out of consciousness and kept calling Jeff's name.

"Jeff is fine, my friend is with him, he'll be okay. Just, relax and stay with me." Rick knew he was lying about Jeff being okay, and it was stupid to tell him to relax, but what else could you say? He decided to just keep talking and make sure the kid didn't pass out.

"Okay buddy, my name is Rick. What's your name?"

The boy just moaned in response.

"Hey, stay with me man, you've got to stay awake. What's your name?"

"Cody," the boy slowly responded. Rick could tell things were getting bad. His breathing was slowing and sounding worse with every breath.

"How old are you, Cody?"

The boy moaned as he struggled to think of his age, "Six... sixteen," he finally answered. His speech was getting weaker, but Rick could begin to hear the wail of sirens in the distance.

"Alright Cody, just hang on, help is almost here."

Just a few seconds later a police car appeared from around the bend. Rick stood up to signal them, waving his hands so the police could see them in the fading twilight. Ambulances shortly followed, and the sound of a helicopter grew louder. Rick backed up and let the police and EMTs do their work.

Police, firemen, and EMTs swarmed around the scene of the accident, calling back and forth on the radio. An ambulance rushed off and took Jeff back into town while police cleared the response vehicles to make room for a life flight helicopter to land on the road. The helicopter didn't even touch down before Cody was loaded in and whisked away. Just minutes from the police's first arrival, both boys were gone. As the firetrucks and ambulances began to clear, Rick could make out a news truck and a local reporter standing in front of a camera, pointing to the overturned pickup and describing the scene.

Rick couldn't believe it; it was all so surreal. He had just come to spend some time to remember his friend, he hadn't asked to be a part of all this. Maybe he and Joe had just saved two boys' lives. Maybe he had just witnessed their final moments. He looked up the hillside from the wrecked truck and made out the little white cross, illuminated by flashing red and blue lights. Rick and Joe walked up the hill and sat in the grass without saying a word.

Rick stared at the little white cross and some dying flowers sitting at the base in the weeds. Poor Shayne, and now this kid Cody and his friend Jeff, just a month later, wrecking their trucks the same way, in the same place. What a tragedy, how unfair life was to take people so young. Rick closed his eyes and bowed his head. He hoped he wasn't right, but he couldn't help but think that in a few more days this hillside would probably hold two more little white crosses.

ONE

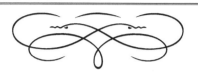

Thursday, July 22nd, 1999

IT REALLY WAS A SHAME TO BEGIN A TERRIBLE TRAGEDY ON SUCH A BEAU-
tiful summer day. Tragedies are supposed to start on a dark moonless
night, or in the middle of a cold winter storm. They're not supposed to
happen in Idaho either, they're supposed to happen in an alleyway in New
York City, or a deserted highway in Death Valley. At least, that's what I
always thought; tragedies don't happen to families like mine, in safe places like Idaho, and they definitely don't start on beautiful summer days.
But ours did.

I started the day by dusting, then vacuuming, in that order of course.
Otherwise the dusting would just move the dust onto the clean carpet,
and I didn't like the idea of that. Usually dusting and vacuuming were
Cody's chores, but by the summer of 1999, Cody had just turned 16 and
he got a *real* job. I'm sure part of Cody's desire to get a job was so that
he could get out of doing housework. "Mom, why do I have to do this?
Cleaning is girl's work!" he would yell, over the sound of the vacuum.

It was a little ironic then, that Cody's first job was working for a
construction crew cleaning up work sites. I guess cleaning up 2x4 ends
and sawdust was better than vacuuming, or at least more manly. As the
summer progressed, his boss, my sister-in-law's father, taught him how
to frame walls and how to cut and install molding. As his boss gained
more trust in him, Cody helped pour foundations and install roof truss-
es. Cody loved every bit of it. He worked from about 7:00 a.m. to 4:00
p.m. and would come home exhausted, but he was always so excited

about whatever project they were working on.

Cody enjoyed his work so much that he decided he wanted to work in construction when he graduated high school. Of course, that was just one of his plans. He also wanted to be a pilot, race motocross, and play football, basketball, and baseball professionally. I just decided to go with the flow. He was just going to be entering his junior year in the fall, and there was plenty of time to talk about careers later on.

As I dusted and vacuumed and wiped down counters and washed cereal bowls, I kept an eye on the girls in the backyard playing on the slip-n-slide. What a blessing they were. We had Kira in 1986, almost three years after Cody, then Brooke came 14 months later. That was not exactly planned, but we were glad to have her! Our youngest daughter, Krissa, was born five years after Brooke. One tough boy, three beautiful girls, and two happy parents; it was about as much as I had ever wanted.

We weren't wealthy by any means, but we were comfortable. We lived in a modest split-level tract home on the west side of Idaho Falls with what seemed like a million neighbors. Our kids loved having so many friends close by to play with, but I would have liked a little more space. The one consolation was that we had no backyard neighbors, just a large open lot with grazing horses.

Having the open lot behind us was nice, until Cody figured he could save a few minutes while mowing the lawn by throwing the grass clip-

Cody's student ID card, sophomore year, 1998-1999

pings over the fence. Pretty soon the horses ate the clippings, got sick, and the owner came to complain. Cody felt pretty bad about that and took a batch of cookies to the owner to apologize. After that, he started bagging the lawn clippings, like he was supposed to from the start.

My husband Kreg left for work pretty early that morning. Summer was kind of a busy time for him since he worked at a tractor and farm equipment dealership. If the farmers were working, so was he. It made for long work days in the summer, but the light work in the winter made up for it. Kreg had started out there sweeping floors, quite literally. In no time the boss saw that he was a hard worker, smart, and honest. Kreg was promoted to work in the parts department, then he became the parts department manager. Kreg liked his job, and he was good at it.

After just a few years at Pioneer Equipment, the owner, Stan Baldwin, took Kreg under his wing and offered to make him the corporate parts manager. He flew us out to Fresno, California, to tour the corporate offices and look at houses, but the city terrified me. We pulled up next to the run-down elementary school and stared at the huge campus surrounded by a 12-foot chain-link fence topped with barbed wire. "You want me to send my sweet little girls to that school?" I asked Kreg with raised eyebrows. He declined the position.

It was okay though, we both really liked Idaho Falls, it was where both of us had grown up and we had quite a bit of family in the area. I was the second oldest in a family of five—two sisters and two brothers— and we loved spending time together, especially when we had a chance to enjoy the great outdoors. Kreg came from a family of two boys and one girl and they had grown up spending nearly every weekend in the beautiful forests and mountains of Eastern Idaho. Camping, hiking, fishing, hunting, their family loved it all.

Church wasn't a major focus for Kreg as a young man, but as Kreg entered his teenage years he finally decided he wanted to serve a mission. He figured if he was going to serve he needed to change his priorities, so he started going to church more often and got some new friends, and that's when we met, in the ninth grade.

I remember being drawn to Kreg's adventurous spirit and love for life. When I was with Kreg, it seemed like there was a whole new world of exciting possibilities out there. Kreg pushed me to see further and dream bigger, and I fell in love, but I tried not to show it.

Kreg and I remained good friends throughout high school but my heart started aching every time I saw him ask another girl out. Finally, on the last day of high school, he asked me to go to the graduation party with him. We sat and listened to The Beach Boys on his cassette player for most of the night and talked about our plans and our dreams. From that night forward we've been inseparable.

We dated for the next year while I went to cosmetology school and Kreg worked to save up money for his mission. Kreg and I talked a lot about marriage and our life together, and one day Kreg asked how I would feel if he didn't go on a mission and we got married instead. There wasn't really an expectation from either of our families that serving a mission was mandatory, so I didn't see a problem with it. I told him that I would support him either way. Kreg thought about it for a long time. We finally decided to go ahead and get married.

We got engaged in July of 1981, about a year after graduation. I'm not sure what my parents were thinking when Kreg came to ask my dad's permission. He was 19 years old, driving a '64 Chevy, making $600 a month at a steam cleaning business with no plans of college. I'm sure my dad was skeptical, but he didn't say anything about career plans or money. My dad, a man of few words, just told him, "Brenda is awful tender-hearted." Kreg replied, "I can handle that." And that was that.

My mother's only fear was that I would drop out of cosmetology school, so I promised to wait to get married until I graduated. Learning how to cut hair has given me a skill I've used for many years to supplement our income. It hasn't ever paid the light bill, but it paid for ballet lessons and baseball mitts for the kids, things like that. I had a few little old ladies that I went and visited in their homes, but most of my clients came to my house. The kids learned early on to take care of themselves and play quietly while I was cutting hair, and I rarely had to get after them about it.

Being a mom is tough, but that was always my goal ever since I was a little girl. Cutting hair was just a little side job for some spending money, but being a mom is where my heart is. I told my grandma when I was young that I wanted 12 kids and I hoped Heavenly Father would save that many spirits for me. We ended up having four, and every one was such a blessing.

I have really good kids, which made my job a lot easier. Each one is unique, and I love each of them in different ways. Krissa, my youngest, was always at my side and we grew very close. Brooke was full of love for everyone and was always surrounded by friends. Kira was smart and determined and helped take care of her younger sisters for many years. And Cody, he was just so fun and kind and active, you couldn't help but love him.

Cody, in a lot of ways, was just like me: very faithful with a clear-cut outlook on the gospel. Right was right and wrong was wrong. Sure, there were times he messed up and pushed the limits, but I knew that if the school was calling because Cody was in trouble, it was because he was sticking up for someone who was getting picked on. Cody had a soft spot for the underdog and made a lot of friends by treating people right and just being a nice guy.

Cody was always active in church, there was never question about his commitment or his testimony. He served in the deacons and teachers quorum presidencies and was kind and respectful, but he was still just a wild teenage boy at heart. If there was a chance to have some good clean fun, he took it.

When he turned 15 and got his driver's license his uncle gave him a beat-up old Chevy S10 Cody named "Old Blue." Just a few weeks later he took Old Blue out into a muddy field near our house and got it stuck. Fearing the wrath of his father, he called his scoutmaster to come pull him out. When his scoutmaster's truck also got stuck, Cody went to a neighbor's house and called Kreg, telling him he needed to come help the scoutmaster, not mentioning a word about his own truck. Kreg arrived and quickly figured out what had really happened, and discovered old ruts and tire tracks all over that field. That's when Kreg learned just how many times Cody had gotten stuck in the mud without us knowing.

Cody inherited a lot of Kreg's fun-loving and adventurous attitude. He loved his truck and he loved the outdoors and he thought he was completely invincible, just like his dad. Cody earned his Eagle Scout award when he was just 13, an accomplishment he was quite proud of. Once when he got pulled over for speeding right after getting his license, the police officer told him to give him one good reason why he shouldn't throw his sorry backside in jail. Cody responded, "Uh, because I'm an Eagle Scout?" and promptly produced his Eagle Scout card from his wallet. The police officer looked at the card, looked at Cody, then shook his head and let him off with a warning. Cody's unassuming and good-natured spirit just had that kind of an effect on people.

It seemed like Cody was always on the run, but somehow he managed to juggle all his responsibilities pretty well. Between baseball in the spring and football in the fall, scouts on Tuesday nights, church on Sunday, construction work during the summer, house chores and lawn mowing, flirting with the girls and watching sports with the guys, dirt bike riding, fishing, homework (when he remembered to do it), and getting the truck stuck, we had a very busy life.

Calm summer mornings were somewhat of a rarity, so I was enjoying every minute of it while it lasted. I knew that once Cody came home from work he would rush into the house like a tornado and devise some grand plan for an adventure. Just after 4:00 p.m., right on schedule, Cody's truck pulled into the driveway. "Well," I thought to myself as the front door flew open, "here we go."

Two

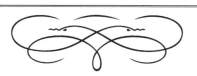

"MOM!" CODY YELLED BEFORE THE DOOR WAS EVEN CLOSED.
"Hey Cody, how was work?" I asked as he stormed into the kitchen like a hungry bear, looking for something to eat. He was a skinny kid, but he sure seemed to eat us out of house and home.

"It was good. Hey, some people are going to the Braves game tonight, can I go?" The Braves were Idaho Falls' minor league baseball team at the time. I assumed he was wanting to go with Jeff, Tyler, or Ben—three of his best friends. What he didn't tell me was that "some people" also included a certain girl from school that Cody liked.

"Well, I guess so, do you have enough cash?" I asked.

"Yeah, I've got enough," he mumbled through the snacks he had scavenged from the cupboard.

"Alright. Dad said you need to mow the lawn today. What time is the game?"

"It's not until later, I can mow the lawn before I go." Cody was a master at speed-mowing. It was usually a 30-minute job, but if Cody had somewhere he wanted to be, he would push that mower like his life depended on it and be done in under ten minutes. That's probably why he started dumping the clippings over the fence. Bagging the clippings would add at least another minute, precious time for a 16-year-old with somewhere to be.

I heard Cody step into the other room and start making phone calls to friends, arranging the night's activities. After just one or two calls, he came back with a new plan.

"Hey Mom, Jeff wants to go fishing," he asked a little more timidly. I knew he wasn't telling me something by the way he talked.

"I thought you wanted to go to the baseball game?"

"Yeah, I did, but Jeff doesn't want to go. He wants to go fishing," Cody said a little hesitantly.

"Oh, where did he want to go?" I kept waiting for the big reveal.

"Oh, you know, just, out to Willow Creek."

"Willow Creek! It's already 4:30! I don't think you'll have enough time if you're going to mow the lawn too." Willow Creek was about a 45-minute drive to the southeast, across town on Sunnyside Road and then all the way out to an old ranching community called Bone. Kreg and I had been learning how to fly fish and had taken Cody out to Willow Creek once or twice.

"I can do it, but Jeff wants to leave right now, so I'll just mow the lawn when I get back," Cody bartered.

"You're not going to get back until dark if you're going all the way out to Willow Creek!"

"We'll be back before that, I promise. I'll mow the lawn tonight." Jeff and Cody had just gotten their own fly rods but hadn't had much of a chance to use them. I wasn't really opposed to them going fishing, but they wouldn't have much time to catch anything.

"Why don't you just both go to the baseball game?" I tried to steer his thoughts toward something more practical.

"Jeff said he doesn't want to go to the game, he's just going to go fishing with or without me. I don't want him to go all the way out there by himself. Come on Mom, I promise I'll mow the lawn tonight right when I get home." Cody was a good kid and always kept his promises. He may have been a little spontaneous, but he never let his mother down.

"Well, call your dad. He's the one who wanted you to mow the lawn so I guess it's up to him." I doubted whether Cody could really do both. Maybe Kreg would let him mow the grass the next day, but it was already pretty long.

Cody thanked me and ran into the next room and dialed Kreg's work number. After a minute or two of explanation and haggling, he got Kreg's approval, contingent upon his mowing the lawn when he got home. Cody rushed down to his room to grab some extra clothes. Cody always wore a plain white t-shirt, but he grabbed another one and a pair of shorts for changing into after wading through the river.

"Thanks Mom, see you later!" He yelled as he zipped out of the house. I watched out the front window for a moment as he jumped into his truck and headed over to Jeff's house. That image of Cody is etched into my memory. I remember exactly what he was wearing, how he looked, how he moved. That was the last time I saw Cody healthy, happy, and full of life.

In a lot of our Sunday School lessons, we hear about someone who has a premonition that something bad is going to happen and is warned by the Spirit. I've heard all the stories where a parent is warned that their child is going to fall off a horse or get caught in a well, and they arrive just in time to save their child. I understand that this is usually the exception rather than the rule, and I wish that had happened to me, but it didn't. It was just another normal day, Cody was just on another everyday adventure, and that evening we'd tuck everyone in, turn off the lights, and go to bed, just like normal. My sense that something was wrong came too late.

Kreg got home around 6:00 that evening, which was really quite early for a summer day. We usually tried to have everyone home for dinner, but summers were a little crazy so I just made dinner at the same time every day and whoever was home got a hot meal and the rest was left in the fridge. Having Kreg home in time for dinner that afternoon was a nice little surprise.

Almost immediately after blessing the food the girls starting telling their dad all about their day. Kira was taking ballet lessons and Brooke was in gymnastics, and both were working hard on their routines. Kira and Brooke almost talked over each other, trying to explain their lessons and exercises and what their friends said and who was being nice or mean to them. Kira was our talker and Brooke was our social butterfly, and when they both got going you had better watch out. Poor little Krissa just sat and watched for the most part, she had just turned seven and lived in awe of her older sisters. Kreg gave each girl his attention and made sure they knew he cared about what was going on in their lives.

After dinner Kreg stared out the window at the long grass and asked about Cody. I explained the whole story about the phone calls and the baseball game and Cody's change of plans, but Kreg didn't seem surprised. Jeff was one of Cody's best friends, and if he was going to do something fun or exciting, Cody just had to be there.

We went about our evening like normal, although a little more calm without Cody in the house, then we said family prayers and put the girls to bed at the normal time. It was the height of the summer and the sun didn't set until about 9:00 p.m., so it was still light outside when the girls were all down and it was just Kreg and me.

That's when it finally kicked in. I'm not sure if it was a mother's intuition, or my normal paranoia about my children's safety, or if it was really the Spirit, but I began to get an uneasy feeling about Cody. I went down to the front room and sat in one of our two green wing-backed chairs and watched out the front window. The skies out to the west were starting to turn orange and pink with the setting sun. Cody might think it was a good idea to mow the lawn at dusk, but I worried about upsetting the neighbors with such noise at that time of the evening. Cody was going to be pushing it.

"Kreg, do you think Cody is okay?" I yelled out to him. He came and sat in the matching chair by my side.

"Yeah, I'm sure he's fine. They were probably just having too much fun fishing and let time get away from them. Cody knows what he's doing, he'll be okay," Kreg responded. I wasn't so sure. Cody was just 16 after all. At least Jeff was with him, that helped me feel a little better.

"I don't know though, Cody promised me he would be home to mow the lawn."

"Well, we'll have to talk about that when he gets home."

"But what if they've got a flat tire or something, or if one of them fell and got hurt?" I asked as the endless list of scenarios started to play through my mind.

"They're smart boys, they can handle it. If something went wrong, Cody knows to call us." But that was in the day before any of the kids had cell phones, and calling us meant they had to get to a phone booth. What if they couldn't get to a phone booth because they were stuck? What if they tried to get to a phone and hitchhiked and someone kidnapped them? My mind wandered as the night grew darker and the call didn't come.

We sat in those chairs and stared out the window for what seemed like forever. The minutes passed so slowly. I wanted to send Kreg out to look for them on the backroads, but I kept expecting Cody to pull into the driveway any second. The best thing, we reasoned, was to just wait and see if they would show up. But the longer we waited, the worse I felt.

The sunset faded into twilight, and then the sky went pitch black. Just before 10:00 p.m. I finally pleaded with Kreg to go look for the boys. Kreg was starting to get worried too, but he was trying not to show it for my sake, and he went and got his shoes. Just then, headlights turned into the driveway.

"Oh thank heaven!" I exclaimed. I opened the door to go meet Cody in the driveway and find out what had taken them so long, but it wasn't Cody, it was Kreg's sister Denise.

"Hey Brenda, sorry to stop by so late, I just came to drop this off." She held something up, but I couldn't see what it was in the dark.

"Oh Denise, I thought you were Cody." I let out an audible sigh and my fear enveloped me once more.

"Where is he? Is everything alright?"

"We don't know, he went fishing this afternoon and he was supposed to be back hours ago." I relayed the whole story to her as we went back inside.

"Hey, Denise, would you mind watching the girls while we drive out that way and check for Cody?" Kreg asked.

"Oh sure, I think I've got your cell phone number, I'll call you if he shows up."

I was so relieved to finally be doing something, anything. I grabbed my shoes and we hopped in the truck and began heading across town, following the route Cody and Jeff would have taken.

Then Kreg's cell phone rang and I breathed a sigh of relief. We must have just barely missed Cody and Denise was calling to let us know he was alright. Reality couldn't have been further from the truth.

Kreg answered, "Hello?"

"Hi, Kreg? This is Jeff's sister, Angie."

"Hi, thanks for calling, have you heard from the boys?" Kreg asked as I got close to the phone and listened in.

"No, but we were watching the news…" her voice started to shake. "There was an accident out on Sunnyside, and they showed a picture of Jeff's truck."

THREE

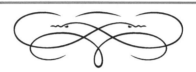

"ARE YOU SURE?" KREG ASKED CALMLY.
"Yeah, it was Jeff's truck, I'm positive. The news said it was off Sunnyside Road just outside of town in the hills. We called the hospital and they said they brought two boys in, but they wouldn't say who." Jeff's sister was on the verge of tears, even across the phone Kreg could tell she was barely holding it together.

"Alright, we're just a few miles from the hospital. Do your parents know?"

"Yeah, they're leaving right now, they said to call you."

"Okay, we'll be there in a minute. It will be alright."

"Kreg…" Angie's voice broke, unable to contain her emotion.

"Yeah?"

"The news said they life-flighted one of them by helicopter. I don't know which one."

"Thank you, we'll hurry." Kreg hung up the phone and stepped on the gas.

I hadn't heard the whole conversation, but I heard enough to know that something terrible had happened. I sat completely still and stared at the road ahead, unable to process the information. Who was hurt? How bad was it? Who got life-flighted? Images of smashed vehicles and ambulances and paramedics rushed through my mind. I felt frozen in place, unable to make sense of the situation.

Kreg remained calm, then put his hand on my leg and looked me in the eyes, "Honey, they think the boys are at the hospital. Jeff's parents will meet us there." Kreg was trying to be strong and control the situation, which made me even more terrified. This was exactly how he acted when Kira broke her leg at my family's cabin in Island Park. She was just three years old, and her leg snapped between the rungs of a ladder. It took almost an hour for us to get to the hospital in Rexburg, and the whole way there Kreg was calm and resolute, and I was panicking.

"Honey, this is bad." I finally spoke as we raced toward the hospital.

"We don't know that yet," Kreg tried to comfort me, but I could tell he was just trying to keep me calm.

"They don't life-flight people if they're alright," I said, my mind racing through the possibilities. I hoped I was missing something, some piece of information that assured us that Cody was okay. Maybe Kreg heard something I missed in the phone call and I was misunderstanding the situation and we were just going to pick him up, but Kreg stared straight ahead, watching the headlights as he sped through intersections. He didn't have anything else. He knew as much as I knew, and what I knew wasn't good.

I buried my head in my hands and tried to control my breathing, but I began to lose it. I put my hands up to my face and tried to mentally digest what was going on.

"Brenda, just wait, we don't know what happened. We don't know who was life-flighted, we don't even know for sure if it was Cody in the crash. Let's just wait and see." Kreg's quick turns and speed told me he feared the worst. I hoped Cody wasn't hurt. I hoped he wasn't life-flighted, but then that would mean that Jeff was life-flighted, and I tried not to wish that either. I just wished I would wake up and none of this was real and it was all a bad dream.

We pulled up to the hospital and I stared at all the lights from the windows on the tall brown building. Was my little boy in there somewhere, scared, waiting for me? We followed the signs for the emergency entrance and parked in ambulance parking right in front of the doors.

Okay, just follow Kreg, I thought to myself. I took Kreg's hand and we hurried inside.

The automatic doors opened in front of us and we tried our best to calmly walk up to the nurse's desk. It was all I could do to not just bury my head in Kreg's shirt and hide from everything that was about to happen.

Kreg began speaking before the nurse at the counter even raised her head, "Hello, you have two boys here who crashed out on Sunnyside, I think one of them is my son, Cody Parmer?"

"Your name please?"

"Kreg Parmer. Cody Parmer is my son, is he here?"

She began typing away at a computer, searching for the name.

"They were the ones in the accident out on Sunnyside, they would have come in just a little while ago." Kreg was becoming impatient.

The nurse looked back at another woman and they stared at each other for a second. They knew something they weren't telling us. "I'm sorry, I don't have a Cody Parmer in our system. Two boys were brought in but they haven't been identified yet. I can't let you see them until we've identified them. If you'll just have a seat..."

"Can I see them so I can identify them?" His request was a mix of frustration and pleading.

"I'm sorry, I'll have to talk to the doctors, once they are able to confirm their names..." She continued on in a long explanation about privacy and minors and how their hands were tied. As she spoke we began to hear cries and moans coming from a room right around the corner. Kreg recognized the voice the same time I did, and we looked at each other.

"That's Jeff!" I said, and Kreg started for the door. He let go of my hand and squeezed between the doctors and nurses who were rushing in and out of the room. The nurse at the counter stood up and began to protest, trying to cut him off, but he got to the door too quickly. I didn't follow him, I didn't want to see whatever was behind that door.

Kreg rushed into the room. There in the bed, hooked up to a million wires and tubes, lay Cody's friend Jeff Smith. He was conscious, but he didn't look coherent. It sounded like he was trying to talk, but the tubes down his throat prevented any of the words from making sense. The nurses were restraining him while anesthetic and sedative were administered. Kreg tried to talk to Jeff and tell him that his parents were on their way and that he was going to be alright. I listened from the hallway and knew that if Kreg was talking to Jeff, Cody must not be in there. Was that a bad sign? I didn't know. Where else would Cody be?

Kreg stepped back out of the room as the nurse tried to lead us toward the waiting area. "This is Jeff Smith, he was with our son Cody, they were in the same truck." Kreg was getting upset now, and the nurse started backing off a little. Then his voice changed and he spoke clearly and sternly. "Where is my son."

She relented. Her reply was calm and slow. "If you're sure that this is your son's friend, then your son is upstairs getting a CT scan. You can't see him yet. As soon as he is available, I'll come get you. I need you to take a seat and fill out some papers." Paperwork? Who cares about paperwork? I wanted to scream at her, but held my tongue.

"Why is he getting a CT scan? Is he okay?" I pleaded.

"I don't know, they haven't told me, but he was in critical condition when the helicopter brought him in. The best thing for you to do right now is sit down and let the doctors do their job. They're doing everything they can do, I promise." Now that she knew who we were, her demeanor completely changed and her tone was compassionate and reserved. That was almost worse. I could tell that she knew how bad it was and felt sorry for us.

At that moment I realized this was not some simple car accident with bumps and scrapes or bruised ribs. Cody might die. For all we knew, Cody might be taking his last breaths in some cold bleak hospital room without anyone he loved beside him. My heart sank and my knees felt weak.

Kreg helped me stumble over to the depressing little waiting area. We sat on an old worn out blue couch and stared at the ugly coffee table in front of us. Jeff's parents, Lyn and Betty Smith, arrived and were allowed to see Jeff for a moment, but then they joined us in the waiting area. We exchanged hugs and cried together, then resigned ourselves to waiting.

Betty was doing about as poorly as I was, and Lyn was trying to comfort her. Betty kept asking questions that none of us could answer. "Who was driving? Do you know who was driving? What happened? Were they wearing seat belts?" Gradually she realized we didn't have any answers for her and she quietly sank into her husband's arms.

We sat in silence for what seemed like forever. What do you say to each other when both boys are on the edge of life or death? I began to pray, but nothing was making sense. My thoughts floated between my own questions about the accident, earnest pleas to Heavenly Father, and what Cody was going through all alone upstairs. I hated knowing that Cody was alone up there. If I wasn't so frozen with fear, I would have stormed right up there, checked every room until I found him, and stayed by his side until it was all over.

After a little while a doctor came in and took Jeff's parents aside and explained Jeff's condition. Jeff was in really bad shape. His lungs had been punctured and the doctors had inserted tubes through his ribs to re-inflate them. His heart had ruptured and wasn't sending the blood through his vessels, it was just pumping into the pericardial sac that surrounded his heart. He had also suffered a broken pelvis, broken sternum, broken collarbone, and broken vertebrae, but those would be addressed when, and if, they could fix his lungs and heart. The doctors were prepping for open-heart surgery but were not very optimistic about his chances. Lyn and Betty sat back down and braced themselves for the worst.

Every possible scenario went through my mind. Was it better that we hadn't heard anything yet, or worse? What was wrong with Cody that he needed a CT scan? Did I really want to hear what Cody's condition was? Jeff's condition was terrible, I didn't think I could stand hearing the same news about my own son. We sat in the little waiting area for more than half an hour. A half hour to contemplate and consider every terrible possibility, everything I'd ever done wrong as a mother, and everything I should have done better. It was my own personal hell.

Someone must have called my parents because they arrived shortly after we did. Kreg's parents arrived as well, along with a few others. Word was getting around. A nurse led them into the waiting room and my mom took me into her arms. My parents tried to tell me that everything was going to be alright, but I knew better. Kreg updated everyone on what we knew, which was not very much, but I could hardly say a word. I sat on the couch and waited, breathlessly, for news I did not want to hear.

"Mr. and Mrs. Parmer?" A doctor in blue scrubs stood at the edge of what was becoming a very full little waiting room, motioning for us to follow. Kreg and I stood up and walked with him a few paces so we could talk privately.

"Your son Cody has been in a very serious accident. It sounds like the truck they were driving in slipped off the side of the road and rolled multiple times, ejecting both your son and the other boy. Cody has experienced a lot of physical trauma. When he came in he was in a lot of pain and was thrashing around, so we've sedated him. This should help him remain still and prevent any further complication of his injuries.

"Our CT scan has revealed several very serious injuries. His pelvis and his arm are broken. His skull is fractured, and his face is fractured in 17 places. His neck is broken at the base of his skull. He has lots of other minor lacerations and bruises all over, but the most critical thing right now is a traumatic brain injury and severe swelling in his head."

With every word the life drained out of me. All of these were injuries that seemed to describe someone who was dead or dying, not someone who could be bandaged up and sent home in a few days.

"Because of the severe head trauma, the fluids and blood from all over the skull are leaking and causing extreme pressure on the brain. This can be very dangerous and could lead to permanent brain damage, so we've inserted a pressure valve under the scalp to monitor the swelling. Because of his neck injury, we fear that there may be permanent nerve damage and possibly paralysis, but we can't be sure just yet. I'm not going to lie to you, he's in really rough shape. If he's going to survive, he will likely have very serious limitations. The one thing he has going

The truck, after having been recovered from the scene of the accident

for him is that he is young and his body is more likely to heal than an older patient."

Kreg nodded, taking it all in. He was trying to be tough, but his resolve was fading. "So what do you need to do? How do you fix those things?" Kreg asked.

"Well, we could fix the arm and the pelvis, and even the neck, but we just don't have the resources here to address the swelling in the head. He needs to see a specialist, and the closest one is in Salt Lake. Because of his age, we're going to recommend that he be transferred to Primary Children's Hospital. They are very good at what they do, and if he's going to pull out of this, they'll be the ones to help him do it." Though he was offering words of encouragement, the fact that there was no one in Idaho Falls who could help him scared me even more.

"So are you going to fix the arm and stuff first? When will that be done?" Kreg asked.

"Mr. Parmer, I wish I could tell you that was our plan, but the head trauma is just so serious that it needs to be addressed immediately. If we take him into surgery for the arm or the neck or the pelvis, it will be delaying his transportation, and those are critical hours we just can't spare. The plane is on its way now from Salt Lake City and it will be here within an hour. He's stabilized now, so we're just going to wait to repair his other injuries until we can be sure…" The doctor paused, choosing his words carefully. "Until we know the outcome of the brain injury."

FOUR

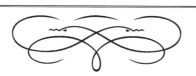

"WHEN CAN I SEE HIM?" I ASKED. THE DOCTOR TURNED TO ME AND took a deep breath.

"We're going to bring him down now and place him in a room where you can be with him, but I'm going to warn you, the swelling is very severe around his face. He's not conscious, you won't really be able to touch him due to the injuries, but you can be with him until the plane arrives." I nodded my approval and he walked down a long hall and got on the elevator.

Minutes later the elevator doors opened again and they rolled Cody out on a large hospital gurney. Several nurses and doctors were with him and they motioned us to follow them into one of the rooms. Kreg and I walked quickly toward the procession of attendants. I couldn't wait to see my son, but as I got closer and finally saw his face, my stomach turned upside down.

The legs, the chest, even the twisted and broken arm, those were Cody's, I was sure. But the face, it was unlike anything I had ever seen. Cody's head was swollen to the size of a pumpkin, several inches of swelling in all directions. His eyes were swollen shut, but his eyelids bulged from his face like golf balls. The whole area around his eyes was as black as tar. The rest of his head was a mix of cuts and bruises of every shade of red, purple, and black. On the side of his head a bolt was screwed through the scalp into the bone, and a bundle of wires led out of the bolt into a machine at his side. Tubes ran down his throat, and monitoring equipment of every kind seemed to be hooked to any available piece of skin.

I had mentally prepared myself to see a broken leg or gruesome cuts;

those things I could imagine, they had some connection to reality. But this, this was so much worse. My beautiful boy's face was disfigured seemingly beyond repair. How could anyone ever recover from this? It was worse than anything I could have ever imagined.

The bed and its trailing assembly of monitoring equipment were set up in a cold, sterile room, and the doctors and employees slowly filed out. It was clear that they didn't really want us all in there, but they weren't going to deny us the chance to be with him, probably because they didn't expect him to live.

Kreg tried to lead me into the room but I planted my feet in the hallway. "I can't go in there Kreg."

"Come on Brenda, Cody needs us, we need to be with him," Kreg spoke softly. We were standing in front of the door and both our parents were right behind us.

"I can't! That's my son! That's my only son! I can't go in there and watch him...and watch him die!" I had barely been hanging on to my wits, but the sight of Cody's face was too much. I lost it, right there in the hallway. I was too confused and frustrated to even cry, but my mind shattered. My legs became weak and I felt like fainting. Kreg tried to comfort me and my dad put his arms on my shoulders. Together they walked me into the room. I caught a glimpse of Cody's face again and collapsed at his bedside, keeping my face below the level of the bed and my eyes closed so that I couldn't see what had become of my precious little boy.

I leaned my head against the cool metal railing and tried to let my mind wander somewhere else, anywhere else, but it wouldn't. I opened my eyes and saw Cody's hand. His fingers dangled almost lifelessly from the edge of the bed. Despite what had happened to the rest of his body, his fingers were just fine. That gave me something to cling to, something recognizable to help me keep my head above water.

I knew they said not to touch him, but his fingers were right there, in front of me, and they weren't injured at all. I softly grabbed his hand and it felt warm, even hot. I could feel the pulse in his fingers. Somewhere in there, despite his appearance, he was holding on and fighting.

Fish. The smell came as I placed my cheek against his warm fingers.

"Kreg, his hands smell like fish," I uttered my revelation and looked up at Kreg, interrupting him. He was talking with our parents and a few others who had rushed to the hospital to offer support.

"His hands smell like fish. They must have caught fish." Kreg nodded but didn't say anything. I'm sure he thought I was crazy, and in that moment I probably was.

My mind imagined Cody and Jeff wading in the river, swinging their fly rods back and forth. Then I imagined them tumbling through the truck like rag dolls. Why would two innocent boys be hurt like this? Why didn't God protect them? I reached back through all the Sunday School lessons, through Young Women and Primary. Why did bad things happen to good people? I knew there must be a good answer, but I couldn't think of it.

"Honey, can you give him a blessing?" I asked. Kreg thought about it for a second, then nodded. He asked my dad to help him. The anointing was quick and heartfelt, and as it concluded I opened my eyes and watched Kreg place his fingertips ever so lightly on Cody's swollen head.

I wasn't sure what he was going to say, I wasn't even sure that I wanted to listen. I knew that death was a real possibility for Cody, a likelihood even, and I didn't want to hear Kreg tell Cody that it was his time to go. But as Kreg blessed Cody to be strong, to fight, and to live, if it was God's will, my heart swelled up. I poured every ounce of hope and faith I had into the words that Kreg spoke and tried as best I could to add my faith to theirs.

The blessing ended and I wiped tears from my eyes. I stood up and hugged Kreg, but I still tried to keep my eyes away from Cody's battered face.

Nurses were constantly walking in and out, checking monitors and taking readings. Family members continued to arrive, and each one needed an update on what had happened. Jeff's parents came to check up on Cody, as they had taken Jeff in for surgery. They looked to be in about the same shape as we were, completely exhausted and emotionally worn out.

After nearly an hour of waiting, the doctor returned to give us final instructions. "Well, the plane has just arrived at the airport. I can see that you have lots of family here, and that's great, Cody will need your support. However, with all the equipment that needs to ride along with Cody, there will only be room for one family member, so you can decide amongst yourselves who will ride with him, and the others will need to find their own transportation if they choose to follow."

I snapped my head to look up at Kreg, my eyes wide with panic. Only one family member? They can't do this! I am not leaving my husband! I couldn't go with Cody alone, I just couldn't face it without Kreg. What if something went wrong? What if Cody died on the way down there, or before Kreg arrived? No, I wouldn't be flying down by myself, but Kreg knew that. He knew I wouldn't be able to handle it, so he would have to go, but I couldn't let him leave me, and I certainly wouldn't be letting Cody out of my sight. There had to be another way.

The doctor continued, "I need to warn you though. The pressure in his head is very sensitive. Even the elevator ride from the third floor down here was enough to noticeably change the pressure on his brain. Over the last hour, the pressure has continued to rise, and the swelling is increasing. We don't know how he will react to the altitude, but we really have no other choice. If he stays here, he won't make it through the night." Kreg put his arm around me and pulled me in close. My world was collapsing in around me.

"An ambulance will be here in just a few minutes, we're going to need to clear the room so we can get your son ready for the flight." And with that, the doctor was gone.

As we stumbled to the waiting room, I tugged on Kreg's shirt. "Kreg, you can't leave me. I can't do this by myself!"

"Brenda, your parents will drive you down, I'll go with Cody and you'll be there in just a couple hours." Kreg spoke slowly and tried to calm me down.

"No. No. They have to let us both go, I'll stand the whole way or sit on the floor if I have to. I'm not leaving my son and I'm not going without you!"

The ambulance pulled up and the flight nurses from Salt Lake City jumped out. While the nurses got a report from the doctors, a man in a Life Flight jacket walked up to us. "Hi, are you the parents?" he asked. We nodded yes.

"I'm the pilot, I'll be taking your son down to Salt Lake tonight. We have one seat on the plane for a family member, do you know who it's going to be?" I shuddered and closed my eyes. There was no way this was happening. They couldn't leave me!

"Please sir, my wife needs to be with our son but I can't let her go by herself." Kreg pleaded.

"I'm sorry," he shook his head and shrugged his shoulders, "There's only one seat."

If I was going to make a case for myself, it had to be now. I opened my eyes and tried to stand tall. I calmed my voice and tried to speak as clearly as I could. "Can I just sit on the floor?" I asked, trying to sound strong, but my voice quivered and revealed my weakness.

"I wish I could, but I can't let you do that," the pilot replied.

Fine, I was going to have to resort to pleading. "Please, I can sit on my husband's lap, I can kneel, I can stand up the whole way if I need to. Please, please just let us both go. You just have to. I can't let him leave, and what if he dies on the flight? What if something happens before I get down there? Please, do you have children? This is my only son. You've got to understand."

The pilot looked down at the ground and shook his head. "This is not a big plane, it's got just enough room for essential personnel and one family member."

I didn't know what else to say, so I just stood still.

The pilot raised his head and looked at me. "I'll tell you what," he began, "the co-pilot's seat is open. I don't usually let anyone ride up there with me, but I can tell you guys have been through a lot."

"Oh thank you," I cut him off, "thank you!"

"But," he came back strongly, pointing his finger at me, "you can't touch anything. Not a thing."

"I promise, I will be so good and I won't say anything."

He stared at me blankly for a second, maybe second-guessing his decision, maybe sizing up my current mental state. Then he nodded. "Alright, let's get going."

The flight nurses wheeled Cody out to the ambulance and we followed close behind. The lobby was filled with family, doctors, and nurses who had helped Cody and were watching him leave. Their faces were all grim as Kreg and I walked out to the ambulance. They didn't expect him to make it. My chin started quivering and I was about to burst into tears. This was going to be the last time my family saw Cody alive, and I could tell they all knew it.

My dad walked up to me and put his hands on my shoulders. "Honey, if you are going to go on that jet you have got to stay calm so they will let you go. Otherwise, you are going to look like you are another patient that they have to take care of and they're not going to let you go. Do you understand? If you want to stay with Cody, you have to stay calm." I nodded my head. Alright. Just stand still and stay calm. Don't think about what's happening, just stay calm. I can do that. Maybe.

We climbed into the ambulance and it was a tight squeeze. Someone closed the back of the ambulance and we were off. It was close to midnight and the roads were fairly empty. As we raced to the airport I began to realize that I had nothing with me. No change of clothes, no purse, no wallet. I had left everything at home. Home. The girls.

"Kreg! The girls! What are we going to do?" I nearly shouted.

"They're fine, I talked to your parents. They'll go stay with them tonight and then in the morning they're going to bring them down in the motorhome. I told them not to say anything until you could tell them about Cody yourself. They'll be fine, don't worry." I was glad someone had some sense to think about the practical things.

We pulled up to the airport and the ambulance drove out among the little planes parked on the ramp. The blacktop was bathed in a dim orange glow from lights on the hangars behind us and the shadows on the ground were long and eerie. We pulled up beside a tiny little jet and stopped.

Cody was unloaded and placed in the plane in a flash, his gurney secured along the far right side of the plane. There were two seats for the flight nurses across from Cody and one seat right behind the pilot for a passenger, and that was it. The pilot wasn't lying, there really was no space for anyone else.

One of the nurses helped me climb over the center console and get seated in the co-pilot's seat while Kreg followed me and sat back-to-back with the pilot. Once both of us were on the plane I let out a sigh of relief. One battle behind us, now we just needed to get to Salt Lake. The cockpit was cramped and I was surrounded by buttons and knobs and gauges. The pilot showed me how to buckle my seatbelt and I turned back to look at Kreg. Cody was right behind me, so I couldn't tell what was going on, but Kreg nodded to me, letting me know everything was okay.

After flipping switches and turning knobs, the pilot started the engines and we were taxiing onto the runway. With a push of the throttle the engines roared and we were airborne. The pilot and flight nurses all had on headsets and were talking to each other, but they didn't give me one. The sound of the engines muffled their voices, but I could make out some words: *pressure, vitals, increasing.*

I turned back and reached out for Kreg's hand. He took it and gave my hand a squeeze. I held onto his hand for the rest of the flight. Every few minutes I turned my head back, checking the expressions on Kreg's face for any increased sign of worry or concern, but he just gave me a reassuring nod every time.

I stared out the window ahead of me. There were so many stars, and all so still. Of course, we were moving at a few hundred miles per hour, but it just looked like we were floating in the midnight sky. The view turned my mind again toward God. I closed my eyes, "Heavenly Father, wherever you are out there, please protect Cody. Just let us get to Salt Lake where the doctors can fix him up. Please just let him live." My thoughts turned into prayers and prayers into thoughts, over and over again. I hoped and prayed the same thing a thousand times. "Just let him live. Just let him make it to Salt Lake." I didn't know what to ask for beyond that, but we just needed to get to the hospital, then we could figure out what the next step was.

The pilot turned to me after some time and spoke loudly so I could hear over the engines, "I talked with the dispatcher in Salt Lake, they said Primary Children's trauma unit is full, there was some sort of an accident and a bunch of little kids were hurt. They're going to take you to LDS Hospital. Don't worry, they've got great doctors there, you'll be in good hands," and with that, he turned back to his controls and kept talking on the radio. It was too loud for me to ask him any questions, but I wondered if that was the right call. Was LDS Hospital the best place to take him? Was there somewhere better? Or maybe this *was* the better option. Maybe, just maybe, God had heard my prayer and was sending us to the right doctors who could fix Cody. I had to believe that was the case.

After about an hour the plane began a steady descent into Salt Lake City. I could see the glow of the city up ahead, and airport runway lights painted a path for us to the ground. The pilot was careful to make a soft landing and we taxied over to a row of hangars. I thanked the pilot again and again and followed the flight nurses as they loaded Cody into the waiting ambulance.

Kreg and I were both exhausted, emotionally and physically. We didn't say much on the ride to the hospital, just held each other's hands and stared at Cody. His face wasn't getting any better. If anything it was getting worse. I wondered about everything else that we couldn't see; had the plane ride hurt his broken neck, arm, or pelvis? Would he be able to walk again? Would he ever throw a football or ride a bike again? It was too early to tell.

We pulled up to LDS Hospital and the driver came back around to open the back door. As both ambulance doors swung open we were shocked to see a whole team of doctors and nurses there in front of us. It looked like the whole emergency room staff was there waiting for Cody. They grabbed the gurney and whisked him off, shouting out pressure levels and calling for medication.

As we climbed out of the ambulance it felt like the accident was brand new again. Their urgency reminded me that Cody was still in very bad shape and every second mattered, but there was a determination in their voices and their actions that comforted me. These were trained professionals who knew what they were doing. After a night of feeling helpless and alone, there was a faint glimmer of hope; someone was finally starting to help Cody get better.

FIVE

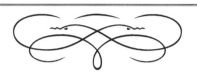

THE DOCTORS MOVED QUICKLY AND WITH PRECISION. WE STOOD IN the back of a large room in the trauma unit and watched them rush in and out, poking and prodding, taking measurements and making notes. There had to be at least a dozen people working on Cody. I grabbed Kreg's arm and held on tight. If anything was going to get me through this horrible night, it was him.

Finally, one of the doctors grabbed the bed Cody was laying on and started pulling. "Okay, we're going up to the CT!" he announced. Several of the people followed the bed while a few others stayed behind and compared notes. We started walking out, trying to follow Cody, but one of the remaining doctors cut us off.

The doctor was nearly indistinguishable from any of the others, covered head to foot in surgical scrubs, a head covering, and a face mask. He pulled down the mask to talk to us and I could see the lines and wrinkles around his eyes and mouth. He seemed a little older than the rest of the doctors and nurses and I hoped that meant he had lots of experience and knew exactly what he was doing. When he spoke, his voice was soft and kind.

"Hello, I'm Dr. Grant. You're Cody's parents?"

"Yes, I'm Kreg and this is Brenda. Can we go with Cody?" Kreg pointed out the door as the parade of people and Cody's bed passed out of sight.

"No I'm sorry, he's going to get a CT scan, or a CAT scan as it's sometimes called. But I promise we'll bring him right back in this room when we're done, alright?" We both nodded.

"Okay, I'm going to be overseeing Cody's care from here on out. We've got a great team of specialists who are going to be working with him. My job is to make sure that Cody gets the best care possible, coordinate all of the surgeries and procedures, and keep you in the loop the whole way. So, before and after every procedure, either I or one of my team will come and let you know exactly what is happening, why we're doing it, and what the results are. Does that sound alright?" We nodded our approval again. He was trying to be very kind to us, but I was too tired and worn out to realize just how nice it was to have a good caring doctor in charge.

"Excellent. Let's have a seat and go over what we know. I've seen the files that came down from Idaho Falls and we've done a preliminary analysis here to verify their findings and make sure we're not missing anything." Dr. Grant took a deep breath, then continued.

"Cody has a long road ahead of him. We don't know the extent of all his injuries yet, but we're going to start working to repair the ones we know about now. First thing in the morning, once all our tests and scans are complete, Cody will go into surgery to repair his broken vertebrae in the base of his neck. If we don't fix that first, any further movement or swelling could damage the nervous system, so that's priority number one." He paused to make sure we were following along.

"If that goes well, we've got him lined up for surgery to fix his pelvis in the afternoon. We may be able to set his arm the next day if things continue to improve. You should know that he's in a medically induced coma, so this is the best time to get in and fix these things because he won't feel any pain and he can begin healing even before we wake him up."

"What about his head, and the swelling and the pressure, they told us that the pressure could kill him? When does that get fixed?" I asked. What use was fixing his broken body if the pressure in his head was going to kill him anyway?

"You're right, the swelling is bad, but to be honest, our specialist has looked at it and there's not much we can do yet. There are a few locations where the cerebral fluid is leaking and pooling just under the skin, and there are a couple of places where the brain is bleeding. Unfortunately, any corrective action we take may just make the situation worse at this point. We're keeping a constant eye on the pressure, and they're taking a second look at his head right now, but we're hoping that these leaks will stop on their own. We just need to wait and see. He'll be getting regular CT scans for the next few days, and the swelling should start receding by then. After a couple days we'll know better what we're up against. Until then, we need to start fixing the things we can fix. If Cody is going to make it through this, he needs a healthy body, so that's our focus right now."

He was trying to be positive, but I didn't like the way he said, "if Cody is going to make it." If Cody was going to die, then just tell me so I can go and be with my son and hold him in my arms, instead of him wasting his final days in surgery. At the same time though, I wanted them to pull every stop and do everything they could to save him. I couldn't decide what to think. It had been such a long tough night that my thoughts no longer made sense, but the late hour made every emotion more powerful and sharp.

"So, what is the final outcome? Do you think he's going to live or be paralyzed or have brain damage?" Kreg was searching for some kind of hard answer, but I didn't want to hear the doctor's response. I closed my eyes and buried my face in Kreg's shoulder.

"Mr. Parmer, I wish I could take all of the negative possibilities off the table, but I can't. Not yet. We're going to do everything we can to get him to a full recovery, but his injuries are very serious, and we probably need to be prepared for anything." I wanted to scream. How much longer until some good news? All night it had been one dire warning after another. It was all one terrible nightmare that I couldn't shake, couldn't wake up from.

Dr. Grant told us Cody would be back down in a little bit, but that it would be a few hours before the surgeon was in so it would be best to get a little rest. It had to be close to 3:00 in the morning by this point, but as tired as I was, I couldn't sleep. My eyes would close and my mind would drift off, then I would snap back awake, searching for Cody. At some point they brought him back in to wait for the surgeon to arrive. Nurses and attendants still marched in and out, but more quietly and less rushed.

Minutes passed, maybe hours, I couldn't tell, then Kreg patted me on the shoulder to wake me up. I had no idea what time it was, but there were more people moving around Cody's bed.

"Mrs. Parmer? Sorry to wake you," Dr. Grant said softly. "I wanted to introduce you to Dr. Richardson, he's an excellent neurosurgeon and your son is in good hands. He's going to take Cody now and repair his neck."

I was still only half awake, but the thought of them taking Cody away jolted me to attention. "How long will it take?" I asked.

Dr. Richardson spoke up, "We're planning on several hours, if everything goes well. It might be noon before we're able to bring him back in, but we'll take good care of him."

I nodded my approval once again, but really, what say did I have in the matter? They were going to take my son and give him to whatever doctor was available and do heaven knows what kind of procedures behind their operating room doors. I didn't know these doctors, I didn't know if they were the best or the worst at what they did, or if their decisions were the right ones. As much as they tried to keep me updated, I was just a spectator in matters that would change Cody's life forever.

After they took Cody for surgery, Kreg and I just sat in the empty room in silence. It was lonely there. In Idaho Falls I hadn't cared if anyone else was around and I paid almost no attention to those who came, but now the solitude was depressing. I wondered how long it would be before my dad showed up with the girls.

The poor girls had probably slept through the commotion and had no idea what had happened. They knew I was worried when they went to bed, but had they heard us leave in a hurry? Kira and Brooke would be okay with Kreg's sister at the house, but Krissa was just seven, what would she think waking up without her mother there? What would they think about Cody's accident? They loved their older brother, he had been their protector and friend, could they handle knowing that he was hurt so badly? Surely I couldn't let them see him, I could barely stand to look at his bruised and swollen face.

"Honey, what do we tell the girls?" I asked Kreg softly, breaking the silence.

"I don't know," he sighed. "I think we just need to wait a little while and see what happens. I don't want to tell them it's going to be okay and then…and then have it not be okay."

I tried to push that thought from my mind, but it wouldn't go. Of course it had to be okay, it had to. For a fleeting moment my mind imagined the girls dressed in their Sunday dresses, walking into the chapel for a funeral, then I dashed the image from my mind. No! Cody was not going to die. The operations would be successful and we would all walk out of here in no time. There was no other option.

Kreg got up to go make some calls. There were tons of people to notify and update, but I didn't want to leave the room. So I just sat there by myself, in an empty hospital room, with my head buried in my hands. There was nowhere to go and nothing to do. My mind couldn't rest, but it also couldn't keep any of my thoughts straight. The accident, the flight, the surgery, the lingering threat of permanent damage—it was a swirling storm of fear, frustration, worry, and pain in my mind.

I had almost no sense of time, hours must have come and gone and soon the hospital was getting busier with people and nurses starting to clamor about. Soon there was a knock at the door. I looked up and saw my dad, escorted by a nurse, standing in the doorway. I jumped up and gave him a hug.

"Hey honey, where's Cody?" he asked cautiously, assuming the empty room was a bad sign.

"He's in surgery for his neck, it's probably going to be a few more hours before they know anything."

"Hey, he made it through the night! That's a great sign!" he offered. I hadn't really considered that. It was morning already? Then he survived his first night. That was a good sign. All those prayers I had said on the plane to just get us to Salt Lake, they were answered. Well, if God was in the mood to answer some prayers, what do I ask for now? It still felt like too much to ask for Cody to be made completely whole, considering his injuries.

The thoughts of the scripture came to mind, "Line upon line, here a little, there a little." Maybe the key was to take each day at a time, each setback or blessing on its own. He had answered one prayer already, now I just needed the surgery on his neck to be successful. But yes, I had received one little miracle. It was a like a tiny ray of sunshine cutting through the darkness of my fear and confusion.

Dad continued, "Well, I've got three very scared little girls out in the motorhome. We didn't tell them what happened, just like you guys asked. We just told them we were going for a ride, so Brooke thought we were kidnapping them all. Kira and Krissa are fine but a little worried. They know something is wrong, especially when we pulled up to the hospital. But you need to come see Brooke so she knows you're okay and that we weren't trying to kidnap her."

Kreg agreed to stay in the room while I went out to see the girls. I made him promise to run and get me if anything happened, then I followed my dad back out to the parking lot.

The sun was just coming up over the mountains and I squinted in the bright light. My parents must have woken the girls up long before dawn to get down here so early. The girls were standing outside the motorhome with my mom, but when they saw me coming, they all started running.

"Mom!" they cried out, as they circled around me in a huge hug. Krissa started crying, and my eyes welled up with tears too. We hugged for a minute, then walked back to the motorhome.

"Mom, what happened to Cody?" Kira had figured it out, or someone had let it slip. Either way, I had to tell them something.

"Cody got in an accident and he got hurt, so the doctors are trying to help him." Kira was 13 and Brooke was 12, and they deserved more of an answer, but I tried to keep it pretty vague for Krissa's sake. Besides, what could I tell them? That he might die? That he might be paralyzed, or have permanent brain damage? No, I couldn't say any of those things. We would cross that bridge when we got there. They couldn't know just how bad the situation really was.

"Can we go in and see him?" Brooke asked.

"We'll see. The doctors need more time to help him, they're working on him right now," I said. The thought of them operating on his spine while I was out in the parking lot was terribly unsettling, I needed to be close in case something happened. "But let's go wait inside, alright?"

I walked with the girls back indoors and asked a nurse if there was someplace where my family could wait. She came back in a minute and led us to a room with several couches and a TV and a few small tables.

"This is one of our family rooms, this is all yours until Cody starts doing better, so anyone you'd like can come and wait in here instead of the main waiting room. We don't usually allow any kids under 14 back in the trauma unit, but you can take them back for a visit once he's out of surgery. After that, we probably only want one or two people back there at a time. The rest of the visitors can stay here in the family room as long as they'd like."

I thanked her and got the girls settled in. Dad and Mom promised to take care of them and go shopping later on to get them some coloring books or activities or something. Kreg came in to join us and the girls cuddled up to him on the couch as he put his arms around them.

One by one, other family members started arriving. My brother Dirk who lived in Park City drove down, and nearly all my siblings from Idaho Falls made the trip down as well. Our private family room was getting quite crowded. Even my Relief Society President and her husband drove down that first day to see how we were doing. Earlier I had just wanted to be alone with my son, but having such wonderful support from everyone was helping to lift my spirits, at least for the moment.

Then Dr. Richardson appeared in the doorway, and my fear returned. The room fell utterly silent as he nodded toward us and spoke. "Mr. and Mrs. Parmer? Can I speak to you in the hall?"

Six

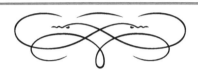

"THE OPERATION WAS A SUCCESS," HE SAID, AS SOON AS WE WERE A FEW feet from the door. Oh what a relief I felt! "One of his vertebrae was broken, so we needed to fuse the bones in that location. We made an incision in the front of his neck and installed a titanium plate across the location of the break to hold it all together while it heals."

Kreg cut in, "So you have to take that back out when he's all better?"

"No," the doctor shook his head, "he'll have it in for the rest of his life. The only reason we'd take it out is if the body begins to reject it, but that's very rare. I don't expect any issues."

"So, everything went alright? There's no permanent damage or anything?" Kreg asked.

"Well, I can only speak for my area of expertise, but no, there shouldn't be any permanent damage to the neck or spine. He's very, very lucky. I have to tell you, I did this exact same operation yesterday. A young boy, the exact same age, came in with a broken neck in exactly the same location. We fused the bone and put a plate in, but the nerves had been damaged and he's paralyzed below the neck. Cody very easily could have been a quadriplegic, in fact, he probably should have been, but we've done all the nerve response tests and everything is responding like normal."

"Oh thank you!" I cried out, both to the doctor and to God who had answered yet another prayer.

"Well, there's a very good team here, and we're all working together to make sure your son recovers. They're bringing him back into the room for now, but he's got another surgery scheduled soon to set his pelvis. You can go in and be with him for now, though." Dr. Richardson put his hand on my shoulder, "Hang in there."

I went straight down the hall to Cody's room in the trauma unit while Kreg went to tell our family the good news. It had been five or six hours since they had taken Cody, and I didn't want to miss another minute.

They wheeled him in just a few moments after I arrived. His neck was wrapped in white bandages and held in a brace. His head was still swollen but the bruises were changing colors and getting darker. In some places the edges looked yellow, or green. I couldn't tell if that was good or not, but it still made my stomach uneasy.

Kreg came back with our three girls. I watched their faces as they looked around and finally recognized that the disfigured boy lying in the bed was their brother. Kira winced and turned her eyes away. I stood up and put my arm around her. Brooke started crying and walked up to Cody's side. Kreg tried to tell her that the doctors were doing all they could, but Brooke's tears kept falling. I felt like crying along with her, but I was too exhausted to summon the tears. Krissa, not really old enough to understand what was going on, but recognizing that something bad had happened, grabbed onto my leg and wouldn't let go. I wished I could comfort them, but I had no words to say. After a few minutes they had seen enough. They told their older brother they loved him and Kreg led them back to the family room.

For the next few hours, Kreg led our family in one by one to sit with me and see Cody. Some handled it well, but others couldn't look at Cody and averted their eyes. Their reactions reminded me that Cody's condition was not just bad, it was horrible. I prayed that his body would heal and return to normal. God had answered several of my prayers for Cody through the night, but I worried that I was coming to my limit. How many more blessings could I honestly ask for? I prayed for a miracle but didn't know what to expect.

After the family all came through, Kreg began bringing back friends and ward members who had driven down to see Cody. It was a three-hour drive, and their sacrifices to see Cody were very kind, but I had no interest in making small talk with anyone. Kreg would explain to each of them what was going on and they would ask questions and Kreg would do his best to answer. He was being so good to everyone, but I didn't want to talk and usually just sat next to Cody and said nothing.

A couple from our ward were in the room when Dr. Grant came to take Cody away again. The sister had sat next to me and tried to ask how I was doing, but she could see that I was in no mood for a long conversation. As she got up to leave, she rubbed my back and said, "God has a plan, this all happened for a reason. It all happened for a reason." I said nothing. What possible reason could there be? I racked my brain for an answer and sent up a quick question to God. I had spent many hours wondering why this had happened, wondering if there was a reason, or if it was all just chance. And if it was just chance, why didn't God stop it? Why didn't we receive the protection we prayed for every morning and night? Had we done something wrong? Had I done something wrong?

Once Kreg and the visitors had left the room, Dr. Grant stopped his preparations and took a seat next to me. "You know, I don't believe that," he shook his head, "what she said about it happening for a reason, that God wanted it to happen."

I turned and looked at him. "What do you mean?" I asked. Even though we were in the LDS Hospital, I knew that many of the doctors and employees were not LDS, so I never really expected to have a spiritual discussion with the staff, but that appeared to be exactly what was happening.

"Several years ago, my daughter was in a really bad accident and was paralyzed from the waist down. She was lying in a bed just like this, and I was sitting there just like you, trying to figure out what was going on. I was barely making it through each day, let alone trying to hold onto my faith and figure out why God would let this happen. My mother came to see us and she told me, 'Son, you know this happened because you need to learn patience.' I couldn't believe she had said that. I told her, 'Mom, if that's the way God works, I'd be happier in hell.'" He paused for a moment, the memory was a difficult one for him to revive.

"You see, I just can't believe that is how God works. He doesn't look down and say, 'Dr. Grant needs to learn patience, so I'll put his daughter in a wheelchair.' How terribly cruel and heartless that would be! My daughter isn't in a wheelchair so I could learn patience, and Cody isn't lying in that bed because he did anything wrong or because you all need to learn some lesson. Sometimes things just happen."

I had no idea Dr. Grant understood exactly what I was feeling, or what I was going through. I thought I was suffering alone, but to know that someone else had been there, and had survived, gave me a tiny bit of hope.

Kreg came back in and Dr. Grant stood up. He switched back into his professional role and began explaining the surgery at hand. "Alright, we're going to take Cody and fix his pelvis now. Because normal body movements shift the pelvis and prevent healing, we're going to hold the pelvis in place so the bone can heal. Several long metal rods are going to be drilled into the bone and stick out of the skin. We'll hold those rods in place with a series of connectors. The final result will be a triangle-shaped contraption that will let it heal correctly. It's going to be another long surgery, but we'll have Cody back to you by this evening."

Dr. Grant then turned back to me and said, "Stay strong, you'll make it through this." He gave me a knowing smile and then took Cody.

Despite the pep-talk, I was a wreck. All the pain and worry and sorrow and fear was starting to meld together into an overwhelming numbness. I couldn't make sense of the situation, and so my mind seemed to shut down. I couldn't hold a conversation with my family, I couldn't read a magazine or watch TV, and I could barely stomach any of the food my family brought me. I just sat and waited, quietly rolling over the worry and what-ifs again and again in my mind.

Late in the evening they wheeled Cody's bed back into the room. Kreg had gone to take care of the girls for a bit and I was all alone. I winced at the sight of the metal rods that pierced his hips and held his pelvis in place. He looked like some kind of medical school experiment, nearly every part of his body had some sort of bandage or contraption wired to it.

Dr. Grant followed the nurses in to give me an update. "Well, I can tell you this, Cody is one tough kid, he did great. The surgery went well, and we're right on track," Dr. Grant said as he flipped through charts and reports. "And even better news, the pressure from the swelling on the brain leveled off around the middle of the day and has now started receding. It might be a few days before we can really figure out what's going on in there, but it's progressing like we had hoped, so that's a good sign."

He closed his folder and stared at me for a second. I must have looked terrible. "I know it's rough being here all day every day. Can we get you anything to make you more comfortable?" I realized then that all his comforting words weren't just platitudes, he had actually been here and he knew what we were enduring.

"I think I'm just tired," I said, shaking my head.

"Would you like a couple pillows or blankets so you can stay in here with Cody tonight?"

"Yeah, that would be good," I replied. I didn't know if I would sleep, but they would help the hard chairs be a little more comfortable.

"Alright, I'll get someone to bring them in for you. We'll be taking Cody early in the morning to set his broken arm. That's really the last thing on our list for now. After that, we'll just have to wait and see how things look." He wished us a good night and left the room.

A dark haired male nurse came in a minute later with few blankets and pillows and set them beside Cody's bed.

"There you go," he said, "it's not the Ritz Carlton or anything, but it will do for now. You're going to spend the night here?" he asked as he pointed to the two small chairs next to Cody's bed.

"Yeah," I muttered, "some of my family are getting a hotel room, but I just don't feel like I can leave."

"I understand. It's good for you to be with him. You know, a few years ago I was in a really bad accident myself. When they brought me into the hospital I was kind of in and out of consciousness the whole time, but they thought I was in a coma. The doctors and nurses all just worked around me and I couldn't see anything or really even feel anything, but I could hear them talking around me.

"I just kept wishing that someone would talk to me and tell me what was going on. So ever since then, I try to talk to my patients and tell them what I'm doing. I don't know, maybe it's crazy and maybe they don't hear me, but on the slim chance that they can, I like to think that it helps." He walked over beside Cody and finished checking the monitors, then added, "I don't know if Cody is awake in there, but if he is, I bet he'd like to hear from his mom." He nodded goodbye and walked out the door.

I sat and thought about what the nurse had said, then Kreg came in quietly. "Hey, your dad took the girls and some of the family down to Little America and got a couple hotel rooms for the night. I think some of them are going to sleep in the motorhome here in the parking lot as well. When did they bring Cody back?"

"Just a few minutes ago," I said, and filled him in on what Dr. Grant had told me. "Hey, Kreg?" I asked.

"Yeah?"

"One of the nurses said it would be a good idea to try to talk to Cody, just in case he can hear us. Do you want to talk to him with me?"

Kreg came over and sat next to Cody with me and put his hand on my knee. "Yeah, that's a good idea. Why don't you start?"

"Alright," I said and took a minute to gather my thoughts. I stood up and leaned over Cody's bed, taking it all in. I held his hand and leaned in a little closer. "Hey Cody, this is Mom. Dad's right here with me. I don't know if you can hear me, but if you can, I know you're probably wondering what's going on. You were in a really bad accident with Jeff last night. Jeff's up in Idaho Falls right now, they're trying to help him get better. We brought you down to Salt Lake City because they've got some special doctors here who can help." That was about all I had planned to say, but it didn't seem like enough.

"A lot of your aunts and uncles came, and your grandma and grandpa are here too. Your sisters came in to see you today, they really care about you." I closed my eyes and could imagine their faces, scared and worried, but I couldn't tell Cody that. I had to be strong for him.

"Cody, I want you to know that I love you so much." I started tearing up but tried to hold it back. "I just need you to get better. I just need you to keep on fighting and not give up. I can't lose you, I just can't. So you just hang in there and fight for your mom, okay? Do it for me, alright?" There was something about the bond between a mother and her oldest son that was powerful and deep. I couldn't describe it, but the thought of losing him tore my soul apart.

"I love you and I'm going to be here all night. Dad wants to talk to you too, then we'll let you get some sleep." I found a part of his forehead that wasn't so bruised and leaned over and gave him a gentle kiss. Then I sat down and Kreg took my place at Cody's side.

"Hey Cody, this is Dad. Man, I wish you were awake. Mom says she thinks you caught some fish yesterday. I guess you must have really figured out how to cast pretty well. That's really great, we'll have to go out fly fishing when you get better." Kreg paused. "Man, I miss you bud. You know the doctors say you're getting better, but for a while there I didn't know if you were going to make it. I'm not really the best at saying my prayers and stuff, but I talked to Heavenly Father last night and promised him that if he would just let you live, I would be better for you and the girls. Your mom's been really good at doing all the church stuff, but I need to do better, and I will. I even told Heavenly Father I'd start going to Sunday School instead of sitting in the hall, which I'm not sure if that was a great idea because that class is really boring," Kreg gave a half chuckle.

"Anyway, I don't know if deals like that even work, but you're still here, so maybe they do. So you just remember that for me, when you get better we'll go do some fishing, and I'll be a better dad, alright? Sleep tight buddy, and hang in there." Kreg sat down by my side and put his arm around me. I'd never heard him talk like that before.

I snuggled into his chest and closed my eyes. Before I fell asleep I said a silent prayer, "Heavenly Father, thank you for keeping Cody alive. Thank you for the good doctors and nurses who are trying to help. And thank you for Kreg."

SEVEN

"I THINK IT'S TIME." DR. GRANT SAID THE NEXT EVENING AS HE CHECKED Cody's charts and looked at the machines monitoring the pressure in his head. "We're going to start lowering the anesthesia. That's going to increase the blood flow to the brain and slowly restore cognitive functions. I'll warn you, when patients—and especially children—begin waking up from this sort of medication, it causes a lot of confusion and sometimes panic. As difficult as it may be, this is the next step in Cody's recovery. We need to figure out what kind of damage the brain has suffered."

Dr. Grant was usually quite positive, but I could tell from his face that he was not yet sure of what the outcome would be, and was trying to prepare us for the worst. The doctors had done all they could, but we were finally coming to a fork in the road. It was time to discover what kind of brain damage Cody had suffered, and if he could recover. As much as I wanted Cody awake, I didn't want to face the reality of what was ahead.

It was Sunday afternoon, three days since the accident. Cody had received the last of the operations, the setting of his broken right arm, on Saturday morning. The bone was shattered so badly they had to install another titanium plate to hold it together while it healed. Fortunately, the swelling of his head had reduced so much that it was almost unnoticeable. Parts of his face still showed light bruises, but he was my sweet Cody once again, no longer a disfigured caricature of my son.

The terror that had gripped me over the past few days had started to fade as Cody's image returned to normal. There seemed to be improvement each day and I tried to focus on that, instead of the looming implications of Cody's head injury. It was an obstacle that I didn't know if

I could handle, so I just refused to let my mind dwell on it. The more I avoided it though, the more it haunted me.

The nurses and my family finally colluded against me and forced me out of Cody's room for a little bit each day. One of the nurses told me, "If you don't get out of this room and go get some fresh air, we're going to have to put you in your own hospital bed! Now go, be with your family for a little bit, nothing is going to happen while you're gone." Finally I relented. My friends and family took turns sitting with Cody while I took a nap or left the room to talk to the girls.

By Sunday evening, many of our friends and family had to return to Idaho Falls for work the next day, but my parents and a few others promised to stay and help. The next few days and hours were going to be critical, and I wasn't sure I could make it without them.

The anesthesiologist came in and adjusted the machine that was administering Cody's medication. We knew it would be several hours before we would see any results, but Kreg and I sat on pins and needles watching Cody and his monitors.

Cody was still in the neck brace and pelvic fixator, and his right arm was wrapped tightly in bandages then placed in a full-arm brace that allowed his arm to bend at the elbow. Wires, IVs, and catheters connected him to an array of equipment, and a long breathing tube ran from the respirator machine down Cody's throat.

A short time after the anesthesia was turned down, Cody's heart rate began to slowly increase and his breathing became more irregular. Something was happening, but I didn't know what any of it meant. The nurses and anesthesiologist starting coming in more regularly, every few minutes, and I started watching Cody's face for any signs of activity.

Then I saw the muscles in Cody's face begin to move like he was waking up from a bad dream. Cody was in there! After Cody had been lying still and lifeless for so long, even the most minor twitches raised my spirits.

"Did you see that?" Kreg asked, grabbing my hand.

"Yeah, I think he's waking up. Look at his chest move, and his mouth," I pointed to his lips, where it looked like he was trying to fight against the ventilator tube. Soon he let out a groan, but the sound was odd as the tube in his throat was blocking his vocal cords from operating properly.

Cody began making gagging motions, and his fingers and arms slowly came to life. The anesthesiologist came in and stood beside us, watching Cody's monitors and his movements. Though he still hadn't opened his eyes, Cody began to fight against his neck brace and the groans came more frequently.

Dr. Grant had warned us about the effects of coming off the medication, but this seemed excruciating. "Is this normal?" I asked the anesthesiologist. He waited a second before answering.

"Yes, but maybe we can help lessen the effects by bringing him out a little more slowly." He pushed some buttons on the medication equipment and in just a few seconds Cody calmed back down and returned to his former lifeless state. "We'll try keeping him at a little higher dose for a while then we'll try again. This should help a little with the confusion."

After an hour or so he returned, and the same process was repeated. The dosage was lowered, Cody began fighting and gagging, and they increased the medication level. By late that evening, they had tried bringing Cody out several times and the result was always the same. Each time I prayed that Cody would be able to make it out and wake up without trouble, but to no avail. Late that night Dr. Grant came to check in on us and told us the game plan.

"Cody's reaction to the medication is normal, and that's a good sign. Eventually we're going to need to let him come all the way out. It's probably going to be difficult to watch, but we can wait until the morning for that. Tomorrow is going to be a big day, try to get some rest." Dr. Grant's characteristic smile that had been missing earlier in the day had returned, giving me a little more faith in the process. If Dr. Grant was okay with what was going on, I guess I should follow his lead.

Kreg left to be with the girls and I set up my normal sleeping arrangement: layers of hospital towels on the floor next to Cody's bed, a hospital sheet over the towels, a pillow at the top, and then a blanket to cover me. The room was too small to bring in a cot or a second bed, and I had grown tired of trying to sleep in the hospital chairs, so I commandeered the materials from an unattended housekeeping cart. I knew the nurses weren't exactly pleased with the arrangement, but they didn't stop me. I never slept soundly, but it was better than leaving Cody alone.

The next morning the anesthesiologist returned and lowered the dosage again, but he stayed in the room to watch. When Cody began writhing and gagging, he called in a doctor. They consulted about Cody's strength and condition and decided it was time to take out his breathing tube.

They snaked the tube out of his mouth and Cody took several deep breaths. He continued twisting and fighting, but not as much as before.

I felt like we had passed over the worst of it, but as the doctors continued to lower the dosage of anesthesia Cody began moaning and wincing in reaction to the pain. Up until this point I had been worried mostly about his brain injury, I had nearly forgotten about all the pain that he was going to feel as he finally experienced the full force of his injuries.

The doctors began administering morphine to help Cody with the pain as they lowered the dosage of the drugs that had held him in a coma. That left Cody in a weird state of semi-consciousness. He opened his eyes a little and started mouthing words, but nothing made sense. Was that the brain injury or the morphine, or was this just how Cody would be from now on?

The what-ifs that I had been holding back were suddenly becoming real, and I could resist them no longer. Would Cody ever walk again? Would he speak? Would he live the rest of his life with impaired reasoning or cognitive ability? Would he ever return to school? Would he grow up and marry and have children? It seemed impossible that after the fractures to his skull, the fluid that had leaked around his head, and the swelling and the pressure on his brain that he would emerge unscathed. It was just a matter of time before I knew what kind of life Cody would have, and the wait was killing me.

Late in the afternoon Kreg and I sat in the chairs along the wall and watched Cody, waiting for any sign of improvement. He seemed to be in and out of sleep, or maybe it was just the medication, we couldn't tell. As the sun set to the west, a narrow beam of light crept through the curtains in an adjoining room, reflected off some glass, and rested on Cody's face. I didn't notice it until Cody's eyes shot open and he gasped, staring straight into the light.

"Kreg!" I yelled, and we jumped to our feet.

Cody sat up in a flash, shot his arms out in front of him, and kept squeezing his right fist like he was hitting the brakes on a motorcycle. He started screaming, "Ahhhh! Dad! Dad! The headlights!" Kreg tried helping

Cody lower his arms, but he wouldn't budge. Cody's blood pressure monitor started to sound an alarm as his heart rate rose rapidly.

"Just calm down buddy, it's okay," Kreg said.

"Dad! Dad! Take the motorcycle!" Cody screamed as he twisted the imaginary handlebars left and right. Nurses started running in and were trying to calm Cody down, but the more they tried, the more upset he got.

"Please! Take the motorcycle, I can't stop!" Cody cried out as he thrashed around.

"Okay, okay, I've got the motorcycle!" Kreg said as he placed his hands over Cody's and pretended to take the handlebars.

"You're lying! Why won't you take it?" Cody shouted, and swung his arms to the right. His injured right arm smashed up against the bed rail and Cody screamed. Almost instantly a steady stream of blood began flowing out of the bandages and running down his outstretched arm. The eight-inch incision along the back side of his arm where they had just operated was torn open and bleeding profusely. As he kept swinging his arms wildly the blood splattered all over his hospital gown, the bed, the floor, and everyone around him.

One of the nurses stepped up to Kreg and spoke quickly, "He's probably allergic to the morphine, I've got some drugs that will knock him out, but I'm only allowed to administer it if he's nauseous." The nurse looked Kreg in the eye and pointed to Cody. "Is he nauseous?" he asked directly. Cody was still flailing around and the amount of blood coming from his arm was frightening.

"Yes, he's nauseous!" Kreg responded, understanding the game. The nurse immediately ran out the door and was back in just a few seconds with a full syringe. He inserted the syringe into Cody's IV and shot the medication into his drip line. Within seconds, Cody was unconscious again. The nurses worked quickly to clean up Cody's arm and stop the bleeding, and a doctor came in to examine the wound and re-stitch the incision.

Kreg sat down next to me and we both stared at each other, breathing heavily from the sudden jolt of activity. Neither of us were exactly sure what had just happened.

"Honey," Kreg said, "Cody's awake! That was him! He was talking and moving and he knew who I was!" I nodded, taking it all in. Cody could talk. He could move. He remembered riding motorcycles. He heard Kreg's reply and responded to it. Of course there were a thousand other things that could go wrong, but half of my fears about Cody's future vanished in a second. As the nurses worried and fretted about Cody's bleeding arm, Kreg and I smiled at each other. It was the best thing to happen in days.

By the next morning the doctors finally got Cody's medication figured out and had him stabilized enough to bring him out of the coma with minimal pain. Cody slowly opened his eyes and began searching the room, obviously confused.

"Mom?" Cody asked cautiously.

"Hey honey, we're right here, me and Dad. And grandpa and grandma and the girls and lots of other people, they're in another room, but they're here to see you." I tried to ease him into the situation as he woke up and struggled to focus.

"What's going on?"

"You and Jeff were in an accident. You're in the hospital, but it's going to be okay."

"Where's Jeff? What happened to him?" Cody became visibly upset.

"Jeff is in Idaho Falls, we're down here in Salt Lake City. Jeff had to have a couple surgeries up there, but we've been talking to his mom and dad every day, and he's doing okay."

"But we were just fishing, we caught... we caught some fish. I don't remember... how long...what time is it?"

"It's Tuesday morning, you got in the crash last Thursday when you were coming home from fishing, so it's been a few days."

"What did they do to my legs?" Cody asked, looking at the rods sticking out of his sides. We spent the rest of the evening explaining to him what the doctors had done for his pelvis, neck, arm, and head. We talked about how we had thought we were going to lose him, how we prayed and prayed, how many ward members and relatives had visited, and how kind the doctors and nurses had been. Within an hour, Cody seemed to be all caught up and completely awake. He seemed to have no recollection past fishing, no idea why they crashed or what had caused it, no memory of the accident or even of his spontaneous motorcycle ride in the hospital bed the previous evening. Besides a little memory loss though, he was back to normal.

Dr. Grant came to see us that morning and ran Cody through a few cognitive tests and checked his reflexes. "I'll say Cody, you sure have done well. I can tell you're a fighter!" Dr. Grant smiled and Cody smiled back. "Now, I know it's summertime, but I've got to give you some homework. There are some very good physical therapists who are going to work with you, and they're going to push you, and you need to do everything they tell you to do. Will you do that?"

"Yeah," Cody nodded and smiled.

"Alright then, I'll hold you to it." Dr. Grant then turned to us and motioned us to follow him into the hall. Once we were a few paces from the door he stopped and turned to us. "I truly am impressed with the progress he's made, he's doing really well. That said, our latest CT scan shows that there is still some leaking of cerebral fluid, which we need to watch. There may also be some underlying mental impairment that we haven't seen yet. His speech is a little slow, which might be connected to the head trauma. We just need to be really careful about watching him and if there's anything that seems out of the ordinary, you need to let us know.

"Also, it appears there might be some damage to his left eye. It might be the nerve or the eye itself or the part of the brain that processes the optical information, I can't be sure, but I know he's lost some peripheral vision. That may or may not come back, we'll just have to wait and see. But, all things considered, he looks like he's going to be fine. I don't say this very often, but Cody's condition is an absolute miracle." He smiled and patted my shoulder and shook Kreg's hand, then went on down the hall to attend to other patients.

Kreg wrapped his arms around me in a big hug that seemed to last forever. We didn't say anything, but in the silence was a mutual sigh of relief. Just days earlier all had seemed hopeless and Cody's life was hanging by a thread. Even after he was stabilized, we never dreamed we would have it this easy. Heavenly Father was indeed watching over us. We had received our miracle.

EIGHT

OUR FAMILY MEMBERS AND FRIENDS WERE ALL TOO EAGER TO SEE Cody and talk with him. One by one they came in and hugged him and told him how happy they were to see him. Cody loved all the attention. He had always loved having lots of people around, and the constant rotation of family and friends lifted his spirits.

The good news of Cody's recovery had completely shifted my mood. Of course, I was still worried about Cody's condition, and very protective of him, but it felt like a thousand pounds had been lifted off my shoulders. I could think clearly and sleep at night, I could eat and talk with my family and friends, and I wasn't deathly afraid of leaving Cody alone for just a few minutes.

After the initial shock of what had happened, Cody returned to his normal 16-year-old self and began joking with the nurses. Many of the nurses loved Cody's positive attitude and seemed to make excuses just to visit and talk with him. I guess in a trauma unit, having someone who is so cheerful and fun is a welcome relief from the pain and suffering that is so much more common.

Cody soon realized the position of power he was in with the nurses and began making special requests. One of the male nurses who checked in on Cody asked him if there was anything he could get for him, and Cody seemed to have it all planned out.

"Yeah, you know what would be really cool? Chocolate milk! Oh man, that would taste so good!" Cody rolled his eyes and made moaning sounds showing just how dreamy it sounded. I was his mother, I had seen that act before and knew exactly what he was up to, but I let it pass.

The nurse just laughed and said he'd see what he could do.

A few minutes later he returned with a large styrofoam cup filled with chocolate milk. Cody made the most exaggerated sounds of satisfaction as he downed every drop.

"Can I have some more?" he asked as he held out the empty cup.

"Really?" the nurse laughed, "That was almost a whole quart!"

"Oh, but it was just so good!" Cody continued to hold the cup out in front of him.

"Okay, just one more!" The nurse shook his head and returned in a few more minutes with another cup, which Cody drank just like the first. That night at dinner Cody asked for more chocolate milk, but they were out.

In the morning when the nurse returned for his shift, he walked into the room and held up a whole gallon jug of chocolate milk with "Cody" written on it in black marker.

"Thirsty?" he asked.

"Yeah! That looks so good!" Cody said, and had another large cup full. For the next several days, a new gallon of chocolate milk would appear each morning and disappear throughout the day.

I was so grateful for the good doctors and nurses. After several days of long shifts, they would come in and let us know that they were going to be off for the next few days and wished us well. We protested when some of our favorite nurses had to leave, but fell in love with the new ones as they rotated in.

A few days after Cody woke up, they decided to move us out of the trauma unit and into a recovery room. We were happy to have made that step forward but sad to leave the nurses and doctors there. We also lost our dedicated family room and all our family had to stay in the general waiting room. Our girls were finally able to come in and see Cody more regularly, which put some of their fears at ease, but the pelvic fixator and all of Cody's monitoring equipment made them a little uneasy.

We spent the next week or so doing mild physical therapy, working to improve mobility in the neck, arm, and legs. Doctors continued to take Cody in for CT scans regularly to check the leaks around the brain, but things seemed to be getting back to normal.

Ten days after we had arrived, one of the nurses helped Kreg move

Cody to a wheelchair, and we went for a walk around the outside of the hospital. It was nice to finally get some fresh air and sunshine, as I had barely been outside at all since the accident. From high up in the Avenues, we could see down into the Salt Lake Valley. It looked like a sea of trees, cradled up against the Wasatch mountains. It was pretty, but it made me miss the fields and hills and rural atmosphere of Idaho Falls.

The nurse with us seemed to read my mind. "Cody's doing really well. I think the doctors were talking about releasing you in a couple days. Would you be nervous to go home, or would that be exciting?"

"Oh, that would be exciting, of course!" I responded. When Cody was still in the coma, Dr. Grant had mentioned that we could expect to be there for four or five weeks. To think of going home in just a couple days made my heart race. Oh, how good it would be to sleep in my own bed, to sit around with the family and talk and laugh! It had only been ten days, but our time in Salt Lake had felt like a lifetime. I had exhausted a lifetime's worth of emotions, at least.

The excitement was real, but then the nervousness came. Cody was still in need of constant physical care. He couldn't walk, couldn't go to the bathroom by himself, and it would be 10 or 11 more weeks before he could get the fixator removed. It would be a lot of work to take care of Cody by myself at home, and I didn't have the slightest clue how to do it.

When we were back inside I pulled the attending physician into our room. "The nurse mentioned that we might be able to go home in a couple days. What do we have to do to make that happen?"

The doctor looked at me like I had just spoiled a big surprise. "Well, we have talked about it, but there's a lot to do before you can leave."

"What do we need to do, we'll start right now." I offered. The doctor then went through a long list of tests that needed to be concluded, physical therapy checks that had to be completed, and training that we had to receive to take care of Cody. Kreg and I committed to doing our part and got started as soon as we could.

We spent the next two days arranging for physical therapists and speech therapists to come to our home and learning our responsibilities for Cody's care. The nurses taught us how to clean the wounds on Cody's neck and arm and how to change bandages. We learned how to clean and disinfect the rods drilled into his pelvis in order to keep him from developing an infection.

By the 12th day, we were ready to go. The only thing we still hadn't figured out was transportation. The hospital gave us a quote for transporting Cody to Idaho Falls by ambulance or plane, but it was astronomical. We had great insurance through Kreg's work, but the transportation from the hospital to our home was left up to us.

We thought about bringing down our SUV or our truck, but Cody couldn't bend fully at the waist because of the pelvic fixator, so he couldn't safely fit in a normal vehicle. Then my dad offered, "What about the motorhome?" He had a point, the motorhome had a bed Cody could lay on for the whole ride, but it was a tight squeeze and we weren't sure Cody could fit through the door with the rods.

Kreg and one of the nurses devised a plan. They got one of the backboards used for transporting emergency victims and strapped Cody to it. Then they measured how he fit on it and took the board out to the parking lot. It was a really tight fit, but by holding the board at an angle, and tilting it upward, they could get it in the motorhome and back to the narrow single bed where he could lie down for the whole drive. It was tricky, but it could work.

Finally, our preparations were finished and the time had come to go home. We collected stacks and stacks of paperwork, said goodbye to all our nurses and doctors, and packed our things into the motorhome. Cody was lifted onto the backboard and half a dozen large velcro straps were used to secure him to the board. Kreg and several nurses walked him out of the hospital to the motorhome. Cody was a little nervous about being tilted and lifted through the narrow door. If the rods in his hips were bumped at all it was excruciating for him, and there was only about an inch to spare as they slid him through the door, but the men took their time and got Cody in safely. The nurses let us keep the backboard, and we set off for Idaho.

I couldn't have been happier to get home. I had my parents and my husband and my patient daughters and my dear son Cody all together. Life was going to be complicated for a while with Cody's recovery, but there was a bright horizon ahead of us. All of us had survived the most harrowing ordeal of our lives, and we were so grateful for good friends and family, kind doctors and nurses, the blessings of modern medicine, the power of priesthood blessings, and a kind Heavenly Father who heard our prayers.

Pulling into our neighborhood felt like crossing the finish line of a long, long race. There were many family and friends there to cheer us on and help us get settled. Our good neighbors had arranged for a hospital bed to be set up in our front room, and they had taken care of our house while we were gone.

Cody watched out the window as we pulled up in front of the house. "I guess I got out of mowing the lawn, huh?" he said with a chuckle, taking a good look at the freshly cut grass that some kind neighbor had mowed. It was a little too soon for jokes like that, but Kreg played along. "Yeah right buddy! As soon as you're out of bed, you're mowing the lawn for the rest of your life!" he replied in a phony stern voice. I just shook my head at them. Yep, things were getting back to normal.

Several of Cody's uncles helped carry him out of the motorhome and into the hospital bed. Our split-level home was terrible for someone with limited mobility, so the only place to put him was in our little living room right inside the doorway. Just up the stairs were the dining room and the kitchen, and down the stairs were the bedrooms. There were just a few feet around each side of the bed, but we put a few chairs around the room for visitors and moved the TV in there to keep Cody occupied.

It ended up being the best place for him because we had so many people coming in and out of the house to see Cody. The physical therapist came three times a week to help him stretch and flex and regain muscle. Cody moaned and groaned about having to do his "stupid exercises," but it was the mental exercises that really wore Cody out.

Cody had lost some ability to retain short-term and working memory, so a speech therapist worked with Cody to restore his mental capabilities. Twice a week they would go through a series of tests and brain games. Sometimes the therapist would give him simple but long math problems, asking him questions like, "what is eight plus four, minus five, plus three, plus ten, minus two," and so on. The better Cody got, the longer the math problems became.

Other times the therapist would hold a picture with hundreds of items up for Cody to see for just a short time, then ask him to draw what he remembered. These games went on for an hour or more. I usually sat in on the therapy sessions or listened from upstairs in the kitchen, and they wore me out, but Cody was totally exhausted after each one. Once the therapist left Cody would fall right asleep and take a nap for two or three hours.

By the evening though, Cody was awake and ready for action. Almost as soon as we got home, one or two of his friends would show up every evening to hang out and watch Nascar or baseball or just sit around and talk. Two friends turned into five, and that turned into fifteen. One night we had 28 kids jammed in nearly every available square foot of our living room and dining room, all there to laugh and play games and talk with Cody. All of the love and friendship that Cody had shared over the years was coming back to him. Kids we never knew came out of the woodwork to tell Cody how much he meant to them and how they wished him well. For a teenager who loved being surrounded by friends, it was a dream come true.

My vision of perfection was coming true as well. Cody's miraculous recovery had renewed our faith and lifted our spirits, and we recommitted our family to scripture study, prayer, and family home evening. Kreg took the lead most nights, and I could tell that he took seriously the promises he made to God in the hospital. He was always a great father, but now he was really taking charge as the presiding priesthood holder in our home, leading gospel discussions and making sure we had family prayer each night.

Often times our commitment to scripture study and family prayer would get tested by the huge number of kids that had invaded our home, but we held strong. Some of the kids were LDS, some were not, but when it was bedtime for the girls, it was time for scriptures and prayers, no matter who was there. A few of the kids decided to leave, but most stayed and listened. After a while they all just got used to it, and nobody ever complained to us about it.

Besides the crowds in the evenings and the hour or two with the therapist during the day, Cody's life was pure boredom. I still had to take care of the girls and make the meals and do the laundry, so I couldn't be with Cody all the time. Daytime TV grew old really fast, and Cody wasn't really the kind of kid who loved to just sit and read. The only thing that really kept him entertained was pestering me.

"Hey Mooooooom!" Cody would yell while I was down in the laundry room.

"What do you need Cody?" I would ask after walking up to the living room.

"Can I get some water?"

"You have some water in your mug right there," I said as I pointed to the large plastic hospital mug he had resting by his bed.

"Oh, yeah, can I get some ice then?"

"Sure Cody." I tried really hard to not get annoyed and just be glad to have my son back, but sometimes it got really tiring.

Cody loved to be in the outdoors or out on some sort of adventure, and being cooped up with mom all day was torture. When his friends began summer conditioning for football, Cody nearly died. He wanted to be out there playing so bad and swore that as soon as he got out of that bed he was going to go play touch football with his friends. I threatened him with his life if he dared to try something like that before he was all better, but he kept dreaming.

When school started in September just after Labor Day, Cody was still confined to his bed. It had been four weeks since we had come home, and he needed about seven more weeks before the pelvic fixator could be removed. We talked with the school and decided to follow the curriculum at home for the first trimester and then reevaluate the situation when he was able to get out of bed at the end of October. Cody's friends would bring his homework and assignments to him each day and take his completed work back to school for us. Kreg was back to work like normal, so I sat with Cody while the girls were at school and went over math or history or science lessons. The school work kept us busy for much of the day, which was a blessing for both me and him.

After what seemed like forever, the 12 weeks were up and it was time to get the pelvic fixator removed. Cody counted down the days with anticipation, like it was Christmas or his birthday. We got permission to go to our family doctor and friend Dr. Lewis up in Rexburg for the removal. The 30-minute drive to Rexburg was much better than having to drive all the way back down to Salt Lake City. Cody was put under and Dr. Lewis unscrewed the rods from the bone and stitched up the holes in Cody's sides. The physical therapy had kept Cody's leg muscles in shape, but we were still told to keep Cody on crutches for at least a couple weeks until he regained his balance.

Cody felt like a free man and would go outside and up and down the sidewalk on his crutches as much as he could. He was still a teenager though, thinking he was invincible and always pushing the limits. One afternoon I had left him home while I ran to pick up the girls from school. As I drove back down our street I could see a group of Cody's friends standing in our driveway, but I didn't see Cody or his crutches. Then I saw it. Racing down the street in the opposite direction was Cody on one of his friends' dirt bikes. Cody got in the driveway before I did and tried to get off the bike, but our eyes met and he knew he had blown it. I parked the car in the street and marched right up to him and his friends.

"Really Cody? You should be more grateful! Now get off that motorcycle!" Cody knew it was better to just say nothing at that point and do as his mother said. You should have seen the look on his friends' faces as I marched Cody on his crutches back up to the house. I think I struck the fear of God into them, and probably for the better because they didn't try anything like that again.

By late October, Jeff had been released from the hospital in Idaho Falls and was on crutches as well. Cody and Jeff had talked on the phone a couple times, but they both wanted to see each other again as soon as they could. Jeff's parents agreed to bring him over to our house, and the two boys saw each other for the first time in three months. I worried about what kind of a relationship they would have, but if anything the accident drew them closer together. They sat and talked for hours, comparing scars and injuries, while Kreg and I visited with Lyn and Betty about their experiences and how close they had come to losing Jeff. Jeff had almost died twice in the hospital and his heart had to be restarted with a defibrillator. What a terrible thing for both boys to have gone through, and what a miracle it was that both had survived.

By the start of the second trimester Cody was ready to go back to school and officially start his junior year. I'm not sure which he was more excited for, to be out of the house and away from mom and dad for a change, or to make sure the girls he liked were still single. From the way he talked after school about girls and friends and dating and the sports teams, you would think he didn't spend a second paying attention in class, but somehow his grades were as good as ever. Cody soon ditched his crutches and began talking about playing sports again. He knew he couldn't play that year, but he talked a big game about how he was going to be the star his senior year. I had to pick my battles, so I let him dream, even though there was no way I was letting him onto the football field again as long as he was under my roof.

As unique as our circumstances were, our life was nearly back to normal. We had dodged a bullet, received our miracle, and were getting on with our lives. Or so we thought.

Just a week or two after he returned to school, Cody came home and was sitting at the dining room table doing his homework while I was making dinner.

"Hey mom, look at this," Cody said with a level voice. I turned around to see him leaning forward on his elbows with his head tilted down at an angle. A quick and steady drip of clear liquid was coming from his nose.

"Ew, Cody, stop that! Not on the table!" I said as I grabbed a few paper towels and walked over to hand them to him.

"No, mom, I'm not sick, and it's not snot," he replied. I could tell he was a little nervous. "And it only happens right at this angle, look," and he tilted his head up just slightly and the dripping stopped. Then he returned his head to the former spot and the liquid quickly returned and started forming a little puddle on the table. I sat and watched in stunned silence, then remembered Dr. Grant's warning about watching for anything unusual.

I reached for the phone, "I'm calling the doctor."

NINE

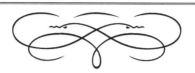

I T TOOK A WHILE BEFORE I FOUND SOMEONE AT LDS HOSPITAL WHO knew what was going on with Cody and was willing to listen to me. They assumed at first that it was some normal nasal fluid, but the more I kept describing what I saw, the more concerned they became. I kept hoping that they would have some normal explanation and tell me not to worry, but I could hear the worry in their voices.

The doctor I spoke with recommended that we drive Cody down and come in to see them. As much as I was concerned about Cody, I wasn't interested in making another late-night trip to Salt Lake at the spur of the moment. I had done that once before and never wanted to do it again.

I asked if there was someone in Idaho Falls that we could see who would be able to diagnose the issue, and they referred me to an Ear, Nose and Throat specialist in Rexburg. I immediately called the doctor and tried to get an appointment, but because it wasn't an emergency and there was no immediate pain, they decided to schedule a consultation for the next day. I wished we could have gone in that evening, if for no other reason than to just alleviate my fears, but I made the appointment.

When Kreg got home I had Cody show him what was going on, and Kreg was just as baffled as I was. The only thing I could think of was that it was excess fluid in the head that was draining through his sinuses. I tried not to act so worried in front of Cody, but I couldn't imagine how this was not a terrible thing. Clear fluid was not supposed to just drain out of your head like that. Something was obviously wrong, and I didn't have the slightest clue how they would fix it. Would they need to do brain surgery? Was it something easy they could fix in a single visit? Was this a symptom of some bigger problem that the doctors in Salt Lake City had missed?

I didn't get much sleep that night, and my tiredness the next day just compounded my worries. Kreg was able to stay home from work to go to the appointment with me, and after we dropped the girls off at school we drove Cody up to Rexburg.

"Well, my best guess is that there is a leak somewhere and the cerebrospinal fluid is draining into the sinuses." The doctor said after Cody showed him how he could get the fluid to drain out of his nose on command. "I couldn't tell you why it only happens at that angle, but we can put a scope up through the nose and try to see what's going on in there." The doctor acted so nonchalant about it all, like it was just some puzzle that needed to be figured out.

"So what does that mean?" I asked, trying to tease any additional information out of him.

"Well, it's not an immediate threat to his health, as far as I can tell. It may fix itself in time, but it's best to just have a look and see." The doctor had Cody lay down as he began gathering the necessary equipment to make an evaluation. He then placed a tiny camera up through Cody's nose and carefully monitored a computer screen that displayed the inside of the sinuses. I couldn't tell what anything was, but the doctor seemed quite interested in one particular spot.

"If you come over here a little closer, I'll show you what we're looking at," the doctor said, as he pointed to the screen. Kreg and I leaned in but still had no idea what we were looking at.

"The images the hospital sent up showed that there were several fractures on the face near the sinuses from Cody's accident, these are all healing nicely. Now look here," he pointed to a spot on the screen that looked red and swollen. "This area here has not joined properly and there is still a gap."

The doctor turned to face Cody and placed his finger right on Cody's forehead, "Right about here, the fracture is still loose. When Cody tilts his head, it shifts the bones in the skull just right and puts just enough pressure on the brain to push that fluid through the gap and into the sinus cavity." The doctor ran his finger down Cody's forehead to the top of the nose, showing us how the fluid would leak through the gap into his nose. He then turned back to us.

"The problem is that it's not just the bone that's holding the cerebrospinal fluid around the brain, there are several layers of matter that act as a protective sac. If fluid is leaking, we've not only got a gap in the bone, and high fluid pressure, but we're also facing a tear in that sac. From what I'm seeing here, I believe this is not an injury that is going to repair itself very quickly, or at all. I'm going to recommend that we seal the sac through endoscopic surgery."

Oh man, not again. Hadn't we had enough surgeries to last a lifetime?

"This is a simple surgery with a very high success rate. We won't have to make any incisions, we'll simply run the tools up through the nose to the point of the leak, then seal it up."

"How soon could we get this done?" Kreg asked.

"If you have the time, we can get it taken care of today."

I let out a sigh, not fully realizing that I had been holding my breath. Seeing the inside of Cody's sinuses had been making me a little sick, but I was glad it was about to be over.

"Of course, let's get it fixed," Kreg said.

"Great. Now, before we get started, I have a few more questions for you Cody, if you don't mind?" the doctor said as he removed the camera from Cody's nose.

"Sure," Cody said.

"Have you been having headaches lately?"

"Yeah," Cody responded. He hadn't said much to me about it, but he had seemed a little off lately.

"And your left eye Cody, it seems to be drifting toward the right. I didn't see anything about that on your charts, is that something you've always had?"

"Uh, no. It's kinda new." Cody said, not sure exactly how to respond.

Kreg jumped in, "They said he lost some of his peripheral vision in the accident. I noticed that the eye was a little off, but I just figured it was all related to the accident. Do you think it's a problem?"

The doctor turned back to Cody, "I don't know, Cody, does it bother you?"

"Well, yeah, at least at school. It makes me look kinda funny." That was Cody, always concerned about what the girls would think about his looks.

"Does your eye hurt, or does it impair your vision?"

"Not really. Well, maybe a little. It's been getting a little worse lately." Cody said. I was surprised that he had been keeping track.

The doctor spun around and faced Kreg and me again. "There's a very good eye surgeon in Idaho Falls, Dr. Ben Hoggan, I'd recommend that you set up an appointment and have the eye looked at again. They can do some amazing things to correct the 'lazy eye,' and that may be contributing to the headaches as well."

Kreg and I looked at each other and smiled, "Yeah, we know Ben," Kreg said. Ben had been a friend of ours back in high school and we had stayed in touch through the years. "He's a good friend of mine. I'll give him a call."

"Alright, well, let's get this leak taken care of and then we'll let Dr. Hoggan work on that eye for you!" The doctor invited us to head out to the waiting room as he started prepping Cody for the procedure. In less than an hour Cody emerged from the back of the office, a little rattled but for the most part he looked fine.

I was glad to have the leak fixed, but now we had to worry about his eye. That night as Kreg and I lay in bed, I complained to him, "I'm just so done with all these doctors and surgeries. Why can't this all just be over with?"

He waited a moment, then replied, "I don't know. We've given him priesthood blessings, we're doing everything we're supposed to do, it seemed like it was all going to be over when we left Salt Lake. I guess I've been asking myself the same question." I was glad Kreg understood how I felt, but a little scared that he didn't have an answer for me.

After all our time in Salt Lake, I still didn't understand why something like this would happen to us, or why we would continue to face problems after doing everything we were supposed to do. Dr. Grant seemed to believe that it was not because we needed to be taught some lesson.

The thought drew my mind to the story of Jesus and the young blind man. People asked Jesus if the man was blind because of his sin, or the parents' sin, and he said neither, but he was blind so that God's works might be made manifest in him. Was that the reason Cody was not protected, so God could make his works manifest in him also? That didn't seem fair, but if it was God's purpose, then hadn't it already been accomplished? The faith of my whole family had been strengthened by the miraculous recovery Cody had made. So why more trials? I couldn't figure it out. My mind struggled with the idea for some time, then I drifted off to sleep.

The first part of the next week we went in to see our old friend Ben Hoggan. He checked Cody's eyes, measured how much of the peripheral vision had been lost, and tested him on a variety of machines. His diagnosis was worse than we thought.

"Well, Kreg and Brenda, I wish I had good news, but it's a little more complicated than I had hoped," Ben started off. "The muscles in the left eye are getting weak, which is causing the eye to wander, or appear lazy. That could be happening for a number of reasons, given the nature of his accident and the head trauma. Now, there's a relatively common surgery to shorten and tighten up those muscles, but because we haven't tracked how quickly the eye has weakened, I'm not sure we want to do that. I think we need to wait, as long as it's not causing Cody any immediate problems, and see where it ends up. If we do it now we run the risk of having the muscles loosen up again, if we haven't found the root cause. Which brings me to another point." Kreg and I listened attentively, Ben's tone told me something was wrong.

"I measured the pressure on the back of the eye, and the left eye is close to normal, but there is a significant amount of pressure on the right eye, which is pushing it out of the socket just slightly." Both Kreg and I turned to look at Cody's eyes to see if we could notice a difference. Cody, not wanting to be the subject of our inspections, avoided our glances and looked down at his feet. He brought his hand up to his right eye and felt around it.

"Yeah," Cody mumbled, "I've sort of felt that for a while, but I thought it was just kind of like a headache or something."

Ben nodded his head, "Well then, this may be related to the cerebral fluid leak and the surgery you just had, and it might just go away on its own. We should probably just give it some time and keep monitoring the pressure behind the eye. Hopefully, as the wound in the skull heals, the pressure will decrease and your eyes will return to normal." That sounded like a positive outlook, but I could tell Ben was reserving his optimism. "If not, then we'll look at surgical options."

Cody spoke up, "Is there any way to make it not look so funny?"

"Not really. You could wear an eye patch to try and train the eye, but that's probably not much better. The five-year-old boys who come in sometimes get excited about looking like a pirate, but I'm guessing that's not your style." Ben chuckled.

Cody didn't laugh, "Uh, no thanks."

We agreed to come back for weekly checkups to monitor the pressure, and I drove Cody home while Kreg returned to work. I knew there was something bothering Cody and tried to get him to open up.

"Hey Cody, so I know this eye thing is no fun. Are you alright with everything?" I expected it to take a while for Cody to tell me what was going on, but he opened right up.

"Mom, I just hate looking stupid. My left eye makes me look like Quasimodo, and now the other one is starting to look weird too."

"Do kids tease you about it?"

"No," Cody answered shyly, "I just, I can see it in the mirror, and sometimes when people look at me I can tell they're staring at my eye. They don't say anything because they're trying to be nice, but I can tell they see it." Cody had always been very concerned with his looks. He commonly spent half an hour in the morning combing his hair until it was just right. Since the accident, I knew that he had been worried about what people would think of him, but his friends had been so good to him that I figured it wasn't an issue.

Maybe now that he was back at school, the novelty had worn off and Cody was having to interact with kids who weren't so kind or accepting. The mother in me wanted to just march into his school and give all the kids a lecture about how they needed to treat him kindly, but I knew that would never work. This was going to have to be a battle he would fight on his own. I had no idea that Cody's eye was going to be the least of his worries.

Cody, Kira, Brooke & Krissa, fall of 1999.
Photo taken after Cody had the pelvic fixator removed and as pressure began
building behind his right eye.

TEN

WE MADE WEEKLY APPOINTMENTS WITH OUR FRIEND DR. HOGGAN to monitor the pressure behind Cody's eyes. The fact that one eye was lazy and the other eye was bulging didn't affect his sight, surprisingly, but it continued to wear on his self-esteem. Week by week the bulge became more noticeable, and Cody became more self-conscious and withdrawn.

After a few weeks his eye looked like it might just pop right out of the socket. Kreg and I felt terrible. Our kids relied on us to protect them and fix their problems when they arose, but this was a problem we couldn't fix.

When Cody was unconscious in the hospital after his accident, Kreg and I were terrified about the potential outcome, but by the time he woke up we had a better idea of what was happening and how to proceed. Though we had been terrified, Cody saw very little of that. This time, Cody was fully aware of the medical dilemma ahead of him, and he knew that neither we nor the doctors had a plan to fix it. Of course, we tried to tell him that it would all be alright and that the doctors would find a solution, but his growing fear and worry told me he didn't really believe us. Maybe if I wasn't so terrified myself, those words of comfort would have been more believable.

Dr. Hoggan didn't seem to have much optimism either. He became more worried at each visit, and our fears about lingering problems in the brain grew day by day. By early November, Dr. Hoggan knew the problem wasn't going away on its own and he recommended we get another MRI. The head of the radiology department at our local hospital was another friend from high school, Dr. Scott Wood, and he agreed to take a look at Cody.

Cody was becoming a pro at the MRI procedure, but he didn't like the idea of doing another one. Cody was sure that whatever they found in this MRI wasn't going to be good either. He was right.

After the procedure was complete and the results came in, Dr. Wood brought the three of us into his office. He greeted us kindly but gave only a forced smile.

"The MRI results are back and we believe we've discovered what has been causing the increased pressure behind Cody's eyes," Dr. Wood explained without the slightest hint of joy. Finding the cause should have been good news, but his reservation told me otherwise. I held my breath. "The MRI revealed a leak in the carotid artery, just above the sinuses at the base of the brain. It's very hard to see, even when you know what you're looking for, but it's there. The leak is allowing blood to seep into the cavernous sinus, right behind the eyes and underneath the brain." Dr. Wood pointed to a tiny spot on the black-and-white plastic film that showed slices of Cody's skull.

"So can we fix it the same way we fixed the last leak?" Kreg asked, always looking for the solution.

"Unfortunately, no. That was a separation in the plates of the skull, this is a tear in the wall of the artery. This is quite a bit trickier. The damaged artery is nearly in the center of the head, there is really no easy way to get to it. Very few people even know how to work on it, because most of the time when a leak like this is discovered, it's after a hemorrhage, not before." Dr. Wood leaned back in his chair.

What did he mean about these leaks usually being discovered after a hemorrhage? Was a hemorrhage imminent? How much time did we have? Was Cody in danger? I wanted to ask Dr. Wood so many questions, but Kreg spoke up first.

"What happens then, if there's a hemorrhage?"

Dr. Wood chose his words carefully, "A hemorrhage occurs when the blood vessel bursts open completely, and there is uncontrolled bleeding. It's a form of a stroke. If blood doesn't get to part of the brain, that part will be damaged, permanently." Dr. Wood paused, but I could tell he was holding back. He wanted to tell us that it could cause death, but he didn't want to say that in front of Cody. His tone became more optimistic, if just for Cody's sake, "But, we've found it in time, and we can fix it before it becomes a problem." I was stunned. I had no idea things were this bad.

Dr. Wood picked up a piece of paper lying on his desk and stared at it. "I made a few calls to some colleagues of mine. As far as I can tell, there are only two doctors who have successfully performed this type of operation. One of them is in Arizona, and the other is at LDS Hospital in Salt Lake City."

"We'd like to go to Salt Lake, if it's all the same," I said as I looked over at Kreg, seeking his approval. Dr. Wood's dire prediction about a hemorrhage had me anxious to get the procedure done. Kreg agreed.

"I figured you'd say that," Dr. Wood replied, as he took the piece of paper and slid it across the desk. "The doctor's name is Dean Jackson, he's an interventional radiologist, that means he does surgery with the help of x-rays, and he's an expert on the brain. I called his office and requested that they hold the next available slot for you, which is about a week from now. You'll need to call them as soon as possible to confirm the appointment. I would clear your schedule to make room for this, time really is of the essence." Dr. Wood looked at Kreg directly, then me, but avoided Cody. The look in his eye sent a message from one parent to another: your child is in danger, don't put this off. Cody didn't seem to notice the underlying tone, and if he did, he didn't say anything.

We shook Dr. Wood's hand and thanked him for his help. I didn't want to ask my questions anymore, especially in front of Cody. His message was clear and I didn't want to know how bad it really might be, or how much time we really had. I just needed to get it fixed and then it would be over, no need to know how bad it might be otherwise.

We scheduled the appointment, made arrangements with the school, and found a place for the girls to stay the night before the operation. It was supposed to be a quick recovery, so we could drive Cody home the next morning if everything went well. The operation was a week away, and I waited on pins and needles, hoping nothing would go wrong with his artery or his eyes in the meantime. Cody's headaches were getting pretty bad and were fairly constant, so the doctors recommended over-the-counter painkillers, which he took religiously just to keep a clear head.

Fortunately the week passed rather uneventfully, and I began packing our bags on Thursday, planning to leave that evening. The appointment was very early in the morning, so we were going to drive down that night, get a hotel, then show up at the hospital in preparation for a long day of surgery. Then I got the call. I figured Dr. Jackson's receptionist was just calling to confirm the appointment, but when she told me she was calling to cancel, I almost screamed. Not out of anger necessarily, but more from the frustration of waiting so long under pressure, and then having to wait some more. I almost boiled over, but I held it together.

"I'm sorry, Dr. Jackson was chopping wood at home and pulled a muscle in his back. He won't be able to complete the surgery tomorrow. It will be at least a week before the next opening. Would next Friday, the 26th, be convenient for you?" Friday, November 26th, the day after Thanksgiving? Of course that's not convenient! Convenient would be having the surgery on the day that we planned it.

"Yes, of course," I replied, biting my tongue, "and if anything earlier comes up, please let us know." I hung up the phone a little harder than usual. My mother taught me to be polite, but the mama bear in me wanted to fight. I resisted the urge, of course getting mad would do no good, but it might have felt good at that moment. I unpacked our suitcases, called the school to cancel Cody's planned absence, and called Kreg to let him know he didn't need to come home early. Another week. Could I survive it? Could Cody? I said another prayer that Cody would be alright until the surgery. God had been very good at answering my heartfelt prayers in the past few months, and I hoped I wasn't asking for too much.

The next week passed more quickly than the first with the preparations for Thanksgiving distracting me. We had planned on having Thanksgiving with Kreg's family, but that was when we expected the surgery to be completed by that point. With the surgery delayed I wasn't exactly in the thankful mindset and wanted to skip Thanksgiving all together, but Kreg insisted that we go, at least for the girls' sake. He was right. They had given up so much and had been so good about the sacrifices we made for Cody, the least we could do was give them a sense of normalcy on a holiday.

We went over in the morning with our bags packed and had a late Thanksgiving lunch at the Parmer's. By all accounts, it was a fairly normal Thanksgiving. The boys were preoccupied with football while the girls played with their cousins and the women worked in the kitchen. Any other year it would have been great, but I was just so worried about Cody and the upcoming surgery that I wasn't very good company.

In the spirit of Thanksgiving, I tried to remember to be grateful for Cody's recovery, but I just wished so badly that the whole mess would be over with. Maybe by next Thanksgiving, I thought, I can really say that I'm grateful that Cody made it through okay.

I forced myself to eat, even though I had little appetite. Once our Thanksgiving meal was over we said goodbye to the girls and the family and hopped in the truck with Cody. We stopped off at home, just to check the answering machine and make sure we hadn't received another terrible cancellation, and then we were finally on our way. Three hours to Salt Lake, a night at a motel, a day at the hospital, then it would all be over.

Cody sat in the back of our crew cab pickup and spent the first hour or so listening to the radio. Cody was an avid Dallas Cowboys fan, and they had started playing their Thanksgiving Day game just before we left Idaho Falls. Cody was dying not being able to watch the game, but listening to it on the radio was better than nothing. As we passed Pocatello and got into the canyons, the station faded out and we sat in silence for a few minutes.

It wasn't like Cody to be so quiet, so I turned around to check on him, "Cody, are you alright? Is there anything we can get you?" I asked.

"No, I'm okay," he responded as he stared out the window. I knew he wasn't okay, but there wasn't much I could say to make it better. Cody then asked, "Do you think it's going to work? I mean, are things just going to keep going wrong forever?"

"Oh no honey, I think they're going to fix it and then your headaches will go away and your eyes will get better and then you'll be just like new," I responded.

Cody thought about that for a second, then asked, "But what if there are more leaks? We thought the last surgery was going to fix everything too."

I hadn't given Cody enough credit. I kept imagining him as my innocent little boy that I had to shield from fear and doubt, but he was in the exact same spot I was. There wasn't any guarantee that this was the end.

There might be many more surgeries. There might be a lifetime of surgeries ahead, how was I to know? Just because Cody had made such a quick recovery at the start didn't mean we weren't in for a long road of pain and heartache. It was a terrible thought, and I tried to ignore it.

I didn't answer Cody's question, because I didn't have an answer. Kreg finally stepped in, "Buddy, if it takes a hundred more surgeries, then that's what it takes, but we're going to do whatever we have to do to get it fixed, alright?" Cody agreed. Kreg just knew Cody so well, there were so many times that he knew the right thing to say when I was at a loss for words.

Cody's questions had gotten my mind spinning again. I couldn't believe that God would save our son from the accident, just to have him die a few months later from a little leak in an artery, or would he? Was this time given to us as a gift, a time to remember, right before he was taken from us forever? No, I couldn't believe that. Say your prayers, read your scriptures, go to church, and God will protect you. I was doing all the things I was supposed to do, didn't God promise to pour out more blessings than you could receive, if you followed the commandments? Well, I was holding out my cup, and he had already poured me a lifetime worth of miracles, but I needed that cup to overflow. I needed the miracle that seemed so selfish to ask for in light of all we had been through. I needed a perfect recovery.

We arrived at the hotel in Salt Lake City well after dark and got our room. My parents were meeting us there, and when they arrived we gathered in our cold little hotel room to give Cody a blessing. Kreg blessed Cody that he would be strong and brave, that the doctor would know what he was doing, and that the surgery would be successful. The blessings always seemed to calm my nerves, and as I slipped under the covers of our hard hotel mattress I ran the words of the blessing through my mind. Each moment I laid there in the dark, an ounce of fear crept in. The mental battle for peace lasted only a couple minutes until I was finally overcome by fatigue and fell asleep.

In the morning the five of us got ready and headed to the hospital around 7:00 a.m., hoping to be plenty early for our 8:00 a.m. appointment. Returning to the hospital where I had spent two of the worst weeks of my life gave me chills, but I had a real hope that this was the last time we would have to be down here under these circumstances.

The nurses checked Cody in and had us fill out stacks of paperwork, then Dr. Jackson came out to introduce himself and explain the procedure. This was the first time we had met him in person, though we had spoken to him in a short consultation over the phone earlier. He was younger than I expected, early forties, with light brown hair and light green scrubs. He was very kind and spent a few minutes just talking to Cody and getting to know him a little bit. I think he could tell that Cody was nervous, so he promised that Kreg and I could come in and see him once they got situated. Dr. Jackson and a nurse took Cody into the operating room, then about 15 minutes later, they called for us to come.

"Cody's right in here," Dr. Jackson announced as we entered a large open room with Cody laying on a bed right in the middle. The room seemed too large for its current purpose, like an operating room scene from the movies. X-ray machines, computer monitors, and trays with instruments were pulled up next to Cody, who was clearly overwhelmed by the situation. I looked him in the eyes and smiled, even though the thought of the procedure made me queasy.

"What we're going to do today is make a small incision near the groin and run a tiny tube up through the artery into Cody's brain. You see this here?" Dr. Jackson pointed to a monitor near Cody. "This is a picture we just took of the arteries in Cody's head, and these different points," he pointed to about eight or ten spots on the image, "are all arteries that have been severely enlarged by the leak at this location," he said as he pointed to one of the arteries in particular.

"We need to fix this leak so that blood can begin flowing at a normal rate and take some of the pressure off these other arteries. We're going to do that by placing two balloons inside the artery at the point of the leak, then inflating them to cut off the flow of blood. It will only take a few seconds, less than a minute, and the artery will begin healing itself, but we have to cut off that flow in order to let it start to heal."

Kreg asked the doctor, "So if it's only a few seconds long, why does the surgery take a few hours?"

"Good question. The arteries are like a maze that snake through your body, so we have to get that small little tube through just the right pathways to get it into position. We are working very close to the brain, so we are going to keep Cody awake during the surgery so that we can make sure we're not affecting his brain negatively. During this process we're constantly taking x-rays and other images to monitor where the tube is and what is going on, so I've got to wear a 120 lb. lead vest to protect me from the radiation. All of these things make the surgery fairly complicated, so we take our time to make sure that we get it right."

I appreciated the explanation and being able to see what was going on, even if it made me a little sick. Knowing that Cody was in the hands of a kind and capable doctor eased some of my fears.

Dr. Jackson then showed us a control room where at least a dozen different monitors were being watched by a team of doctors and radiologists who would be assisting remotely, safely shielded from the radiation in the operating room. They would watch the doctor's every move and ensure that things were going according to plan.

The doctor then let us see Cody one last time, and led us back out to the waiting room. I turned to wave goodbye to Cody as we walked out the door and the look on his face broke my heart. His expression was scared, and the corners of his mouth drooped down like he was about to cry. He reached his fingers out to me to wave goodbye, but they lingered in the air as if to say "don't leave me here mom, don't leave me." There was nothing I could do. I waved again and walked out the door.

We never received a timeline for the surgery, we just knew it would be a few hours. They started around 8:00 a.m., and by noon I was getting worried. Kreg and my mom and dad talked about work and family and life, but the longer we went without hearing anything, the quieter they got. I bowed my head and prayed over and over again that Cody would be strong like the blessing had promised, and that the operation would be successful.

Just after 1:00 p.m., more than five hours after the surgery began, I saw Dr. Jackson hobble down the hallway with his head down and his hand supporting his lower back. He was still wearing that heavy lead apron and his steps were labored. He saw us, but avoided our eyes as he came down the hall. Kreg and I stood up and walked to meet him at the entrance to the waiting room.

"I'm sorry, the surgery wasn't successful today. We're going to need to try again in a week or two."

"What do you mean? Is Cody okay?" Kreg asked, fearing the worst.

"Yes, he's fine, but we had a complication in the surgery. We placed the first balloon successfully and inflated it, then when we began to inflate the second balloon, the first one popped, I'm not sure why. It's incredibly rare for that to happen, but it did. I've spent the last several hours fishing out pieces of the balloon from his artery and it's all clear now, but we'll have to try again another day."

All of my willpower and strength faded in a flash. Fear and heartbreak washed over me like a flood. My legs gave out and I collapsed to the floor on my knees and curled over at the doctor's feet. "Please! You have to finish it! Please, just go back and finish the surgery! Please don't send him home like this!" I pleaded with him as tears began to well up in my eyes and muddled my vision.

In all the surgeries and procedures Cody had been through, I had never felt like this. Something was wrong, it was terribly wrong, and it needed to be fixed. I had seen the pictures of the artery and they all looked like they were ready to burst. I knew that once that happened, Cody was probably dead. But even more than a practical understanding of the problem, my gut told me that this placed Cody in a terrible position. If it didn't get fixed now, something bad was going to happen. I had to plead with all my might to get him to go back in.

Kreg and Dr. Jackson lifted me into a chair. All the while I kept begging him to go back in and finish the surgery.

"Mrs. Parmer, believe me, I wish I could, but it's just not going to happen today. We're working in his brain and I have to be completely 100%, and the weight on my back and the time we've already spent, it's just too dangerous to try again right now."

"But those pictures, what if the arteries burst?" I pleaded. Kreg rubbed my back, trying to calm me down, but I would not be consoled.

"Look, Cody has been like this for several months, he'll be fine for another week or so. It's just not safe to try again today. The earliest time available is about two weeks out, December 10th, we'll try it again then and we'll get it done. That's really what's best for Cody. I'm sorry." Dr. Jackson knew it was no use arguing with me, so he turned and left. He was doing his best, I could see that, but it wasn't good enough. I needed more, I needed something he couldn't give. I needed another miracle.

ELEVEN

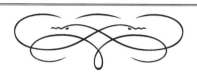

THE SURGERY HAD FAILED, BUT WE STILL HAD TO WAIT IN THE HOSPI-
tal for another eight hours before we could go back to the motel.
Doctors were concerned that if Cody raised his head he might suffer complications, or that too much movement might tear open the major artery
in his groin. We had expected this recovery to be a time of celebration,
but instead it was overwhelmed by worry.

I felt like I was hanging off a cliff, just holding on by my fingertips,
and I could feel myself slipping. At any moment I would lose my grip and
slip off the edge into despair and frustration and anguish, a fall I wasn't
sure I could recover from.

I prayed and begged the Lord to take this cup from us, but the analo-
gy drew the suffering of the Savior to my mind. Faced with an impossible
task, he asked for the same thing, but he knew it was unavoidable and he
stood up and walked out of the garden to face what was coming head on.
Somehow I sensed that something terrible was waiting for us as well, but
I doubted I was strong enough to face it.

A nurse led us into the recovery room where we could sit with Cody.
As we entered I rushed to his side and tried to keep from crying for Cody's
sake, but he was nearly as depressed as I was.

"Mom, it didn't work," Cody said as I took a seat beside him and
held his hand. Cody was overcome by disappointment. "He was almost
done, then he said 'Darn it!' and I knew something was wrong, and they
couldn't fix it and they had to stop. Why didn't it work mom?"

"I know Cody, I know."

"Why didn't it work? It was supposed to work." Cody said again and again. He was trying hard to hide his fear and frustration, but I knew my son, and I knew he was at his breaking point.

Kreg tried to comfort Cody and told him that it would be alright, they would get it next time. The glances I shared with Cody told another story, however. We both knew, somehow, that there was much more on the line than just a wasted week or two of waiting. We had all seen the images of his arteries, a burst in any one of those eight or ten places could kill Cody in an instant. For eight long hours we sat in the recovery room, powerless to ease the threat that loomed over us.

I had endured Cody's many surgeries before, but this felt different. A broken arm can be set, a pelvis can be held in place until it heals, titanium plates can repair a neck, but what do you do about a brain? Even if one of those other surgeries went terribly wrong, you might lose some functionality, maybe even be unable to walk, but you don't die in an instant or lose your ability to think and reason. Being trapped in a body that has physical limitations would be terrible, but at least you're still you.

My mind kept replaying the images from the monitors in the control room, every angle and view said that something was terribly wrong. What was to prevent those arteries from popping unexpectedly, just like that balloon did? If the doctor couldn't predict when his own instruments would work or fail, how could he say when a leak might rip open into a hemorrhage and Cody would bleed out?

After Cody had come home from the hospital in August, I had convinced myself that nothing could be more torturous than those few days when I didn't know if Cody would live or die. I was wrong, this was much worse. Cody was walking a razor's edge, and we had to pretend like nothing was happening. I couldn't grieve over the threat, I couldn't even really talk about it because there was nothing left to say. The one doctor who could do something about it had told us to go home, and there was no one in the world we could turn to for help. It even seemed like God had left us on our own.

"Why didn't it work?" I asked my mom after Cody had fallen asleep in the hospital bed. I had no answers for Cody when he asked me the same question, and my mother had no answers for me.

"Why wouldn't Heavenly Father let that work?" I asked again under my breath, confused by the whole situation. "We had a miracle before, we know it's possible. A balloon is a simple thing. He could have just held that balloon together, and everything would be over by now." I leaned forward and rested my aching head on the side of Cody's hospital bed. No one even tried to answer my question. As I prayed and asked God my questions, no answer came, and no comfort either. Were the heavens turning a blind eye? Of course God knew what was at stake, so why not let a simple operation proceed as planned? We were doing everything we were supposed to do, we found the problem, the doctor was doing his best, and still it had failed. What had we missed?

"Didn't we give him a blessing?" I asked Kreg after some time.

"Yeah," Kreg said and shrugged his shoulders. He shook his head, "I don't know honey, I don't know." Then silence. Nobody knew what to say, nobody had any answers, and there was no reason to continue asking them aloud.

Once the eight hours had elapsed, we took Cody back to the hotel for the night, then drove home the next morning. I had hoped that a night's rest and a little distance from the situation would settle my fears, but it didn't. As we drove home Kreg tried to convince me that the only thing we could do was move on and wait the two weeks until the next surgery. He was right, that was the sensible thing, but it didn't help to ease my mind.

We arrived home on Saturday and tried to carry on like normal, pretending that Cody wasn't in immediate and grave danger. Dr. Jackson had told us that normal everyday activities provided no additional threat, but I wasn't taking any chances. Cody was under mother's orders to take it easy and relax as much as possible, so I sat him in front of the TV and handed him the remote. As long as he was within earshot and not doing anything crazy, I felt like I could at least manage my fears.

Cody called Jeff and they spent the evening watching sports. They sat and talked and yelled at the TV like old times, and I was glad to see that the accident hadn't hurt their relationship. Jeff still had complications from the accident as well, but he was back at school and recovering as well as could be expected. Luckily for him, none of his injuries included damage to the brain and his physical injuries were mostly behind him. Doctors saw nothing preventing him from making a full recovery. I could only hope that we would eventually get to that stage with Cody as well.

We attended church on Sunday like always and Cody helped bless the sacrament. Being at church with his friends helped him to forget about his problems for a while, and it gave me some time to think and pray. I made sure to thank God for what he had already given us, but prayed with all my heart that we could overcome the obstacles that blocked Cody's recovery.

I could tell after church that Cody was exhausted so I encouraged him to go take a nap. Truth be told, we were all exhausted. It had been a very long and difficult few weeks with the first operation canceled at the last minute and the second operation a tragic disappointment just seconds before it was completed. Even the girls were getting worn out from all the stress and frustration they could see us going through. We were all just ready to move on. If we could just survive two more weeks, we could make it.

That evening I checked the kids' backpacks and made sure that all the homework assigned over Thanksgiving was done and ready to be turned in. I hated that they assigned homework over holidays, but our kids were pretty good about getting it done. Kira had finished all her homework the day she got it, like always, so I didn't have to worry about hers, but Brooke, Krissa, and Cody needed a little more oversight.

"Hey Cody, did you get all your homework done?" I yelled downstairs, staring into his empty backpack.

"Yeah, I've got it," he said as he came upstairs, carrying his books and some loose papers. "I didn't know if you were going to have me go to school tomorrow or not."

I hadn't really thought about keeping him home, maybe Kreg had said something. "Why wouldn't you go to school tomorrow?" I asked.

"I don't know, just because of the operation and everything. I don't know if I'm just tired or if I'm getting sick or what. I thought that nap was going to help, but I'm still exhausted."

Every procedure we had been through left Cody tired in the days afterward. I assumed this was still the case, but my heightened level of fear made me pause and think. "Okay Cody, I'll leave it up to you. If you don't feel good in the morning, you can stay home and I'll have one of your friends pick up your new assignments. But don't just use that as an excuse to get out of school!" I said facetiously as I wagged my finger at him. Cody loved school, if for nothing else than the simple fact that it let him hang out with all his friends all day. I wondered how he kept his grades up because from the way he talked it sounded like school was just one big party all day long.

"Yeah, okay, I'll let you know," Cody said as he stuffed his books in his backpack. He took a drink of water then went down to bed.

After the kids were all in their rooms Kreg came into the kitchen to talk to me. "Hey Brenda, the Killians called earlier and wanted to see if we were still planning on going to *The Forgotten Carols* tomorrow night with them."

"Oh geez. I totally forgot." I moaned, walking over to the calendar sitting on the counter. Sure enough, there it was, *Forgotten Carols* on November 29th with the Killians. We had bought tickets for the show months ago before we had any clue about Cody's leaking artery or his operations. "I don't know honey, I wasn't even thinking about it. I don't know if I want to leave Cody home alone."

"I know, I told them that as well, but they said they would have Tauni come over and hang out with Cody and the girls, just to keep an eye on them all." Kreg was one step ahead of me, he knew me all too well. Tauni was Cody's same age and they were good friends. She was a smart and capable girl, I knew I could trust her with babysitting the girls, but if something happened to Cody, there wasn't anyone in the world who would be prepared for that.

"I don't know, Cody's just so…fragile right now." I thought out loud.

"I know, but you're sending him to school, right?" Kreg asked.

"Yeah, I think so, if Cody feels well enough to go."

"I'm sure he'll be okay. Look, I told them we were going to go unless I called them back. If he's not doing well tomorrow then we'll stay home, but I think it would really be a good idea for us to go and get out of the house." He came and put his arms around me. His big hugs always had a way of making me feel protected. "We just need to take a step back and let it go for a night," he said as he kissed my forehead.

"Okay," I said softly. The thought of 'letting it go' for even a few moments frightened me. I had been on guard for so long, I wasn't sure how to let it go anymore, but the stress was going to kill me if I didn't do something. I took a deep breath. This would all be over in just a couple weeks.

I got up early in the morning to get the kids ready and could hear that the shower was already running. I walked in to check on Cody and his bed was empty. Maybe the nap really had done him some good, at least it got him out of bed without a fight. I went upstairs and made pancakes, then helped Krissa with her hair. After his normal long shower and even longer hair styling session, Cody came upstairs to shovel down some pancakes before his ride came to pick him up.

Cody had been getting rides to school with friends since he had started back at school in October. Cody's truck still sat in our driveway, but I had forbidden him from driving after the accident and wasn't sure when I would lift that restriction. Probably never, if I had my choice.

It was just starting to get light outside when Cody's ride pulled up. He threw his backpack on and ran out to hop in the car, "Bye Mom!" he shouted as he left. No mention of a headache or tiredness, no mention of staying home from school. That must be a good sign.

Dusting, vacuuming, dishes, counters, sweeping, mopping, laundry, paying bills, and tidying up kept me busy through most of the morning. At least it kept my mind off my problems. If I wasn't busy, I was worrying, so I tried to stay as busy as I possibly could. By the time the kids got home from school, I felt like I had earned the right to leave for the evening, but then Cody walked in and nearly collapsed into the first chair he could find.

"Cody? Are you okay?" I asked as I walked down from the kitchen to the living room. His backpack was lying on the floor just inside the door and he sat slouched in the chair with his eyes closed.

"Mom, something is wrong." He said, finally opening his eyes and staring at me with a frown and puppy dog eyes. Cody was usually really tough, but he looked like he was five years old again and needed to cuddle up on his mom's lap.

"What's wrong Cody?" I asked as I held my hand up to his forehead, checking for a temperature.

"I just don't feel good. I've got this really bad headache and it won't go away when I take the pills. And then, in the middle of the day," he stuck his tongue out and moved it around a little, like he was checking for something, "my tongue started going numb, or tasting funny, like metal or something, and then my nose started feeling tingly and going numb, and I didn't really feel hungry so I didn't eat anything at lunch, but my stomach kind of hurt, so I tried to eat something during the last period and then I felt a little sick to my stomach, like I was going to throw up, but I didn't. But my head hurts the worst, it just feels like my head is going to explode or something." Cody finally took a breath and sunk back into his chair.

This couldn't be good, not at all. "Do you need to lay down? Do you really think you're going to throw up?" I asked. "I don't know," he moaned as he put his head back and closed his eyes again.

"Alright, I'm going to get you a garbage can, if you get sick to your stomach, throw up in there. You can go lay down if you need to, but I'm going to call the doctor." Cody remained seated in the green wing-backed chair and I put a small garbage can on his lap. The couch was much more comfortable for laying on, and the fact that Cody didn't even want to move to the couch to lay down had me worried. What in the world could it be? I was always suspicious of hospitals and contracting some infectious disease from another patient; maybe he caught something there? But the metallic taste in his mouth, wasn't that a sign of something? And what was causing a numbness in his mouth and nose, surely that wasn't just from some flu, at least I had never heard of that being a symptom before. It had to be something going on in his brain.

I got out my notebook with Dr. Jackson's phone number and dialed his office. A receptionist answered and said that Dr. Jackson was not available, but that she would take a message. I explained who I was and that it was incredibly urgent and I needed to talk to him now. She insisted he was unavailable to come to the phone, but she would have me wait on the line while she took my message to him and asked for his opinion. It took far too long for her to return and I was beginning to get upset.

"Mrs. Parmer? Are you still there?" she asked after several minutes of silence.

"Yes, I'm here."

"I told Dr. Jackson exactly what you told me. He said that none of those symptoms are things that would be caused by the surgery that we performed here. It's possible that he has a cold or flu, or that the pressure in the head may be causing other complications. He recommended to keep your son on some over-the-counter headache medicine until the symptoms subside, and if they don't get better in a day or so, take him to your local family doctor for a checkup. We'll still plan on the surgery for the 10th, but for now, don't worry, he'll be okay."

That was not what I was wanting to hear. Something was wrong, and I knew it. I hung up the phone and went to talk to Cody again when the phone rang. I rushed to pick it up, hoping it was Dr. Jackson, reconsidering and moving up the surgery.

"Hello, this is Brother Kentner from the Skyline High School Seminary, is this Sister Parmer?"

"It is," I replied. A call about homework or discipline was not exactly my greatest concern at the time.

"I'm calling about Cody, did he make it home alright?"

"Yes, he's with me right here."

"Okay, good. He just didn't seem to be doing well today in class and I had him lay his head down on the desk for a while. I know you've been through a lot, so I wasn't sure if this was something normal or not, or if it was related to his accident or the recent surgery. I asked him if he wanted me to call you and he said no, but when I saw him getting into someone's car at the end of the day he still looked really sick."

"Yeah, he told me he didn't feel well. I'm not sure what it is though."

"Okay, I'm glad he made it home alright at least. If you need anything, please don't hesitate to call. Cody's a great kid and we really love having him in our class."

"Thank you very much, I appreciate you calling me and letting me know." We said our goodbyes and hung up the phone. If a teacher from school took the time to call a parent about a sick kid, it must be really bad. I immediately called Kreg and told him what was going on. He brushed it off at first, but then as I explained further he said he would leave work in a few minutes and come home to help.

Once I was off the phone with Kreg, I heard Cody start to groan downstairs. "What's wrong, Cody?" I said from the kitchen, not trying to sound alarmed.

"My head, it hurts," Cody moaned. I walked downstairs once again.

"When was the last time you took some aspirin?"

"I don't know, before lunch?" Cody said.

"Well, I'm going to give you two more and we'll see if that helps." I got Cody the medicine and a glass of water and went back to the phone and dialed Dr. Jackson's office again. I told them that it seemed like it was getting worse, and something must be wrong with his head. The receptionist put me on hold again, then returned with pretty much the same instructions as the first time.

"If it's getting really bad," she told me, "you'll need to go into your local emergency room and they'll be able to help. There's nothing we can do from here at this point."

I was so mad. What was the ER going to do? They didn't know Cody's full situation or have the resources in Idaho Falls to fix his artery. I figured the next best thing was to go see Dr. Hoggan, the optometrist who had been measuring the pressure behind Cody's eye. Maybe if the pressure was really bad, he could convince Dr. Jackson to move up the surgery. I called the office and had them clear a spot for me in about 15 minutes, then I called Kreg and told him to meet me at Dr. Hoggan's office. I helped Cody into the car and left Kira to watch over Brooke and Krissa.

Kreg and I showed up to Dr. Hoggan's office at nearly the same time. Kreg questioned Cody about what was going wrong, then helped Cody walk into the office. Dr. Hoggan greeted us at the door, "Come on in, let's take a look at this eye and see what's going on." Finally, a doctor who acted concerned about what was happening!

Dr. Hoggan laid Cody back in an examination chair and took out his pressure measurement instrument. Cody's eye still looked terrible. It was probably worse than ever, but I wasn't really paying attention to how it looked much anymore because I was so concerned about the operation in the brain. Dr. Hoggan placed the small tool at the top of Cody's open eyelid and pressed through the skin onto the eyeball. The instrument gave him a reading, and he wrote it down and tested it again and again to make sure the readings were the same.

"The pressure is still increasing, but it's at a steady rate, the same kind of increase we've seen before. I'm not going to say that's a good thing, because any additional pressure is going to have negative effects, but it might mean that nothing is necessarily out of the ordinary for today. My advice would be to just wait for the surgery to fix the artery and don't make any major changes to your normal activities. If these symptoms don't get better over the next day or so, we can talk to some of the other doctors about nausea medicine or something else to get you feeling better. Okay?" He patted Cody on the knee and stood up. "Sorry you're not feeling well Cody, get some rest and I think you'll be alright."

Kreg and Cody and I thanked Dr. Hoggan for seeing us on such short notice and walked back out to the car. What else was there to do? I trusted Dr. Hoggan more than Dr. Jackson, but they both said the same thing. Maybe it was time to just take Cody home and lay him down so he could get some rest. If nobody else seemed as freaked out about this as I did, maybe I was just being a little overprotective. Kreg gave me a hug and told me he was going to head back to work to finish up a few things if I didn't need him at home. I agreed and let him drive off.

Cody hobbled into the house once we got home and laid down on the couch to watch TV. My schedule had been thrown off and I had to rush to get dinner on the table. I abandoned my original dinner plans and threw some spaghetti in a pot. I tried to help the girls with their homework until the spaghetti was ready, then had them set the table. It was going to be a pretty basic meal, no frills, but at least everyone would be fed.

Kreg walked in right as dinner was about to start, and Cody followed him up to the kitchen and sat at the table with us.

"Are you feeling better Cody?" Kreg asked as the girls put the last few items on the table and sat down.

"Yeah, I think it's a little better. It doesn't feel numb anymore. I don't know what it was." Cody sounded a little embarrassed that we had made such a big fuss over him.

"Are you hungry? I thought you were feeling like you might throw up?" I asked, hoping to prevent any nasty messes.

"Yeah, I'm really hungry actually. This smells really good." Cody still didn't look very healthy, but at least he was feeling a little better. We blessed the food and ate while the girls each gave us a full report of their day. I was amazed by how much each of them were growing up. Spending so much time focused on Cody had really forced them to mature, and it seemed like life was passing us by in an instant. I was sorry I couldn't devote just as much time and attention to each of them, but I committed myself to make it up to them once Cody's surgery was all over.

"I'm going to go change, the Killians are going to be here to pick us up at 6:30," Kreg said.

"What? You're still planning on going? Cody's sick!" I said, surprised. I had just assumed after all the calls and appointments this evening that Kreg had already canceled.

"I'm fine mom, you can go, I'm feeling a lot better," Cody interjected.

"Oh, I don't know about that. You don't look better," I told him.

Cody smiled a goofy oversized grin. "Look better now?" he asked.

Kreg cut in, "He's fine honey, everyone said it will be alright. Let's get ready and if he's feeling bad again by the time they get here we'll tell them to go by themselves." I could tell Kreg was going to get me to go whether I liked it or not. I looked at the clock, just half an hour to get ready. Kreg was watching my expressions as I thought about it and he knew that he had won. Was I that easy to read? Probably.

"Okay, but Cody, if you don't feel well, just tell us and we'll stay home. I don't want you getting sick with Tauni here, okay?"

"Okay mom, but I promise, I'll be fine."

TWELVE

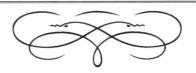

TICKETS TO *THE FORGOTTEN CAROLS* WERE HARD TO COME BY, WHICH is partially why I felt obliged to go. We hadn't been able to get any tickets for the Idaho Falls performance, and we were lucky to get tickets to the showing in Pocatello, nearly an hour away. I also didn't want to back out on Lisa and Earl at the last minute, we had been friends for a long time and they were so fun to be with. Lisa and I had served together in the Young Women's organization several years back and we got along really well.

They had been really good to us when we were in the hospital with Cody after the accident and had come down for a few days to see us. While they were there Earl had helped give Cody a blessing before one of the operations, and Lisa had sat beside me while I waded through my grief. They were true friends. I hoped that an evening with them would help me reset my mind and give me strength for the next couple weeks.

The show was great and I loved the music and the message, but it kind of caught me off guard. Even though Christmas decorations had been up in stores for a while, I wasn't thinking about Christmas at all. December 10th was my new holiday, and everything revolved around that date. A successful operation to fix Cody's artery would be the best Christmas gift ever, and I wanted it more than I had ever wanted anything else. If anything, the show made me feel bad that I hadn't really been preparing for Christmas much and wasn't really in the mood to do any decorating or Christmas cookie baking until after the operation. I considered putting up a box or two of decorations the next day while the girls were at school, just for their sake.

As we drove home Kreg turned his cell phone back on and checked for messages. We had told Cody and Tauni to call us if there were any problems, but there was nothing in Kreg's voicemail. That didn't necessarily mean there weren't problems, it just meant they didn't have time to call if there was an emergency. I wanted to call home but Kreg convinced me not to waste any of the minutes on his phone plan, he was certain they would have called if there was a problem.

We finally pulled up in front of the house and I was happy that there was no sign of any emergency. My mind had imagined ambulances or police tape stretched across our lawn as we drove home. I worried about stuff like that all the time even before Cody had his accident, but the events over the past few months had validated my fears, at least to some extent. We all got out of the car and walked in to find the kids sitting in front of the TV, finishing up a movie. It was a school night, so I had Kira put Brooke and Krissa to bed at the normal time, but told Kira she could stay up with Cody and Tauni.

"Hey guys, how was it?" Kreg asked as the kids put the movie on pause. Tauni got up and walked our direction, but Cody stayed sitting down and didn't really look at us.

"I don't think he feels well, he's not really acting like himself," Tauni said quietly as she got closer. My heart sank, I knew we shouldn't have gone to the show. I shouldn't have left her here to watch Cody when he wasn't feeling well.

"Oh, I shouldn't have left you here alone, he said he was feeling better. I'm so sorry," I apologized to Tauni. She brushed it off and told me it was no big deal, she just felt bad for him. Earl and Lisa said their goodbyes and rushed off to get Tauni home to bed. After they left I went down to talk with Cody. He was still slumped into the couch and hadn't moved.

"Son, you've got school tomorrow, you really need to go to bed." I wondered if I was really going to send him to school after how bad this day had gone, but he needed to get some rest either way.

"Mom, I just feel like my head is going to explode. Like really, explode," he said as he put his hands up against the side of his head and squeezed his temples, trying to relieve some of the pressure. Kreg came downstairs and heard us talking.

"Come on Cody, you're just tired. Let's get you to bed." Kreg walked over to the couch and helped Cody up. His room was just down the hall and I followed Kreg and Cody as they walked.

"Did you guys have fun with Tauni tonight? What movie were you watching?" Kreg asked. Cody just held his head and didn't answer. He walked to his bed and sat down on the edge, putting his elbows on his knees and his head in his hands.

"Do you need some aspirin or something? When was the last time you took some medicine?" Kreg asked. It was terrible to see your child in so much pain and not be able to do anything about it. Hopefully some aspirin would help him get to sleep.

"I can probably take some more, I had some right after you left," Cody said. Kreg patted Cody on the back and left to go upstairs for the medicine.

"You just need some sleep buddy, you'll feel better in the morning," I told him, hoping I was right.

"Mom," Cody said with a long pause, "I need a blessing. I really need a blessing right now." His plea was urgent and his breathing was getting fast, like he was about to throw up.

"I'll go get Dad," I said and turned to walk out of the room.

"No, you can't go! Just stay here. Don't go," Cody said, his breath was becoming more and more labored. I started to panic and didn't know what to do. Should I get a trash can for him to throw up in? Should I yell for Kreg? Do I need to sit by him and talk to him, or will that make it worse?

Kreg came down just then with a glass of water and some aspirin. "Here you go," Kreg said as he held out the pills. Cody took them in his hands and hesitated for a moment, thinking about swallowing them, but then set them on the blanket at his side and put both hands against his head again.

"Babe, he said he needs a blessing," I told Kreg. He stood there for a second and stared at Cody. I could tell he was working it over in his head, wondering if he needed to call someone over or just give him an emergency priesthood blessing right then.

Cody sat straight up and had both of his hands on the top of his head.

"Mom, I cannot even explain to you how bad this hurts. It's like the top of my head is going to blow off. It's not right. Something's not right. I just don't feel right." I looked at Kreg, hoping he had some sort of answer. This was getting serious, and I had no idea what to do.

I looked back at Cody and time stopped. His hands fell limp to his side and his eyes rolled back in his head so all we could see were the whites of his eyes. His head tilted back slightly and his stomach muscles tightened, then his jaw dropped open and he began vomiting blood. Cody's body went limp and he collapsed sideways on the bed, his eyes still rolled back and his jaw open. His body convulsed again as he let out a second stream of deep red vomit onto the blanket and the floor. Then he was completely still.

Kreg was instantly by his side, calling his name and lifting him into a sitting position so he didn't choke on his own vomit. There was no sign of breathing, there was no response from Cody, there was no life in him. I was sure my son had died right in front of me. I couldn't move, my life had ended in that second.

"Cody! Cody!" Kreg yelled as he got him upright.

Then Cody's body convulsed again and the last of the blood and vomit trickled out. Cody's eyes rolled back down slightly so I could start to see the color in his eyes again, but Cody was limp in Kreg's arms. Cody coughed and gagged on the vomit once, then twice, then he was silent for a second. What had just happened? I realized then that Cody was still alive, but for how long?

Kreg yelled to me, "Brenda, hold him! I've got to call Ben!" I heard Kreg call to me, but my body wouldn't move. Kreg let Cody collapse on the bed and ran to grab the portable phone in the hallway.

"Cody! Come on Cody!" I yelled, willing him to wake up from across the room, but there was no reaction. He was as limp as a rag doll and seemed completely lifeless, except for the occasional convulsion of his stomach muscles resulting in a dry heave. I wished I could do something, but I couldn't move, so I just kept yelling.

Was this how it was going to end? Was I going to watch him die, slumped over on his bed, covered in blood? I began to shake, terrified of the possibility, or rather the probability, that I was going to lose my son in the next few moments.

How could I go on with an emptiness in our family that could never be filled? I couldn't, there was no way. I began to cry out in my heart the quickest and most simple prayer I could muster, "Please God! Save him!"

Kreg ran back into the room with the phone pinned between his ear and his shoulder and propped Cody up once again.

"Ben, I've lost him! I've lost Cody!" Kreg cried into the phone as Dr. Ben Hoggan finally picked up. Ben had been the last doctor to see Cody, maybe he knew what to do to save Cody, but I doubted it. Kreg continued after a moment, "I was talking to him and his eyes rolled back and he threw up blood and he's not conscious! What do we do?" Another pause. "No, it will take too long for them to get here, I'll take him." Kreg dropped the phone to the bed and scooped Cody up in his arms.

"Brenda, let's go!" Kreg shouted as he ran past me. "I'll hold Cody, you drive!" Kreg was halfway down the hallway before I finally was able to move my feet and follow them upstairs. Kreg opened the door with Cody still in his arms and ran out to our Chevy Yukon parked outside. I grabbed the keys, slammed the door behind me, and ran barefoot and coatless into the cold night to catch up to them.

It was thirty minutes until midnight on a Monday night, and there were very few cars on the road. We had already had a few inches of snow that year but the roads were clear and dry, so I pushed the Yukon as fast as I dared, barely slowing to check for traffic at the red lights. I almost wished a police officer had seen me so that he could race ahead with his sirens and lead us to the hospital, but the streets were empty, so I raced on.

I tried to focus on driving but I kept turning around, checking on Kreg and Cody in the back seat. Kreg kept trying to call to Cody and get him to respond, but to no avail. "Kreg, what's wrong with him? What's happening?" I cried out.

"I don't know, I don't know! He's still breathing, I think, just get to the hospital! Ben said he would call and tell them we were coming!" Kreg was acting nearly hysterical, which didn't help me gain my composure. I couldn't see a way that this would end well at all.

Finally we arrived at the hospital. I tore through the hospital parking lot and slammed on the brakes in front of the ambulance parking. "I'll go get help!" I shouted as I jumped out and ran across the cold concrete and through the automatic doors.

"Help, help, help! My son is in the car!" I shouted to a nearly empty emergency room waiting area. One of the few nurses there slowly walked over to me and asked what was the matter. "My son! He's bad, he's really bad! Come on!" I begged. She turned and began walking over to the wall. I couldn't believe it, why wasn't she rushing out to the car? Hadn't Dr. Hoggan told them we were coming? "What are you doing? Come on!" I yelled.

"I'm getting a wheelchair, just calm down, it will be okay," she replied.

"No! He doesn't need a wheelchair, he's really really bad, he's unconscious, come on!" The nurse selected one of the wheelchairs lined up against the wall and began walking toward me, making gestures for me to keep my voice down. I wanted to scream even louder, how could she work in an emergency room and not respond quickly to an emergency? A male nurse seemed to understand my urgency and ran past me out to the car, but the first nurse seemed more concerned about the wheelchair than what was outside.

"Ma'am, any patient who needs assistance coming in is required to be in a wheelchair," the nurse tried to explain to me. I wasn't having any of it. Right beside me was an empty hospital gurney, ready to go. I grabbed it and started pulling it out the door while the nurse gave me a scowl for defying her. The male nurse from outside raced back in and yelled some instructions to the few nurses who had come from the back to watch the commotion, then grabbed the gurney out of my hands and we ran for the car together.

Kreg and the male nurse loaded Cody's limp body onto the gurney and pushed past the first nurse, still holding her wheelchair. The nurses from the back seemed to suddenly recognize who we were and jumped into action. Cody was taken into a large bright room right off the main entrance. Kreg and I stood helplessly against the wall as the nurses worked to hook up IVs, breathing tubes, heart monitors, and other equipment. Several doctors soon entered and began shouting out orders for medication or tests. Cody didn't seem to be responding well to any of the tests, and the doctors seemed to be getting frustrated. Nurses and doctors rushed in and out of the room, bringing new trays of equipment required for each additional procedure or test.

"Kreg? Brenda?" The call came from just outside the doorway, it was another friend of ours, Dr. Len Nicholls. We hadn't even recognized him in all the running around. He walked over to us and spoke quietly so he wouldn't disturb the nurses and doctors working on Cody. "Ben called and said you were bringing Cody in. From what it looks like here and what Ben told us, it appears that Cody had a brain hemorrhage. We're prepping an operating room now. The neurosurgeon on call tonight is Dr. Stone, and he's getting things ready as well. He'll be here in just a few more minutes. I'm sorry this has happened, we'll do our best to take care of him."

"What's going to happen? Will the surgery be able to fix it?" Kreg asked guardedly.

"I really can't say. I know it doesn't look good, but we can't really know until the neurosurgeon goes in to find the problem. They'll run a bunch of tests, then determine the best course of action after that. We'll know better what's happening after those tests. I'm so sorry, I wish I had better news." Dr. Nicholls excused himself and went back to work.

We stood at the back of the room watching them work on Cody for several more minutes until Dr. Stone arrived. He didn't announce himself, but it was obvious he was in charge from the moment he arrived. Most of the nurses stopped what they were doing and began taking orders. After just a moment in the room Dr. Stone looked at us and pointed, "Get them out."

A nurse walked over and calmly escorted us just outside the doorway and closed the door. It was the most horrible feeling to be sent away. I figured the only reason they were so adamant was because they didn't expect Cody to live.

Once the door was closed behind us we were left alone in the hallway. The waiting room with the old blue chairs and ugly coffee table was available out front, but we wanted to be as close to Cody as possible. There were no chairs in the hall, so Kreg hopped up on an empty gurney that was sitting right across from Cody's room. I hopped up next to him and stared at the door just feet in front of us, trying to hear what was going on inside the room. We sat and waited, staring at the door across the hall, not knowing how long it would be before the door opened again, or what would happen when it did.

Neither of us said a word. I put my elbows on my knees and rested my head in my hands, trying to block out the world. Why had this happened, what more could I have done? Maybe I should have pushed Dr. Jackson more, we could have made it to Salt Lake by the evening if we had left right after school. Or maybe we should have taken Cody to the emergency room that afternoon, instead of to Dr. Hoggan. Could they have prevented this? Would they have seen some sign we had missed? I kicked myself for going to the musical. I should have stayed home with Cody, but then again, what could I have done to prevent this?

I felt vindicated in my frustration about Cody's condition. Why had nobody listened to me? Everyone was trying to tell me it would be okay, but Cody and I both knew how bad it was. We had both seen it coming, though we never said as much openly. And even though we had pleaded with the doctors to do something, anything, none of them took any action. Maybe they couldn't, maybe there really was nothing that could be done.

Maybe the only one who could have stopped it was God, and if he chose to let this happen, then what did that mean for Cody's outlook? Hadn't we already prayed for protection, and hadn't Cody received blessings? If so, was God ignoring us now, or was he letting this happen on purpose? And for what purpose? My mind constructed questions faster than they could be answered, or even fully contemplated.

After a few minutes Kreg stood up and grabbed the phone next to us on the wall and dialed my parents. "Hey Marvin, it's Kreg. Cody had a brain hemorrhage and we're here at the hospital waiting…No, we don't know anything yet…Alright, thank you, and could you call someone and have them go over and spend the night with the girls? I hope they're still asleep, but we left in a hurry and they might have woken up…Thank you, see you soon." Kreg called his parents as well to give them the news, then sat back down. I nodded my thanks at Kreg, grateful for his awareness and foresight while I wallowed in grief.

In just a few minutes my parents arrived and met us in the hallway with hugs and tears. Kreg stood up to talk to my dad and fill him in while my mom took the seat beside me and held me in her arms as I cried. Having my mom there opened the floodgates that so often I held back because I was trying to be tough, as a mother should be. But once I was a daughter again, in my mother's arms, I became a weak little girl, unable to control my emotions. "He's not going to make it, Mom. He's not going to make it!" I sobbed into my mom's shoulder, then sunk into her lap. She tried to comfort me, but I was inconsolable. I stopped trying to ask questions or make sense of it, I just sunk deep down into my pain and let it fully engulf me.

I spent nearly an hour lost in my misery before the sound of an opening door jolted me back to reality. I sat up and tried to compose myself. There was the doctor, head to toe in green operating scrubs, walking toward us.

"You're the parents?" he said abruptly.

"Yes," Kreg responded before I could clear my throat to speak.

"We're going into brain surgery, I need to go get my team. It's going to take eight hours. If he lives, he'll be a vegetable." And with that, he turned around and left.

Thirteen

WE ALL SAT THERE STUNNED, NOT JUST BY THE PROGNOSIS BUT BY the cold-hearted delivery as well. Had Dr. Stone really just said Cody was going to be a "vegetable" without so much as batting an eye? And that was only if he survived the operation? I was so stunned by the lack of compassion that it took me a moment to understand exactly what was happening.

I turned and looked up at Kreg and our eyes locked, a million thoughts passed between us without a single word. I turned to my mom and dad, each one staring at me, waiting for my reaction. I silently leaned back against the wall.

Was that all the information we were going to get? What were Cody's odds of survival? What exactly did being a "vegetable" mean? Was there any chance of a miracle where Cody came through unscathed? I couldn't believe the doctor had been so cold and calculated, without taking any of our emotions or feelings into account and without answering any of our questions.

A nurse stepped out of the operating room and walked over to where the four of us were waiting. "It's going to be a long surgery, can I help you to the waiting room?" she asked.

"Can we wait here? If something happens I'd like to know as soon as possible," I said, my frustration being the only thing holding back my tears.

"Well," she looked up and down the hall, "it really is probably best if you wait in the waiting room, there will be a lot of equipment and people moving up and down the hall and we're really supposed to keep this area clear." I nodded in agreement and stood up. Kreg took my arm and we walked down the hall beside the nurse.

"That doctor was so rude. He didn't even talk to us, he just told us Cody was either going to die or be a vegetable. That was so mean," I scoffed, hoping the nurse would take the rebuke to her superiors.

"Yeah, Dr. Stone is very...blunt. He just tells it like it is, no sugar coating. But I promise you, he's a very good surgeon. He may sound kind of harsh but he does his very best work on every patient, regardless of the situation or their odds of recovery. Your son is in good hands." The nurse opened the door to the waiting room and let us pass through. I nodded my thanks and the door closed behind us.

It felt like a terrible case of deja vu, back in the old ugly waiting room where we had sat waiting for Cody just after the accident. It was after midnight and there was hardly anyone there, so I wandered over to a stuffed armchair with floral print and sat down. The chair was probably 20 years old and looked like it might be something you would find at a garage sale or at Goodwill, but it was still fairly comfortable. I pulled my knees up to my chest and turned sideways in the chair, tucked in between the arms and leaning against the back. Nestled in my little cocoon, I sat and waited, and waited, and waited.

My family tried to make conversation but I wasn't listening. It seemed as if my mind was shutting down to protect itself from the inevitable announcement that Cody had died. The only other option, according to Dr. Stone, was that Cody would be completely unresponsive. Was that option any better? Maybe it was worse. I couldn't decide.

Across from my chair was a big industrial clock hanging on the wall. I watched the seconds tick away and the minute hand spin around again and again. We sat in silence for some time, then Kreg came over to talk to me and see how I was doing.

"Hey honey, can I get you some water or something?" Kreg asked.

"No," I said softly. It was the only word I could muster.

"Okay, do you want to eat? I can go get you a muffin or a banana or something."

"No."

Kreg stopped asking questions and leaned back in his chair, rubbing my leg and trying to show me he cared. I wasn't trying to be rude, but I could not, for the life of me, conjure any other response. I couldn't sleep, couldn't speak, couldn't even think straight. Family members began arriving to offer support for us and Cody and I couldn't even fake a kind greeting or carry on in small talk. All I could do was sit and stare at the clock and wait for the worst news of my life.

I didn't know when it was going to come. Every time I heard a door open my heart skipped a beat and my chest felt tight. I braced myself for the doctor's arrival, but it was just a nurse, or a janitor, or someone else being admitted or released. With each click of the door I grew more nervous, knowing that the next click might usher in the news that my son had died on the operating table.

The clock ticked on and on, minute after minute, hour after hour. As the morning came I made 8:00 a.m. my deadline. That would be eight hours, or close enough, from the start of the surgery, and that was when I would know. The clock became a countdown in a cruel scenario where the only two outcomes were death or devastation. I wanted neither, but I knew one of the two were coming. The appointed hour came and went. Each additional minute was terrifying, and the clicks of the door opening and closing rattled my fragile mind.

I remembered the promise of Helaman in the Book of Mormon that the devil would send mighty winds, shafts in the whirlwind, hail, and storms to beat upon the righteous and sweep them down into the gulf of misery. I felt like I had endured all that and the gulf of misery was wide open, waiting for me to slip, but I held on. Christ was the answer, the only way to make it through the storm. Hour after hour I held on to my hope in Christ with an iron grip as the storm continued to beat down upon me, praying each moment that I could find relief before the winds and waves of grief would overtake me.

Nearly nine hours after the surgery began, the door clicked open and Dr. Stone walked toward us. I held my breath and tightened nearly every muscle in my body, bracing for impact. Our corner of the waiting room, full of friends and relatives, went silent.

"The operation was a success," Dr. Stone said, just as coldly as he had given his original prognosis. What did success mean? That Cody was not dead, but left mentally disabled? After an initial gasp from the crowd, he continued "We removed a section of the skull and cleaned out the hemorrhage, the pressure has been greatly reduced. We won't know his condition until he wakes up. He will remain in recovery for at least one hour, then we'll move him to the ICU. At that point you can go in and see him." He nodded to us and turned to walk back into the operating area.

Once the large wood door had closed behind Dr. Stone, the waiting room around me buzzed to life. Everyone was discussing and theorizing exactly what the doctor's report meant. My mother sat next to me and leaned in, "Isn't that great news? The operation was a success!" I wanted to rejoice with her, but I still felt burdened by the possibility that Cody could be brain dead.

"I don't know, I just want to see him. I just need to be with Cody and then we'll see." It was the first coherent sentence I had spoken in hours. Even though I wasn't at all optimistic about the situation, the possibility of a better outcome than I had imagined allowed my mind to begin functioning again.

An hour came and went without any update, then a nurse arrived to bring us back to see Cody. Only a few would be allowed in at a time, so naturally Kreg and I went first. I clutched Kreg's arm and we shuffled our tired and grief-stricken bodies behind the nurse as we weaved our way back to the ICU.

The nurse stopped outside a door where Cody's name was written on a whiteboard on the wall. I paused, not sure what to expect, then at Kreg's urging we stepped through the doorway. The first thing I noticed was the thick layer of white gauze bandages covering Cody's head. There seemed to be yards and yards of it wrapped tight to form a protective covering all the way around his skull from the ears upward. A breathing tube was supplying air and multiple IVs and sensors ran everywhere. Cody's hands were tied to the bed. I didn't understand why, until I saw his arms pulling at the restraints. Movement! I didn't expect to see anything like that so soon.

The nurse could see I was startled. "He's trying to wake up right now, the sedative is wearing off. We're going to be doing some tests to check his cognitive status, but you can stay here with him while we do it."

I pulled a seat up next to Cody and took his hand, rubbing it between mine. Cody's head began to sway left and right, as if he was waking up from a bad dream. His eyelids opened slowly and then closed again, appearing heavy. In a minute or two he began moving his lips and throat, apparently conscious of his breathing tube and fighting against it. The more Cody seemed to wake up, the more he seemed to be upset with his restraints and limitations. I had seen this before, when he was waking up in the hospital right after the accident; the confusion, the struggling, it definitely didn't look like Cody was brain dead.

"Kreg, I think he knows what's going on," I said.

"It sure looks that way, doesn't it," Kreg responded curiously.

Surely this had to be better than the two options Dr. Stone had given me. I had labored for more than eight hours under that threat, and now it seemed like Cody's mind was still in there after all. I began talking to Cody, trying to soothe him and explaining the situation. He turned to me and his eyes met mine and we held the glance long enough for me to realize Dr. Stone had indeed been wrong; Cody was conscious, if only just a little. He tried to speak but only muffled groans escaped his mouth.

"Honey, he's trying to say something," I said to Kreg.

"Maybe he could write something. Is there a pen?" Kreg asked as he checked his pockets. I looked around the room and found a pen and small pile of yellow scratch paper cut into three inch by four-inch sections. I grabbed the pen and put it in Cody's hand, then held the paper so he could write. Cody's hand began moving, but at the angle I was sitting I couldn't recognize any letters. After a few labored seconds, Cody stopped writing. I turned the piece of paper so Kreg and I could read it more easily. The letters were hard to make out, but there it was, "please untie me."

Kreg grabbed my arm and squeezed, "He can write!" Kreg burst out. But it wasn't just the writing that excited us. Writing meant that he understood the situation, he knew language, he could develop thoughts. After being told he would be a "vegetable," this was the best thing we could have imagined! Kreg hugged me and I hugged back. The reality of it all took a second to set in, but my spirits lifted and I felt like I had been given a new lease on life.

I bowed my head and prayed softly, "Thank you Heavenly Father, thank you, thank you, thank you."

Kreg tried to explain to Cody what was going on, and it seemed that Cody understood, at least enough to stop fighting the arm restraints. It was apparent that he wasn't comfortable or happy, but there wasn't much we could do to help him. We sat and waited and talked a little bit, then Kreg stood up to use the phone on the wall beside us.

"Pioneer Equipment, how can I help you?" I heard the familiar voice of Kreg's manager from the other end of the phone. It was early morning and they were probably wondering where Kreg was.

"Hi, this is Kreg. Hey, I'm at the hospital again with Cody, he's had a hemorrhage and they're not sure what's going to happen with him. I'm not going to be in today, can you guys take care of things without me?"

"Oh, I'm so sorry Kreg, that's terrible. Yeah, we can cover for you, no problem…hold on a second…hey Kreg, Mr. Baldwin is here and he'd like to talk to you."

I looked at Kreg with a little bit of worry on my face. Stan Baldwin was the owner of the company and he wasn't usually at their store in Idaho Falls. The fact that Kreg was missing on the day that the owner came by was probably not a good thing.

"Kreg? Stan Baldwin here!" His booming voice and Texas accent carried well enough for me to hear. "What's going on with your boy?" Kreg gave Stan a condensed version of what had happened, then waited for the response.

"Kreg, I'm so sorry. You have been such a good employee for us, you've really turned around our operation here in Idaho Falls and I've appreciated your advice for our other stores as well. You're an indispensable part of our family here, but you need to be with your family right now. You take as much time as you need, don't worry about coming back to work until things are taken care of there. We'll keep your paychecks coming just like normal. Our insurance should take care of all the medical bills, but if they try to stick you with anything else, you just call my secretary and she'll take care of you. Now you go on and see to your son, alright?"

"Thank you Mr. Baldwin, that's so kind of you. I'll call to check in when I can, and I will be able to take care of some things by phone, but I appreciate that. Thank you very much."

"I hope your boy gets well soon. Keep me updated, alright?"

"Will do. Thank you sir," Kreg said, and they said their goodbyes.

"Could you hear that?" Kreg asked me.

"Yeah, that's really nice of him," I said. We were making ends meet, but even the co-pays from the first set of operations were difficult to fit into our tight budget. Knowing that Stan was okay with Kreg taking some time off was incredibly relieving. And to have them continue to pay Kreg while he was gone was more than I had hoped for.

"Wow. I can't believe that," Kreg said as he sat down, the surprised look not leaving his face. I leaned on his shoulder and closed my eyes. Things were starting to look so much better than they had just a few hours ago.

The nurses arrived and began administering tests to check Cody's reflexes, so Kreg left me alone with Cody in order to go share the good news with all those outside in the waiting room. One by one he brought our family back to see Cody. They were so excited and happy and we shared hugs and they spent time talking to Cody and encouraging him to be strong and get better as quickly as possible. After about an hour Kreg returned and sat with me at Cody's bedside. Cody appeared worn out from all the interaction and his eyes began drifting, so we tried to talk quietly in case he was trying to go to sleep.

A nurse came back in and began administering reflex tests again. She began to act confused and kept running the tests again and again.

"Is something wrong?" I asked.

"I don't know, he doesn't appear to be responding like he was just a half hour ago. We just need to keep an eye on him." She made a note on the chart and then left. Kreg and I began paying closer attention to Cody's reactions. Over the course of the next half hour we noticed he wasn't shifting in his bed or fighting the restraints anymore, and his eyes began rolling aimlessly. Where Cody had been able to respond by squeezing our hands to signal yes or no, he no longer had any reaction to our voices or commands. We called the nurse back in and told her what we had seen. She ran the tests again, then said she would call Dr. Stone. The worried look on her face told me that things were not good. I wondered if I had celebrated too soon.

The nurse returned just a minute later. "Dr. Stone is out for a moment, but he ordered an MRI and he'll be back shortly," she said as she prepared Cody for a trip up to the radiology department. We waited in Cody's room for 20 minutes, then they finally returned. Dr. Stone followed Cody's bed into the room. I almost didn't recognize him at first, he was dressed in gym shorts and a sweaty t-shirt and had obviously been out running when they paged him. He wasted no time and gave us the news in his matter-of-fact style.

"He's suffered an embolization, meaning there's a blockage in one of the blood vessels in the brain. There's no sense in opening it up again because it will just keep bleeding and it won't stop. The specialists in Salt Lake may be able to fix it, that's his only hope. The nurses will arrange transportation." He started walking out the door, then stopped and turned back. "Good luck," he added, then left.

Another trip to Salt Lake while Cody's life hung in the balance. Did we have to do this all over again? I pulled the yellow note out of my pocket. "Please untie me." I read it over and over. Cody was in there, somewhere. I had seen it in his eyes, but this piece of paper proved it. He was in there, he would fight, and he would make it. After all we had been through, after all the miraculous comebacks, he just had to pull through. It would be too cruel, too unjust if God just let him die now. He had to make it, he just had to.

FOURTEEN

I T TOOK NEARLY FOUR HOURS FOR THE LIFE FLIGHT JET TO ARRIVE IN Idaho Falls. It seemed like we were back at square one with Cody. He was unconscious, the pressure in his head was threatening his life, and we were waiting for a jet to take us to Salt Lake. When the nurse tried to tell us that there was only one seat on the plane for a parent, I just brushed her off. I knew the magic words that could get us both down there.

The ambulance pulled up and the emergency room doors opened to a cold blast of air. Someone had run back home to grab my shoes and purse, but I hadn't thought to ask them for a coat and the frigid night air made me shiver. Two life flight nurses and a paramedic hopped out of the back of the ambulance and came inside to get Cody. They consulted with the hospital's nurses for just a minute and began wheeling Cody out with us in trail. One of the life flight nurses saw me shivering and took off his coat.

"Here," he said, "can you hold onto this for me?" he asked with a smile as he threw the coat over my shoulders. I smiled back thankfully, then put my arms in the sleeves and zipped it up. It was a nice heavy coat with the nurse's name embroidered on the front. 'Taylor.'

They loaded Cody into the back of the ambulance, but there was only one seat left. "You can ride back here," Taylor said, pointing to Kreg, then he told me, "and you can go hop in up front, it's warmer and more comfortable up there." Kreg jumped in the back and I walked around to the passenger door and climbed in the cab.

"Code three?" the driver asked before I could even close my door.

"What?" I asked him.

"Do you we need lights and sirens?" he asked, a little more urgently.

"Yes!" I said affirmatively. Every second we waited meant another artery could burst. The driver flipped a few switches and the lights and sirens started up as we sped out of the parking lot.

"So what's his condition?" The driver asked.

I tried to explain it as best I could, but it was hard to summarize so much so quickly. "He had a hemorrhage in the brain and then…and they took him in for surgery and they tried to fix it but it…it didn't work, so they've got to try again in Salt Lake."

"Huh, so is he stable right now?" The driver questioned as he looked both ways before speeding through a red light.

"Not really, he could die at any moment if another artery bursts."

"But his BP is holding?"

I thought for a second. BP, that must be blood pressure. His blood pressure monitor looked about the same as it always had before we left. "I don't know, I think it was fine. Normal, I guess"

I turned and peeked through the little window at the back of the cab into the area where Cody was lying. They didn't seem to be doing anything back there, just sitting, so I wasn't too worried.

The driver turned to me and gave me a funny look. "Where did you get your EMT cert?" he asked.

"I'm not an EMT," I said, then realized that the jacket must have thrown him off, "I'm the mom!"

The driver let out a frustrated grunt, "Well, that explains a lot!" He shook his head and slowed down just a bit, but he left the lights and sirens on, thankfully.

When we arrived at the airport I thanked the driver for getting us there quickly, to which he laughed and wished us luck. I walked up to the pilot while they unloaded Cody and told him I had ridden in the co-pilot's seat before and I would really appreciate it if he let me ride up there again so both Kreg and I could go down together. The pilot didn't put up a fight, just nodded his approval and let me climb in. In just a few minutes we were off.

The night was clear but the moon was nowhere to be seen, leaving the stars looking bright and the ground beneath us almost perfectly black, except for the headlights on highways and little clumps of city lights. It was about 10:00 p.m. and neither Kreg nor I had slept throughout the day or previous night. We'd been up for about 40 hours, and it was definitely taking its toll. The constant buzz of the engines and the slight vibrations tried to lull me to sleep, but every time I started to nod off I would jolt back awake and turn to grab Kreg's hand. Cody's situation was bad, but there was no way to know what was going on in his head, so we just had to sit and wait.

We landed at the Salt Lake City airport without incident and got another ambulance ride to the hospital. I was hoping for a flurry of activity from the emergency room staff once we arrived, just like we had received right after Cody's accident, but the nurses who received us were less rushed and didn't seem to be too nervous about Cody's condition. They wheeled Cody into a room in the ICU and we took a seat next to Cody while the nurses checked vitals and made notes. After just a few minutes they wheeled Cody out to go take a new brain scan, but promised to be back in less than half an hour.

Kreg and I sat quietly in the room until Cody returned. It was near midnight and we were both running on fumes, but it was impossible to sleep. My limbs felt weak and my eyes were groggy but I knew I had to be strong and stay awake for Cody. I didn't want to miss anything. When they wheeled him back in he looked so peaceful. His eyes were closed and his arms were lying loose at his side. His chest was slowly rising and falling as the breathing machine pumped air in and out of his lungs.

How many times had I sat by his bedside now, waiting for the doctors to perform some lifesaving operation? It seemed like we had been through it all too many times to count. In the back of my mind I wondered how long we could go on like this before something happened that could not be repaired. We had been so blessed, but it seemed like Cody's body just didn't want to heal, no matter how many surgeries or blessings we gave him. I knew we couldn't go on like this forever. The sleepiness, the emotions, and the frustration all combined to tear down my hope for any kind of positive recovery.

A doctor in a long white coat soon walked in to greet us. I was too exhausted to stand, but Kreg got to his feet and shook the doctor's hand.

"Hello, I'm Dr. Pike. I'll be overseeing your son's care for the next little while," he said, getting right down to business.

"Last time we were here, Dr. Grant was overseeing Cody. He's pretty familiar with our situation, is he still around?" Kreg asked. Dr. Grant had been so kind to us, I hoped that he was available to help us again and was glad that Kreg had asked.

"I'm sorry, he's on another assignment right now," he said, then moved on without any further explanation. "In about ten minutes, we're going to take Cody in for surgery. The brain scan was really bad, the hemorrhage and embolization have caused some serious damage to the arteries and the brain matter. We're going to try to get the bleeding stopped, but it's going to be difficult. Even if we can get this fixed, and I'm not saying that we can, his odds of long-term survival are very low. I wouldn't get your hopes up. I'm sorry, I wish I had better news, but this is one of the worst cases of brain damage I've seen in a long time. Most patients wouldn't have survived this long. I'll give you a few minutes alone with your son."

Kreg sat down and put his arms around me and I collapsed into his embrace. The rollercoaster of emotions was taking its toll. It was just too much to handle. If my sweet 16-year-old boy was going to die, then why put him through all this? I didn't want him to bleed out in surgery, why couldn't they let us just say our goodbyes and be with him while he passed peacefully from this life? I wanted to ask Kreg if we should just let him pass away here with us, rather than sending him in to die in surgery, but there was no good way to say it, so I just tucked myself closer into his chest and silently began to cry.

They came to take Cody away before I was ready. As the nurses entered I knew it might be my last time seeing Cody alive, so I stood up and walked to his side. I picked up his hand and held it while I stared at his face, trying to remember every curve and line.

Cody was still so young, but so close to becoming a man. I could see a hint of light brown stubble on his chin. Would he ever give his daughters scratchy kisses with those whiskers, like Kreg had given our girls? Would he grow up to be the construction foreman that he had dreamed of becoming, calling out instructions and commands with a deep booming voice? Was there any hope of a normal future for my son? Probably not. I couldn't see any way out of this. Maybe Dr. Stone had been right, and Dr. Pike too. Maybe this was it.

The nurses began pulling on the bed and I let go of Cody's hand. I tried to take a mental picture of him one last time, but there were too many nurses around him and I couldn't get a good look. I followed them into the hall and watched as they slowly passed through a large set of double doors. "He's gone," I said to Kreg. He rubbed my back but said nothing.

A nurse came along and led us to another family room. It wasn't the same one we had been in months earlier, but it might as well have been. A half dozen couches and chairs lined the walls. My parents told us they would wait to come down until the next day at some point, so it would just be us for a while. Kreg and I took a seat on one of the couches and I laid down, resting my head in his lap. He ran his fingers through my hair and told me everything would be okay, and I began to drift in and out of sleep.

There was a knock on the door that startled me awake and I checked the clock. It was 5:00 a.m.

"Hello?" I looked at the door and saw someone begin to poke their head in.

"Come in," Kreg said, just waking up himself. I sat up and tried to fix my hair.

"Hi, sorry to disturb you, I'm Dr. Richardson, I worked with your son several months ago."

"Of course, come on in," Kreg said. Dr. Richardson had fixed Cody's spine on our first emergency trip to Salt Lake and I recognized him immediately.

"I hoped to see Cody again under better circumstances, but unfortunately, here we are again." Dr. Richardson seemed genuinely saddened by the fact that Cody was back in the hospital. I was amazed that a doctor in a major hospital would remember a patient like our son, and feel a personal concern for his wellbeing.

"I just finished up with your son's procedure, and I wanted to come in and let you know how it went."

"Yes, please, sit down," Kreg said again, waving him in. Dr. Richardson stepped out of the doorway and took a seat next to the couch where we were sitting.

"The operation was a success, my part of it at least. Dr. Jackson is on his way in to finish up the embolization, but we've got the bleeding stopped." That seemed like good news, but I couldn't tell if any of it would matter. Would this help his brain heal, or was the damage already done, and we were just prolonging the inevitable? It seemed too difficult to regain hope again, just to have it stolen from me again in a few days or weeks. I held my breath as the doctor continued, trying not to get excited.

"We removed the same piece of skull they cut out for the surgery in Idaho Falls and were able to reach the problem area from there. We cleaned out the hemorrhage, once again, and relieved the pressure, but we didn't want to put the bone piece back just yet, so we've left that out. It's being stored in a freezer for later, but having that piece removed will let the brain expand a little bit if the pressure starts building again." He stopped for a second and took a look at us, sizing us up. We must have looked terrible, it was our third day in those clothes, we had little sleep, and the worry and frustration was etched onto our faces.

Dr. Richardson sat forward in his chair and tried to give us a little pep talk. He seemed to be genuinely concerned with Cody, and with making sure that we knew and understood what was going on. "Look, I know things seem really bad right now, but we just won't know how bad it is until he wakes up. Your son is young, amazing things can happen with a young brain. Just hold on, don't give up yet. Alright? Dr. Jackson will be in here in a little while to finish up the surgery. He's still got to fix that one artery from the inside, then take care of the embolization, then we should be done. Just hold on until then."

Dr. Richardson stood up and shook our hands then walked out the door, closing it behind himself. I turned to look at Kreg. He had hope in his eyes, but I couldn't believe in it anymore. It was too much back and forth, up and down. One doctor says Cody will die, the next one says don't give up. What was I supposed to believe? Was I supposed to listen to this doctor but not the other? As much as I wanted to grab onto the hope, I just couldn't make my brain accept it. Maybe Cody would pull through, maybe, but it was a one-in-a-million shot, and it seemed like we had exhausted our good luck.

"Oh babe," Kreg said out of relief, pulling me into a big hug. I didn't want to say anything to pour water on the fire, but I just didn't feel the same hope he did. Kreg probably sensed my reluctance, it was almost impossible to hide my emotions from him.

"There's still a chance. Don't give up, there's still a chance," he told me, pulling me in closer. The battle in my mind between hope and reality began to spill out, and my tears left faint stains of mascara on Kreg's shirt. I cried until my mind stopped fighting itself, but I was no closer to a resolution.

A short time later another knock came at the door, this one softer than the first. We looked up and saw Dr. Jackson walking into the room. My face was still red and I tried to wipe away the remaining tears and makeup. Dr. Jackson stopped in his tracks and stared at me, and tears began to stream down his face.

"I'm so sorry," he said through his broken composure. "I should have listened to your mother's intuition. I made the best medical call that I could make at the time, but you were right, you were right. We should have finished the surgery." He shook his head and wiped away some tears. Kreg and I were stunned and didn't know what to say. Dr. Jackson continued, "I'm so sorry. All we need is twenty seconds in there with the balloons to fix the artery. We'll get it done this time, I promise. I'm sorry." He stood there for a moment more in silence, then turned and left us alone again.

I had never seen a doctor as remorseful as he was, let alone one who cried about their patient. But his sadness also told me that this was indeed a terrible setback, one that was traumatic enough to cause one of the best brain surgeons in the country to break down and cry. It helped my heart a little to see his compassion, but it solidified my growing fear that the end was near for Cody.

Cody was in surgery for nearly five more hours and I was growing restless. It had been more than ten hours since I had seen Cody and each minute was more and more difficult. I didn't know why they were even doing the surgery anyway, if there was almost zero chance he would recover. What use was it to get him stabilized if his brain had already been damaged so much that he wouldn't wake up? And even if he did wake up and had to survive on a breathing machine and a feeding tube with no cognitive ability whatsoever, that was no way to live. If Cody was going to be brain dead, there was no use in keeping his body here. We might as well let him pass on and return to Heavenly Father. At least in death there would be no more pain for him, no more hemorrhages, no more surgeries.

Kreg obviously didn't feel the same way. He was holding out hope for a recovery that I seriously doubted was even possible. Any talk of letting

Cody die was quickly turned around and rejected. Kreg wasn't going to give up on Cody until the doctors had done everything under the sun to fix him, but I couldn't wait that long. My heart couldn't take it.

Dr. Jackson returned at the end of the surgery to give us an update. The tears were gone and he had regained his professional demeanor. "The surgery went well, no complications. The carotid artery seems to be holding for now, which is as good as we can hope for at this point. We've repaired every problem that we know about. Now we just have to wait."

"What happens next, what are we waiting for?" Kreg asked.

"Honestly, we don't know. There's really no way to tell what's going to happen when there's a brain injury. It's just such a complex organ, and there's so much we don't know about it yet. We'll keep Cody sedated for a little while, but we'll know a lot more when he comes off of that medication and tries to wake up. Until then, we wait."

We were finally allowed to go back in to see Cody, but his condition didn't look much different, aside from a new dressing of bandages around his head. He wasn't moving or shifting around, and I suspected he was already gone. I couldn't imagine that anyone could survive what he had been through. I held his hand and tried to talk to him. Maybe, even if his brain was gone, his spirit could still hear me. "Hey Cody, it's Mom. I'm sorry this is all happening to you. You don't deserve this. I'm so sorry Cody."

We waited by his side for several more hours before my parents arrived with the motorhome and our three girls. They knew the routine and set up shop in our designated family room with movies and coloring books and games. Kreg's parents soon arrived as well. They had been spending the winter in Arizona, but started on the drive to Salt Lake as soon as they got word about the hemorrhage. Kreg's sister Denise and her husband Tracy, and his brother Bret and Bret's wife Tami also arrived from Idaho. Our little family room was filling up quickly.

In the late afternoon my dad came in and gave me a hug and spent a few minutes standing at Cody's side, patting his hand softly and examining all the machines and contraptions that kept Cody alive. My dad was a man of few words, so the silence wasn't unusual. His time and attention meant the world, even if there were no words spoken.

After a few minutes he came and sat in the chair next to me. "Honey, I've got a room we can use at the Ronald McDonald House just down the street. I want you to go down…"

"No," I cut him off, "I'm not leaving Cody."

"Honey, you need to go down and just take a little rest. Take a shower, maybe take a nap. We've brought a suitcase of clothes for you."

"Dad, I don't want to go." I stood my ground.

"Brenda, listen to me." If my dad was this adamant, I knew he was serious. "You're going to kill yourself if you don't take a few moments to get cleaned up and clear your mind. Cody needs you to be strong. The girls need you to be strong. Kreg and I will stay right here and you and Mom can go for just a little bit, then you can come right back."

I hated the idea, but I knew he was right. A shower would be nice, and I did need a new change of clothes. Kreg came in and continued working on me until I finally relented. Kreg and I would take turns going down to the room for showers, then coming right back.

As my mom and I drove down the Avenues to South Temple and headed east, I became nervous. The Ronald McDonald House was only a couple minutes away, but it felt way too far from Cody. When any moment could be his last, every moment apart was torture. We walked in the

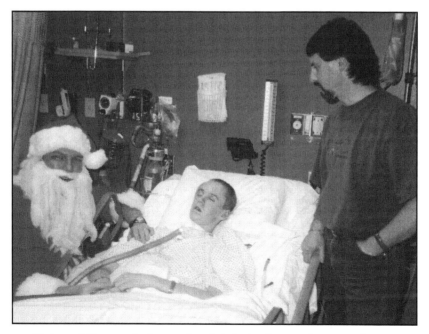

Cody and Kreg in the hospital in Salt Lake City, with a special visitor

front doors and introduced ourselves and they showed us to our room. In the gathering areas and hallways and kitchen and through open doors, all I could see was the pain of injury or disease inflicted on families with sick children. It was a terrible feeling, being in the middle of so much pain and suffering. Of course, some of the families were trying to make the best of it, but they looked worn down and exhausted. I figured I didn't look much better.

I gathered my things and went to take a shower in the community bathroom. The hot water felt good and relaxed my aching muscles. It also reminded me that I had avoided sleep for far too long. I could have stayed in that hot steamy shower for an hour, but I needed to get back to Cody.

As I got dressed in a fresh change of clothes, I checked my old pockets for anything that I needed to keep with me. I reached into the right front pocket and pulled out a little yellow piece of paper. 'Please untie me,' it read. Had that only been a day ago? It seemed like forever. Cody had only been unconscious for a little over 24 hours, but so much had happened in that time. I didn't know whether the paper was still evidence of Cody's will to live, or if it was a memory of a consciousness that would never return. I paused for a moment, staring at the paper, examining the long loose strokes. No matter the outcome, that paper was important. I slipped it into my new pair of jeans and packed up my things.

After I got dressed I returned to our room to fix my hair and put on my makeup, leaving the shower available for one of the other 20 or so families who needed to use it. My mom offered to sit by the phone while I took a nap, but there was no way it was happening. I had already been away from Cody for too long.

"I don't want to come back here," I told my mom as we left, "it's too sad here." She just nodded.

It was dark by the time we got back to the hospital. I stopped at the family room and promised to come talk to the girls in a little bit, after I checked up on Cody. I walked back to the ICU by myself and found Dr. Pike there with several nurses. He didn't look happy, but then again, he never looked happy.

"What's going on?" I asked, my eyes darting from doctor to nurse, and finally to Kreg, whose nervous expression told me everything.

Dr. Pike turned to me and stated coldly, "We've got a problem."

FIFTEEN

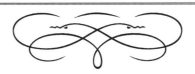

I KNEW I SHOULDN'T HAVE LEFT CODY'S SIDE. IT WAS A MISTAKE, I SHOULD have just stayed.

"Mrs. Parmer, as I was just telling your husband, Cody has developed another leak in the brain. The pressure from the hemorrhaged artery being sealed has caused another weak artery to start leaking. We expected as much, there's no real way to fix them all. His brain is already so weak and damaged that going in again will probably just cause more harm. So, we're just going to leave it."

"What does that mean? He's just going to bleed out?" I asked, wondering if this was the end. Oh, how could I have been so stupid to leave the hospital at a time like this?

"No, not necessarily. It's a slow leak, and it will probably be absorbed by the body. But it could lead to another hemorrhage later on," Dr. Pike continued.

"So what do we do?" I asked, unsure of how dire the situation really was. His doom and gloom attitude suggested that Cody was near death, but the substance of his report was fairly tame, compared to everything else we had gone through.

"Just wait, I suppose. If he makes it through the night, we'll continue with the operations as scheduled. I'll be here until the early morning, then Dr. Richardson will be in and he'll make the determination to proceed or not." Dr. Pike closed the chart and stepped out of the room, followed by the nurses. I was beginning to really despise the man. He seemed so nonchalant about everything, assuming the worst and not seeming to care in the least bit for our son.

I plopped down in a seat next to Kreg. "I don't like him," I whispered as soon as I was sure Dr. Pike was well out of earshot.

"I know, he's not very...pleasant," Kreg agreed. We talked about Cody and Kreg filled me in with some of the details Dr. Pike and the nurses had given him before I returned. Despite Dr. Pike's morbid tone, it really didn't seem like much was going on. A minor leak in the brain might be something that could heal itself, but it wasn't life threatening, not at the moment at least. I was just glad to be back.

That night I made my customary bed out of blankets and towels on the floor next to Cody. My dad canceled our reservation at the Ronald McDonald House and got a couple rooms at the Little America hotel where we would have some more privacy and a few more beds. Kreg and my parents went down to the hotel to get the girls situated, but I stayed next to Cody. If I could help it, I wasn't going to leave his side until he was better.

The hum of hospital machinery seemed to sing me to sleep. The ventilator machine made a slow pumping sound that combined with the hum of fans keeping electronic equipment cool. The heart rate monitor was turned down, but I could still hear the faint beeps. Every so often an anesthesia machine would purr as it injected a tiny dose of medicine into Cody's IV. Sleep was coming quickly, but I hadn't yet said my evening prayer. I figured that one of the hundred prayers I had said that day should count, but then reconsidered. I needed every blessing I could get, not only for Cody, but for my family, and myself.

I got up on my knees and formed the words in my mind. "Heavenly Father, it's been a long day. I don't know what to do, I don't know what to think. I need your help. If Cody is in there, if there is any way that he can survive and come out of this okay, please let it happen. But if Cody is already gone..." Even in my head, the words wouldn't come. I didn't know what to ask for if Cody was gone. God knew what was best though.

"Just please help us, help Cody, help my poor girls to know that I love them, even if I can't spend enough time with them. Bless Kreg, I know this is difficult for him too but he has to be so strong for everyone else. And Father, please help me." My eyes began tearing up and I covered my mouth to keep from sobbing. "I don't know how much more I can take. I'm at my limit. I can't do it anymore, I just need this to be over soon.

Please help us. In the name of Jesus Christ, amen." When the prayer was over I collapsed onto my makeshift bed and curled up in the fetal position. Ask and ye shall receive, knock and it shall be opened unto you, that was the promise, and it was about the only tool I felt I had left. I figured that if I never gave up asking or knocking, something would finally turn around for Cody.

I was asleep within seconds, but despite how tired I was, I couldn't sleep soundly. Nurses and doctors came in and out, Kreg returned from taking the girls to the hotel, and I woke several times afraid and disoriented. Morning came almost as a relief. Kreg had slept in a chair that was even less comfortable than my makeshift bed, and he was up before me. He brought me back some food from the cafeteria and we ate quietly alongside Cody. Slowly, the hospital was waking up and things were coming to life.

"You're awake!" It was Dr. Richardson at the door. He caught me with my mouth full, so I politely nodded and smiled. "Well, I thought about Cody all night and came to check up on him as soon as I got in. I'm really glad he made it through the night, that's a great sign and it means we're on the right track!" Even though I wasn't really sure what to believe about Cody's outcome, Dr. Richardson's optimism was contagious.

Dr. Richardson was dressed in blue scrubs and looked like he was ready to head into surgery. He walked over to Cody's side and stood there, looking at him for a moment. "He looks like a baseball player. Does he play?"

Kreg and I stood up and walked to Cody's side as well. "Yeah, that's a pretty good guess! He was the pitcher last year, but he can play almost anything. He plays football too," Kreg said.

"I figured as much, he looks like a pretty active kid, he probably keeps you on your toes, eh?" He turned to look at me.

"Yeah, more than you could imagine!" I was glad that he was taking the time to remember Cody's face and try to understand him. Maybe it didn't make any difference in the end for Cody's condition, but it sure helped me to know that the doctor cared.

"Well, I didn't want to wake you, so we waited a little bit, but we're ready to take Cody in to put the bone plate back in his head."

"You're going to do that now?" I hadn't prepared myself for Cody to leave, but he seemed stable, and I was glad Dr. Richardson was going to be doing the operation. "Okay, well, take good care of him," I said.

Dr. Richardson put his arm around my shoulder and gave me a hug and said, "Oh don't worry, this is nothing big. We'll have Cody back in just a few hours. Later this afternoon though, we're going to take him off of the sedative and we'll see what kind of response we get. Hang in there!" He patted Kreg on the back and then got a few nurses to help him wheel Cody out.

"Aren't they just night and day?" Kreg asked when Dr. Richardson left.

"What do you mean?" I wondered.

"Dr. Pike and Dr. Richardson. They're doing the exact same job, but their attitude, their outlook, everything is just so different."

"Yeah," I replied, "I wish Dr. Richardson were here all the time instead of Dr. Pike."

As soon as the girls arrived we moved to the family room to spend a few hours with them before Cody's operation was complete. The girls had a handful of activities for the day and jumped right into coloring and crafts. Then, one by one, my siblings began arriving—Dirk and Margaret, Vicki and Corey, Kip and Mac, Carrie and the kids—as each of them arrived they wrapped me up in warm hugs and kind words, and I felt so thankful that Heavenly Father had given me such a great support system. They had come just as soon as they were able to, leaving work and school and lives at home in order to travel to Salt Lake and care for my girls and give us moral support.

We had learned just how important that support system was when Carrie's husband died in an avalanche a year earlier. Everyone came out to help, and Kreg and I stayed in their house for two months so we could be there full time for her and her five kids. That experience brought us all closer together and formed a bond that has held our family together through the toughest of times. It was just natural then for everyone to band together and come down for Cody's sake, but their sacrifices and support still overwhelmed me and I knew how much they were giving up to be there.

We talked for some time about Cody, about the doctors' predictions and what might or might not happen. I told them about the mean Dr.

Pike and the sensitive Dr. Richardson, about how I didn't want to leave the hospital to stay in a hotel or even really want to be away from Cody. My sisters and sisters-in-law gathered around to help me make decisions about how to schedule time with Cody and time with the girls. They made a list of people who would watch Cody while I was taking a nap or sleeping, and issued the assignments. They even pulled together a couple couches and designated them as my official sleeping quarters in the family room. Life was still rough, but my dear family was making it as smooth as they possibly could.

A few hours later the nurses brought Cody back to his room. The surgery had gone well and the portion of his skull they had removed was back in place. I finally started escorting family members in one-by-one to see him. The ICU didn't allow more than two visitors at a time, so when I came in, Kreg had to leave. Sometimes we could sneak a visitor in with Kreg and I, though a few of the nurses would give us dirty looks for breaking their rule.

Dr. Richardson came in that afternoon at the end of his shift and started running Cody through a set of reflex tests. He checked his pupils, ran an instrument along Cody's feet, and pressed on several pressure points. I could see Cody's toes flexing and muscles responding to the various tests and hoped that was a positive sign.

"Cody is responding well to the tests, but his coma is no longer medically induced. He's on his own now, so there's no telling now when he'll wake up, or what state he'll be in when he does. But these response tests tell us that he's still in there, his brain is still functioning at the primary levels. Just keep praying for him, it's up to Cody and God from here on out." Dr. Richardson gave me a little side-hug and shook Kreg's hand and left for the day.

After dinner Dr. Pike came through and made the rounds at the beginning of his shift. He checked on Cody and ran through the same tests that Dr. Richardson had done, working with the feet, eyes, and pressure points. He checked the charts again and ran through the tests a second time. "It looks like we have another problem," Dr. Pike concluded.

"What's that?" I asked.

"Cody's temperature is rising quickly. Based on these readings, it looks like his body is rejecting the bone that was put back in during the surgery."

Kreg asked, "So what do you do?"

"We'll monitor it for the night, the temperature might recede. If his condition gets any worse we'll have to remove the bone again," Dr. Pike concluded.

"What about the tests? The response tests for the brain activity?" I asked, hoping that the tests had changed his mind about Cody's overall outlook.

"Unfortunately, Cody did not respond to the neural tests, indicating that he has no brain function. This confirms some of my earlier conclusions, and we'll need to start discussing end-of-life options fairly soon," Dr. Pike said without any emotion. My jaw dropped open. How was that even possible? I had seen the positive responses myself, earlier in the day. Had things gone so wrong in just a couple hours that Cody was now doomed to die? I collapsed into one of the chairs and Dr. Pike left the room.

"I saw it, I saw the tests work!" I told Kreg.

"I know, but I was watching when Dr. Pike did his tests, and he's right, there was no response," Kreg said in disbelief. We sat in silence for quite a while before Kreg got up to go talk to the family. Though I had planned on sleeping on the couches in the family room that night, I made my bed beside Cody once again, not wanting to leave the room.

Dr. Richardson came early in the morning on Friday to take Cody into surgery again. They removed the piece of skull that was causing the fever and sewed up his scalp for the third time in four days. When they brought Cody back after the surgery I spoke to Dr. Richardson about the neural response tests and what Dr. Pike had said. He promised that he would try the tests again in the afternoon, after a few more appointments he had.

When Dr. Richardson returned, I went and got Kreg so we could both be there with Cody for the results. We held our breath as Dr. Richardson performed the response tests once again. When he ran an instrument along the bottom of Cody's foot, I saw the toes curl. I saw muscles contract as he pressed on pressure points. The response was there, we all knew it.

Dr. Richardson set down his tools and covered Cody back up with a blanket. "Okay, everything looks as good as it can be right now. He's responding normally to the tests. I'll put it down in the notes on his chart here, but you be sure to tell Dr. Pike what you saw, alright?" We agreed, and he moved on to other duties.

That evening, once again, Dr. Pike came in to start his shift and we told him about the tests. He took out his instruments and ran the exact same tests in the same way. No response. "I'm sorry, I can only tell you what I see. Cody is exhibiting no signs of brain activity and there is no response to the most basic neural tests. There is some minor muscle movement from the muscles being touched, but that's not the type of nervous system response we're looking for. I have no other option than to formally declare that your son is brain dead. I know it's not what you wanted to hear, but that's the truth." Dr. Pike recorded his findings in the charts and walked out.

"How is that even possible?" Kreg asked. "Cody responded to the tests just this morning, I know it. Why isn't it working now?" Kreg asked as he stood and leaned over Cody's body.

"It's because Cody knows I don't like Dr. Pike, so he won't respond to him." I patted Cody's leg and glanced at his still and lifeless face. Kreg looked at me to see if I was joking, but I wasn't. Cody was in there somewhere, listening to us, I just knew it. It was the only explanation, the only way I could make sense of the situation.

The next morning during the shift changeover, Dr. Pike and Dr. Richardson came in together to try the tests again and discuss their results. Admittedly, they didn't go very well, at least not as well as the last time Dr. Richardson had tried, but there still seemed to be a little response. The two doctors argued over the meaning of the muscle movements and tried the tests again and again. Dr. Richardson was adamant that Cody's brain was still functioning, Dr. Pike was adamant that it was not. They excused themselves to continue their discussions in private while Kreg and I tried to figure out what it all meant.

Dr. Pike came back that evening with a slip of paper. "Mr. and Mrs. Parmer, we need to talk about Cody," he said as he handed Kreg the note. Written on it was a room number, a date and time. "We need to discuss end-of-life options. We'll have a meeting on Sunday afternoon in that room. I know you have a lot of family here, so you can invite anyone you'd like, it's a conference room. We'll have a lot more to discuss there, but primarily, you need to decide whether Cody will be an organ donor or not. What you decide will determine how we take care of his body from here on out."

Dr. Pike left and I burst into tears. Kreg took me in his arms and held me tight. Part of me already accepted that this was probably the end, but another part was still holding on. In either case, having to deal with the practical decision to end my son's life was more than my mind could handle. Kreg sent my mom and sisters in to comfort me as he shared the news with the relatives in the family room. My family seemed to have known this would be the likely outcome and didn't appear too surprised, just concerned for my sanity and welfare.

We spent the next couple days waiting and sobbing. I refused to leave Cody's side and found it difficult to eat or even talk to anyone else. My heart just could not process what was happening, even though my mind understood the implications of the looming decision. My family would send someone to sit with me throughout the day, but I was poor company. Kreg spent all night in the room with me, watching over me and Cody and sleeping little if any. I would catch him throughout the day, sleeping while he was standing up with his arms folded and his head bowed down. Poor Kreg, he was my rock, but I could tell it all was wearing on him as well.

Sunday morning came and the meeting loomed over us like a dark cloud. What were we going to do? I knew that Dr. Pike would tell us to end life support, but was that really the best decision for Cody? If his spirit was still in his damaged and sick body, I was never going to give up. But if he really was gone, I couldn't justify holding on to him, no matter how much I wanted to. There was just no way to know which doctor was right. How was I supposed to choose life or death with almost nothing to go on? It was an impossible task.

SIXTEEN

K REG SAT WITH ME IN CODY'S ROOM SUNDAY MORNING BEFORE THE meeting. "Honey, do you think Cody would want to donate his organs?" he asked.

"No, I don't want him cut into pieces and mangled up. That's just too cruel. He's just a boy, just let him be," I said, halfway through tears.

A nurse was in the room checking on Cody's vitals and interjected, "I'm sorry to butt in, I know this is a hard decision, but donating organs can do a lot of good. I'm assuming you are LDS?" We nodded yes. "Just recently we had a missionary come in. He was brought home from his mission after an accident and was on life support, and the family elected to donate his organs. I was here that night and saw a bunch of the receiving families come in for the surgery. His heart went to one family, his lungs to another. Two different people got new kidneys. They sent his skin to a burn center, his bone marrow was used, lots of the arteries and valves, even his corneas. It was really remarkable. I know it sounds strange to donate the organs, but there were over a dozen families whose loved ones were able to survive because of this one missionary's final gift. It was really touching. I would really recommend that you consider it, if you can."

But I couldn't. I knew Cody was young and his body was healthy, but those organs were meant for him, not for someone else. I just couldn't agree to the doctors chopping him up, as much as I knew it was probably the right thing to do.

At 4:00 p.m. the time came to head up to the conference room. We all decided to go, and it was the first time Cody would really be on his own. I kissed him on the forehead before we left, not knowing what would happen or if I could even survive what they were about to tell me. We walked through the halls and up the elevator to a conference room with a big table and at least twenty chairs. At the last minute I grabbed Kreg's arm, "I can't do it. I can't go in there. I know what Dr. Pike is going to say and I just can't do it."

Kreg looked around. There was a small waiting area outside the conference room and he led me to a chair and sat me down. "Alright, you stay right here then. I'll let you know what happens. Okay?" Kreg asked. I nodded yes.

My younger sister Vicki sat down next to me. "I'll stay with Brenda," she told Kreg. The rest of the family entered the conference room and closed the door. I buried my head in my hands and folded over in my chair. Vicki rubbed my back but didn't say anything. That was probably best, considering my state of mind.

As the rest of the family took their seats inside the conference room, Dr. Pike introduced himself and then pulled out a set of MRI images, CT scan printouts, and charts.

"Cody's hemorrhage this past Monday was massive. The lack of blood flow to the brain during that time killed a significant portion of his brain cells, almost half of his brain, in fact." He placed a large black and white film on the board behind him. It was a top-down cross section of Cody's brain, and the whole right side was dark.

"This large dark area here is dead brain matter. This is one of the worst results of a hemorrhage on a surviving patient that we've ever seen in Salt Lake City." He then pulled out a stack of charts and proceeded, for the next twenty minutes, to describe each and every way in which they had examined Cody's situation, and why it was so bad.

"As you can see, we also have a history, over the past several days, of negative brain activity at the most basic levels, showing that there is no connectivity from the brain to the rest of the body. These are the conditions that constitute an individual being deemed 'brain dead.' Cody's brain has ceased to send messages to control his body. He is alive only because of the life support equipment that is in place. He could remain in this state indefinitely, but it is impossible to recover from a situation like this." He paused for a moment to let the news set it.

"As difficult as it is, we need to accept the fact that this is the end for Cody. This is not a decision we take lightly. I have shared these charts and images with several other experts, and all have come to the same conclusion. Our professional recommendation is that he be removed from life support. Mr. Parmer, we discussed earlier the possibility of organ donation. Have you made a decision?"

"No, not really. I don't think my wife is interested in that, but we still need to talk about it a little more. How much time do we have before we have to make a decision?" Kreg replied cautiously.

"I haven't reviewed your insurance, but most plans will only allow a short period of time on life support after this determination has been made. We will need your decision as soon as possible, so we can arrange for the surgeries and organ transportation, if that's what you choose," Dr. Pike concluded. "For the rest of the day, I will advise the nurses in the ICU that your visitation restriction is lifted, you can have as many people in there as you would like, as long as you don't disturb the other patients and you keep the door closed. I will let you talk amongst yourselves, you can stay in this room as long as you would like." Dr. Pike then collected his things and left. I heard him leave as I sat in the hallway but kept my head down so I wouldn't make eye contact.

Back in the conference room, the family talked and came to the conclusion that it was indeed time to let Cody go. It was really the only available option. "I can't tell her," Kreg said to the rest of the room. "I can't go out there and tell Brenda that we need to let Cody die."

"I'll do it. You can stay in here and I'll go talk to her." It was my brother Dirk who volunteered. He was always the tough one and had been my protector many times, but now it became his job to softly deliver the most terrible news of my life. He got up and left the conference room.

Vicki and I were sitting only a few feet from the door when Dirk came out. I was curled up in a ball on my chair with my arms wrapped around my knees. I lifted my head to see who it was and could tell by the expression on Dirk's face that it wasn't good. I got up from my chair and started walking away quickly, trying to get away from the awful news that was going to follow.

"Brenda, come here. Come on," Dirk caught up to me and I started staggering, my knees about to give out. Dirk caught me and held me up.

"Brenda, it's time to let Cody go. They've done everything they can do. It's time." I broke down crying and Dirk walked me back to the conference room and inside the heavy wooden door. Through my tears I could see everyone else sobbing as well.

Cody was such a good boy, so kind and friendly, the world needed more of those kind of people, not less. I didn't understand. How could God take such a good person away from a family that loved him and cared for him? Cody had been blessed with so many miracles, only to end up brain dead after some stupid artery burst in his brain. I couldn't take it anymore. This was the worst moment of my life, and God had left me alone with no way out.

After many tears we slowly made our way back to Cody's room. Everyone was packed into his room, sharing stories about Cody and memories they had. I sat on a little round rolling chair and pulled up close to Cody's side, wanting to wake up from this nightmare but knowing it wouldn't end. Kreg stood behind me and had his hands on my shoulders, trying to comfort me though I could tell he was holding back tears as well.

All I could think about was what our family would be like without Cody in our lives. From four kids down to three in the flip of a switch. Three kids seemed so small, too few. Our family had been just right, and now it would have a gaping hole. And to lose our only son! Cody was my buddy and my friend, but he also protected his mom when Kreg was away. I relied on him for so much, his place could never be filled. I wondered how Kreg would handle it, losing his fishing buddy and sports partner. They did so much guy stuff together, and now Kreg would be all alone in a family of girls, with a wife who would be grieving for the rest of her life.

Somebody finally broached the subject of a funeral. We hadn't made any plans, but one of my sisters got out a piece of paper and we began talking about songs that could be sung or who should give the eulogy. We decided that his scoutmaster should give one of the talks, as he had been such a good friend of Cody's. We began assigning prayers and decided on a cemetery. Then Dr. Richardson arrived.

"I heard about your meeting," he told us. "I'm sorry I wasn't there. Dr. Pike is the lead doctor and I'm sure he's only saying what he believes, but I have to disagree with his assessment." You could hear a pin drop in the room. "I know it looks bad, I know he showed you some really terrible charts and images, but believe me when I say that it's not the end. The brain can do amazing things, especially with someone like Cody who's so young, and his body is healthy." Dr. Richardson was giving this pep talk all he had.

"It's a tough decision, I know, but I'm not giving up hope yet. I've seen miracles happen in some really terrible situations. Just…think about it. It's up to you, but I'd say you should wait. Wait and see what happens over the next week or two. Maybe I'm wrong, but there's plenty of time to wait and see." Dr. Richardson looked directly at me. His eyes were pleading with me to listen to him, to not give up hope. I had appreciated his caring and kind words, but I didn't understand the depth to which he really cared about Cody until I saw him plead with us to keep him alive. He apologized for interrupting our family time and excused himself.

No one spoke for quite a while, waiting for Kreg and me to say something. Kreg didn't speak, and I didn't know what to say. How could I possibly make the decision to end my son's life? And yet, I couldn't just let the doctors and nurses poke and prod and operate on him forever. Dr. Pike said he was already gone, so what use was there in waiting? Kreg would have to make the final decision, there was no way I was going to be able to decide on my own.

I turned to Kreg who was standing behind me and stated quietly, "I don't believe it anymore." Kreg looked confused. "I don't believe that scripture that God will not give you more than you can handle. It's not true. I can't take this anymore. I can't do this back and forth one more second."

Kreg started shaking his head, "Oh honey, you don't mean that, we'll get through this…"

But I did mean it. I wasn't upset at God, and I never stopped believing that he was real, but his promises and blessings seemed to pass by us somehow. We had been abandoned and forgotten, we were alone and sinking in the storm. This was indeed so much more than I could bear, so much more than we deserved, and so much more than we were capable of overcoming. And there was no help in sight, no way out, no solution or option that could fix it.

I turned to Cody and he truly looked lost. The charts didn't lie, Dr. Pike had done the tests again and again. It was done. Finished. Cody was gone and he wasn't coming back. No amount of wishing or hoping or praying was going to fix it. And instead of him just dying naturally, we had to be the ones to flip the switch and cut off his air, his food, his medication. It was cruel. It was torture. It was too much.

Kreg was trying to be strong for me but I knew he felt it too. I could see it in his eyes. The pain, the struggle of the impossible choice, the burden of our whole family's emotions on his back. It was too much for him to bear as well, though he had to maintain some sense of composure for all our sakes.

I gave up trying to make decisions and buried my head in my hands. Then, in the middle of our solemn and painful silence, came a knock on the door.

Seventeen

I HEARD THE DOOR OPEN AND LIFTED MY HEAD TO SEE WHO IT WAS. "Excuse me, is this the Parmer family?" It was a middle-aged gentleman with light colored hair parted down the side and a navy-blue business suit.

"Yes, I'm Kreg Parmer," Kreg said, awaiting an explanation.

"Hi, sorry to interrupt you, my name is Craig Zwick, I'm from the Church. I'm a member of the First Quorum of the Seventy, and I was in your stake in Idaho Falls this morning for a stake conference. Your stake president told me about your family, and about Cody, and a little bit about what you've been through. I'm here with my wife, would you mind if we joined you for a moment?"

"Of course, come in!" Kreg motioned for them to enter, but there wasn't much space. People shuffled around to make room for him and his wife, both still dressed in their Sunday best. It was a dramatic contrast, our family was worn out and exhausted and our tear-stained faces could not hide our grief and pain. Elder Zwick and his wife, however, were beacons of light, composed and confident, with kindness radiating from their compassionate smiles.

Elder Zwick went around and shook hands with everyone, reaching over and around people to make sure he didn't miss anyone. As he shook my hand and smiled at me I could feel of his strength and optimism. There was a spirit of hope and comfort I hadn't felt in a long time. I wanted to soak up his warmth, but the depression that had filled my heart was still too overwhelming.

After he had gone around the whole room he stood at the foot of

Cody's bed and addressed Kreg and me directly. "Brother and Sister Parmer, I want you to know that your bishop and your stake president are aware of your struggles and they care about you deeply. Your stake presidency, the high council, your entire ward and stake, they are aware of how difficult this is and they wanted me to send their love and support. You have a great network of caring saints who are waiting to assist you when you go home." We nodded our agreement. It was true, our ward and stake had been so helpful and kind to us and had remembered us in their prayers and meetings often.

Elder Zwick asked how we were holding up and we were completely honest: we were in a nearly impossible spot and it was terribly troubling. He listened as we told him about the original accident, the hemorrhage, the surgery in Idaho Falls and emergency ride to Salt Lake City. We explained how Cody was responding sometimes and not others, but how the latest tests had shown that he was brain dead, and how Dr. Pike advised us to cut off life support. That brought us up to our present time, planning the funeral but unsure and unable to actually say goodbye to Cody.

Elder Zwick took it all in, listening to every word. "That's an incredible story. You've been through so much, I can't begin to imagine how hard it's been for you. As Janet and I were driving down we called a friend of ours who works here and asked if he knew you. As it turns out, our friend is one of Cody's surgeons, Mike Richardson. He told me about Cody and said that he had been through a lot and wasn't sure what was going to happen, but that Cody was a fighter, and that your family was one of the most remarkable and supportive families he had seen in here," he nodded toward my parents and siblings.

Elder Zwick turned to Cody for a moment and watched him, leaning against the bedside railing. Cody looked terrible. His body was thin and weak and while his bandages hid the gruesome marks of surgery, you could tell it had been an extreme measure to open up his skull. Elder Zwick then turned back to us.

"I hadn't planned on giving Cody a blessing when we came here, but I can feel of the incredible faith in this room. Brother Parmer, would I have your permission to give Cody a blessing?"

"Oh, of course!" Kreg gave an overwhelming response. Who would turn down a blessing from a general authority?

"I know his head must be really tender, we'll just lightly place our hands on his head here. Would you anoint, then assist me in giving a blessing?" Elder Zwick asked Kreg. Kreg agreed and gave the anointing, then Elder Zwick placed his hands on Cody's head and began to pronounce the blessing.

The power and authority with which he spoke was incredible, it was like nothing I had ever before witnessed. The blessing was confident and direct, and the words he spoke tore the depression from my heart and replaced it with a measure of hope and strength and faith that I hadn't believed possible. Elder Zwick's blessing was the miracle that God knew we needed, and that we were too tired and exhausted and depressed to even ask for.

The words of the blessing were specific and precise. He blessed Cody's neurological system that it might recover, then blessed his brain, his skull, his eyes, and every bone in his body. He blessed him that he would regain his ability to walk and talk, and promised that these blessings would come on this side of the veil and would not be reserved until after death. Through Cody he blessed Kreg and me, Cody's friends and family, and even blessed Cody's friend Jeff with understanding to accept God's will in this situation. He blessed the physicians that they would be able to work beyond their natural capabilities for Cody's benefit.

He continued, "I bless you to look forward to your great future, and not to look back at what might have been. Harbor no bitterness about what has happened, but focus on what you can become, and what God will do through you. Cody, your recovery will be long and hard, but you will recover. These blessings are promised to you by your faithful friend, your Father in Heaven. In the name of Jesus Christ, amen."

I opened my eyes but strained to see through the tears that clouded my vision. I wiped my eyes and could see Elder Zwick rubbing Cody's arm. "What a neat kid. He has so much faith," Elder Zwick remarked.

Cody did have incredible faith, and I was amazed that Elder Zwick could sense Cody's spirit, even though there was no outward manifestation of any life or activity. Elder Zwick then went around and shook everyone's hands again.

He stopped in front of me after shaking my hand and told me that he had a meeting with President Hinckley coming up soon. He promised to put Cody's name on a special list of people to pray for, and told me that President Hinckley would read Cody's name out loud and call down the blessings of heaven for him. I thanked him so much for his blessing and his visit and told him that he would never understand how much it meant. He took my hand and held it between his, patting the back of my hand softly. "He'll be okay," he said, smiling.

He told us he would try to check in on us at a later time, and then said goodbye and left. The room broke into a hushed roar as soon as he left, everyone eager to express their amazement at the blessing that had been pronounced.

I grabbed the small yellow pad of paper that we had been using to plan Cody's funeral, ripped off the plans and threw them aside, then took the pen and began writing down everything I could remember about the blessing. Everyone else in the room helped fill in little details until we were sure we had nearly all of the promises correct. The words were personal scripture, blessings that seemed as powerful as if God himself had appeared to us and issued them in person. To us, they carried the same weight.

My brother-in-law turned to Kreg and put his arm around him. It had been several years since he had been active in church, but he told Kreg that if the blessing that had been issued really came true, he would make the necessary changes and come back to church, no doubt about it. Kreg just smiled. With the power of the spirit that had been felt during the blessing, there was no possible way to doubt that it was the work of God.

The mood in the room had changed in the blink of an eye. Where before we had been inconsolable, we were now full of faith and hope and strength. The blessing had been a catalyst for all of us to renew our faith and our prayers, to resolve to be worthy of God's blessings, and to have the strength to endure. In that moment, we chose to believe. Yes, we knew it would be a long road as Elder Zwick had promised, but now the ending was clear. Cody was not dead, he would recover. He would walk and talk and serve Heavenly Father and be an instrument for good in this world. Armed with incredible blessings from God and a promise of recovery, we were ready to face anything that stood in our way.

The feeling of the Holy Ghost remained in the room to such a degree that no one wanted to leave. We stayed and talked for as long as we could.

When our tired eyes and full hearts could take it no longer, people finally began to shuffle out. Some of my family who had stayed several days had to return to work on Monday, so they said their goodbyes and began their long drive back to Idaho Falls. A few stayed to help, and they returned to the family room with the girls to gather their things and head to the hotel for the night.

After the last family members headed out, Kreg and I were left alone with Cody in his room in the ICU. It was hard to find the right words to say. So much had changed with that one visit, it was a complete course reversal from the previous week. We stood at Cody's bedside and no longer saw a body lying lifeless, waiting to take its final breath. Instead we saw our son, the boy we had raised and taught and prayed for and worried about for 16 years. He was there, trapped somewhere inside a bruised and beaten body. In order to make it through, and we knew he would, he needed his mother and father to fight for him and help him and protect him.

"We can do this," I told Kreg, as he held me in his arms.

"He said it will be a long road to recovery," Kreg said, not disagreeing, but reminding me to stay strong for the long run.

"I know, but it will be okay. We can do it."

A long road to recovery. How long could it be? A few months; four, six maybe. That seemed like a long time, but it was manageable. If Cody was going to be all better in six months, I could do it. I could endure whatever came my way in order to help him make it back.

Though my faith was strong and my heart was in the right place, I had no idea just how long Cody's recovery would be, and there was nothing that could have prepared us for the work that lay ahead.

EIGHTEEN

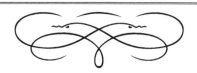

MONDAY CAME AND IT FELT LIKE THE SUN WAS RISING ON A NEW phase of life. My spirits were lifted, my heart was full, and my optimism was at a new high. We were ready to begin this journey toward recovery, no matter how long it would be, and we weren't going to be looking back. I thanked Heavenly Father every moment for sending Elder Zwick to bless Cody and give us hope.

After the blessing the difficult things were no longer so difficult, and things that had bothered me were instead an inspiration. The nurses coming in and out of Cody's room at all hours now seemed like angels, rather than instruments of pain and suffering. The Christmas decorations that had started appearing around the hospital were no longer signals of a future without a complete family, they were messages of hope and peace. Even my feelings toward Dr. Pike began to soften. He was merely following protocol and trying to give us the best medical advice possible. How was he to know that God had interjected on our behalf and promised that our son would live? When he arrived later that morning to check in on Cody, we decided to tell him about our plans.

Kreg and I had discussed together how we were going to tell Dr. Pike, but I let Kreg make the announcement. As Dr. Pike checked Cody's charts and equipment, Kreg broke the news.

"Dr. Pike, we've come to a decision. We appreciate what you've done for us and for Cody, and we know that you've put a lot of work into giving us all the options and information about Cody's health. Our family had a long talk last night," Kreg turned to look at me for a moment. He wasn't going to say anything to him about the blessing, but we both knew it wasn't the family talk that had made up our minds, "and we decided that we're going to wait for Cody to get better."

For a split second I could see a look of shock on Dr. Pike's face. He was obviously not expecting that response, and it hadn't been one of the options he presented. His recommendation was to end life support, and the options were to donate his organs or not donate his organs, there was definitely no talk of waiting for a recovery. Dr. Pike stared blankly for a moment, apparently gathering his thoughts.

"You do understand that we have determined there is no brain activity?" Dr. Pike stated clearly.

"Yes, we understand."

"And you understand that any type of normal recovery is simply not possible?"

Kreg hesitated a moment. There was no use in arguing with the doctor, our reasons for believing in a recovery wouldn't make any sense to him anyway. It was better to just go along. "Yes, we understand what you're saying, but we're willing to wait and see if something changes."

"Okay," he said slowly, obviously disappointed, then appeared to resign himself to our decision. "Hmm. Well, we have a lot to consider then." He nodded his head, rolling over the next steps in his mind. "I'll get you some more information in the next few days." He closed the chart he was reading, put it back in the slot on the wall, and moved on to his next patient, giving us a polite smile.

"Thank you," Kreg said to Dr. Pike as he left.

I looked at Kreg and sighed. That was more difficult than we thought it would be. It almost felt like we had let him down or offended his pride in some way, but in the end all that mattered was Cody's recovery, and our loyalty was with our son.

Knowing that Cody would recover was reassuring, but not knowing when was agonizing. I had hoped that the blessing would have provided some immediate jolt of life, but Cody's condition was the same on Monday as it had been on Sunday, and the few days before that. Cody had plateaued, but we didn't let our faith waver. The promise had been made, and I was going to hold God to that promise for as long as it took.

We began making long-term plans. Cody might be in the hospital for several more weeks, or months even. Kreg would eventually need to go back to work, but we decided the girls should probably go back to Idaho Falls as soon as possible so they could go to school and have some kind of a normal life. My sister Carrie took Brooke and Krissa back to her house and my sister Vicki and her husband Corey took Kira to their house. Brooke and Krissa were looking forward to the company of a house full of cousins, but Kira needed some room to herself to deal with what was going on.

The girls had given up so much and had spent more than a week cooped up in our little hospital family room, it would be good for them to get out of the hospital and back to a somewhat normal schedule. I felt bad for everything they were having to go through, but I knew my family would give them the time and attention I just couldn't provide at the moment. Carrie and Vicki promised that one of them would bring the girls down on Fridays and then take them back to Idaho Falls on Sunday nights so they could return to school.

With the girls gone and most of the family back to their normal lives, Kreg and I were left mostly to ourselves for the next several weeks. The days were long and dull, and we became experts at hospital life. We knew the nurses, the shift changes, the meal schedules, every vending machine option available, and the best places to take a walk or find some peace and quiet. Kreg grabbed a spare wheelchair from the hall and learned how to balance on two wheels, then started trying to figure out how to do spins and tricks. We used nearly every diversion possible to stay sane, but the monotony and boredom were overwhelming.

By the middle of December Cody had stabilized, but he still wasn't improving. The doctors performed a tracheotomy and inserted a plastic device called a cannula into his neck to make breathing easier. Cody could breathe on his own for a short time, but it was slow and labored, so they usually had him hooked up to a breathing machine.

The doctors finally decided to remove the bandage around Cody's head to let the wound heal. A nurse was sent in to remove the gauze and Kreg and I watched intently, hoping that everything was healing normally. The upper layers of gauze came off quickly, but the lower layers had been soaked through with various fluids from his healing scalp. The bandage became crusty and difficult to remove, but the nurse finally peeled the last layers away to reveal the bare head.

The newly grown hair was matted down and sweaty all over, but the wound itself was caked with a dark sticky substance. The missing bone plate left a horseshoe-shaped indentation in his scalp about the size of a hand. The incision was plainly visible, it began in front of his right ear, then ran over the ear toward the back of the head and made its way in a C shape back up to his forehead. I had been excited for Cody to have the bandage off and look more normal, but the condition of the wound made me queasy and I had to leave the room until she was done.

The nurse took a wet cloth and began cleaning around the incision, but as she wiped the hair where his bone was missing, the skin sunk into the hole and the pressure on the head caused more dark matter to squeeze out of the sutures. The nurse took a step back, apparently startled, and put her rag back in the bowl.

"What is that?" Kreg asked, suddenly worried at the nurse's reaction.

"I don't know, I've never seen anything like that," she said frankly, "I'm getting a doctor." She returned a few minutes later with a doctor and they examined the wound.

"That's dead brain matter," the doctor said calmly. "The hemorrhage killed part of his brain and the body will eventually clean it out internally, but it looks like some is coming out of the wound. As soon as the wound heals completely you won't see any more leakage. You can continue to clean it, just be soft." The nurse carefully returned to her job, obviously uncomfortable with having to clean it up, but doing her job nonetheless.

Kreg came out to tell me what all the fuss was about, but I made absolutely sure that Cody was totally cleaned up before I went back in the room. Even after all the time we had spent in the hospital, I still got queasy from the sight of blood or vomit, let alone dead brain matter. Even the mere thought of Cody losing part of his brain made me nauseous.

I knew that Cody's brain injury was bad, but knowing that his body was actually getting rid of part of his brain wasn't just sickening, it was sad. What did that part of his brain do, or what memories did it hold? I knew it wasn't an exact science, and that the brain could transfer responsibilities to other parts after a while, but it still seemed like a pretty big deal to physically lose almost half of your brain. I tried not to dwell on it. The blessing promised a recovery, and that was all that mattered.

Cody looked much better without the bandage. Even though it made no real difference in his overall condition, it made me feel better seeing him closer to normal. His hair was still fairly short since they shaved it before the surgery, but it was starting to regrow and cover the incision. Cody's mouth was hung slightly open and his lips glistened from the vaseline the nurses applied to keep them from drying out. His eyelids were cracked open a bit, just enough to see the color of his eyes, but he still looked like he was sleeping.

There were plenty more tubes and monitors and sensors underneath his blanket, but those were hidden. The only visible medical device was a long blue tube that ran from his trache to a breathing machine on the wall. I tried to imagine what he would look like in a month or two, when all this would be over and he would be asleep in his own bed and I would come in to turn off the lights. I longed for those days so much that it hurt. I just wanted us to be home, and to be a family again.

Just a week before Christmas Dr. Pike came in to talk to us again about Cody's condition. "How is Cody doing today?" he asked as he entered the room.

"Pretty good," Kreg replied, "I think. He seems to be breathing a little better today." Kreg seemed to notice stuff like that, or maybe he was just trying to be optimistic, I couldn't tell.

"Very good. Well, it looks like Cody's condition is fairly stable and we have no more pending surgeries for him," Dr. Pike spoke cautiously, as if he were leading up to some bad news. "I think it's time for Cody to move downstairs to the rehabilitation ward." Dr. Pike looked at each of us, evaluating our responses.

"Oh, that's great!" I said. Anything to move Cody's progress along was good news to me. Of course we would miss the nurses in the ICU, but getting Cody some help with physical therapists would be a step forward. Besides, it might break up the monotony.

"Good. I'm glad that will work out for you. I'll get the transfer request put in and we should probably have a bed ready for him by tomorrow morning. It's been a pleasure to work with you and Cody, and I wish you all the best." Dr. Pike held out his hand for Kreg and they shared a firm manly handshake. Dr. Pike then turned to me and approached me cautiously, knowing I hadn't always been his biggest fan. I stood up and held out my hand. He took it and smiled, and we shook hands.

"Thank you Dr. Pike, for everything you've done," I said.

"Oh, you're welcome," he said, a little surprised. I could tell there was more he wanted to say, but he was hesitating. "Listen, I want you to know that I'm sorry. I shouldn't have called that meeting or made those suggestions so soon. It was a little premature. Dr. Richardson was right, there is a small chance that Cody could get better. It was your decision from the start, and I'm glad your family seems so happy with the decision you've made."

I smiled as kindly as I could, it must have been very difficult for him to admit that he had been hasty in his call to terminate life support. For as much as I had disliked him in the past, I knew that he had only been doing what he thought was best, and his apology made my respect for him grow immeasurably. I reached in and gave him a hug, and he returned it softly.

"Thank you," I said again. He smiled and wished us luck once more, then he was gone.

"Well that was unexpected," Kreg said as soon as he was sure we were alone again. He was right, I didn't expect the apology, nor did I expect my reaction. It felt good though. It was comforting, and healing, to be able to forgive.

The next morning, as promised, a team of nurses came to move Cody down to a room in rehab. It seemed like every nurse in the ICU turned out to say goodbye to Cody and Kreg and me, and I held back tears as I thanked the nurses for their help and their kindness. It was kind of silly, we were just moving downstairs, but it felt like we were moving across the country. Eventually we headed down the hall, trailing behind Cody's bed and waving goodbye to the nurses left behind and the people we had come to love.

The elevator took us downstairs and we walked through a few sets of doors until we entered the rehabilitation unit. The walls in the hallways and patient rooms were painted forest green and it seemed like there was exercise and therapy equipment everywhere. Cody was wheeled into a room that felt much emptier than the one we had just left. The absence of so many monitors and racks of equipment made it feel much more open, but I had grown used to all the equipment that had surrounded him upstairs. I felt a little nervous without Cody's every move being monitored, but if the doctors didn't feel like they needed to monitor everything anymore, I assumed I had nothing to worry about.

The new nurses showed us around the unit and told us about their programs and equipment. They also brought in a cot for us to use at night, which was a welcome improvement from the makeshift sleeping arrangements we had been enduring for the past few weeks in the ICU. It was a little uncomfortable to be moved and not know any of the nurses or staff, or know their expectations, but all in all we were happy.

We settled in for a long stay and got to know our new nurses. They started Cody out with a simple routine of stretches which mostly consisted of a therapist moving his legs and arms back and forth. I wasn't sure it was accomplishing much, but I trusted that the therapists knew what they were doing. Day after day, nurse after nurse, stretch after stretch, we held on, but nothing seemed to improve.

Finally the girls got out of school and came down to Salt Lake to stay with us for the Christmas break. We lost our family room when we left the ICU, but moving to recovery also meant that Kira and Brooke and Krissa could finally join us in Cody's room all day. They would sit on my lap as I sat beside Cody and I would read them stories or listen to them talk about school.

Despite my best efforts to keep the girls entertained, it was still quite boring for them. Thankfully my parents or visiting siblings would try to keep them occupied for most of the day with little outings or activities. Margaret taught the girls how to play monopoly and marbles, and my dad would take them on walks to throw quarters in the fountain and make wishes. For the most part, I kept my vigil at Cody's bedside, though I wasn't so afraid anymore to let him be alone for a short time. No longer living under a dark cloud of death and destruction did wonders for my state of mind and my ability to handle the world around me.

At night my parents would take the girls up to my brother Dirk's house in Park City. Dirk and Margaret didn't have any kids yet, but they had a nice home and enough room for the girls to sleep comfortably. Even though it was a bit of a drive, a nice bed in a real home with an aunt and uncle that loved them was a real blessing.

Everything went smoothly most of the time, but some nights Krissa refused to go home with Margaret and wanted to stay with Kreg and me at the hospital. I could hardly refuse, so Krissa and I snuggled up on the cot and tried to get some sleep. As soon as the lights went out and everything got quiet Cody would start snoring so loudly that Krissa would have to put a pillow over her head just to fall asleep. After a few uncomfortable nights in the cot, Krissa decided that the soft bed at her aunt and uncle's house wasn't so bad after all.

Dirk and Margaret really helped the girls get into the Christmas spirit. While they were up at the house Margaret let the girls help her decorate for Christmas. One day when they were at the hospital she took the girls to a gift tree in the lobby where they selected a family in need and chose a present to buy for them. The girls had fallen in love with marbles, so they decided to buy a big bag for one of the families. Margaret's efforts were working; soon the girls were singing Christmas carols and making long wish lists for Santa.

Though the girls were finding joy in the holiday, it was hard for me to really get in the Christmas spirit when we were cooped up in the hospital all day. There was no tree to decorate and no Christmas cookies to bake and frost with the kids. We wouldn't be attending the ward Christmas party or driving around to look at lights and decorations like we loved to do. Christmas was coming, but it didn't feel the same and I definitely didn't feel ready.

As we reviewed the girls' Christmas wish lists, I felt bad that I didn't have a chance to really find something special and meaningful for each girl. Instead, Kreg took care of most of the presents that year and got a few books and toys for the girls, along with a few more practical gifts. A friend at work had wholesale access to some high-end audio equipment, so Kreg bought a CD player for Kira and a stereo for Brooke. Krissa had been asking for Winnie the Pooh stuffed animals, so Kreg found a store that had the ones she wanted and picked out a few. On Christmas Eve, with all the presents wrapped and waiting at Dirk's house, Kreg sat down with me at Cody's bedside to have a talk.

"Babe, I think we both need to go up to Dirk's house tomorrow morning for Christmas with the girls."

"What? No, I'll just stay here and you can go. One of use needs to be with Cody." The thought of leaving Cody alone had never crossed my mind. Since the short trip to the Ronald McDonald house nearly a month earlier, I hadn't left the hospital at all.

"I talked to your mom and dad, and they'll stay here with Cody while we go, it will just be for the morning so we can open presents and spend some time with them, then we'll come back."

"No, I can't. I can't leave, Kreg. The girls will be fine, you and Dirk and Margaret and my parents can do it, just go and have a good time and come back down when you're done." Even though I no longer feared the thought of Cody dying while I stepped away, I just couldn't bear the thought of leaving him alone without one of his parents there. We'd been through so much, it felt terribly mean to leave him in such a bad condition, especially on Christmas.

Kreg took my hand and held it in his. "Honey, I know you want to stay, but Cody will be fine, and nothing has happened in weeks. No emergencies, no progress, just the same thing day in and day out. He won't know if you're gone for a few hours, but the girls are going to remember this Christmas for the rest of their lives." He waited a minute for that to sink in.

"Brenda, you've been a terrific mom to Cody, you're more dedicated than anyone I've ever seen. No one will ever say that you're not doing everything you can for him. But we've got three other girls who need their mom. They've sacrificed and given up just as much as we have, and they need to know that you are still there for them, and you still care about them. It's Christmas morning, you need to be with them."

Kreg had been really good about supporting me in whatever decision I wanted to make with Cody's care. He had been my rock through it all and had handled everything when I couldn't even function. This was the first time he had really pushed me to do anything I didn't want to do. If he was seeing the big picture where I couldn't, then I needed to trust him.

I sat and thought for a moment. Kreg had a point, it wasn't fair to the girls to make them sacrifice any more than they had to. They had been so patient with me through all of Cody's medical problems over the past six months, and they had taken a back seat to whatever Cody needed. They deserved better than I had been able to give, but I was in a better place now, mentally, and it was time to stop waiting to be a mom to them again.

"Okay. We'll both go." It was all I had to say. Kreg put his arm around me and kissed me on the forehead. It would break my heart, but it would be worth it.

Our Christmas Eve was quiet and serene. Snow had just started to fall and we watched the tiny snowflakes glisten through the window in Cody's room. Even though we weren't much in the Christmas spirit, the snow helped create a peaceful evening. The girls had already gone up to Dirk's house for the night and Kreg and I and my parents were sitting in Cody's room sharing memories. A faint sound of Christmas carols was heard from down the hall, and we stopped talking so we could listen. When the carol stopped, we heard footsteps coming our way, then four college students appeared at our door.

"Hello, I hope we're not disturbing you," one of the carolers said hesitantly.

"No, not at all, the music was beautiful!" Kreg replied. Music has been a big part of our lives; Kreg especially loved singing and always appreciated good musical talent.

"Oh good. We're an a capella group from BYU and we'd love to be able to sing a Christmas carol for you tonight, if that's alright?"

"Of course! Please do!" Kreg answered with a wide smile.

The four students, two girls and two boys, were nicely dressed and obviously very well prepared. The quartet's leader hummed a note, then they started singing softly in perfect unison. The music they made was magical, honestly one of the most peaceful and beautiful pieces of music I have ever heard. Their four voices combined perfectly in a sweet rendition of *Still, Still, Still.* It was nearly impossible to keep from tearing up at the beautiful music they made, but the words of the song touched my heart even more strongly.

"*Still, still, still. One can hear the falling snow. For all is hushed, the world is sleeping. Holy Star it's vigil keeping. Still, still, still. One can hear the falling snow.*" The scene was perfect, with the snow softly falling outside and my husband and parents beside me, Cody with a promise of recovery, and beautiful voices filling the room. The next two verses spoke so deeply to our hearts that we have never forgotten the feeling that evening.

"*Sleep, sleep, sleep. Tis the eve of our Savior's birth. The night is peaceful all around you. Close your eyes let sleep surround you. Sleep, sleep, sleep, 'tis the eve of our Savior's birth.*

"*Dream, dream, dream, of the joyous day to come. While guardian angels without number, watch you as you sweetly slumber. Dream, dream, dream, of the joyous day to come.*"

I held Cody's hand as the group finished their angelic lullaby. The lyrics seemed to be written for us. The night was indeed peaceful, and Cody quietly slept as snow fell peacefully outside. Just as the carol taught, we were truly looking forward to the joyous day to come; not only Christmas day and the celebration of Christ's birth, but the promised day of recovery for Cody. God had sent angels at Christ's birth, and he had sent angels—nurses, siblings, doctors, parents, life flight pilots and paramedics, ward members, a general authority and his wife, and BYU carolers—to bless and protect our family in our time of need.

I was completely overcome by the spirit of gratitude and memories of all our many blessings seemed to flood my mind. God had been so good to us, we had received more blessings than we ever deserved, and Cody was still alive. As difficult as our present situation seemed, I knew that God was looking over us, he wasn't going to leave us, and with his help we would find a way through our trials.

NINETEEN

THE LIGHT DUSTING OF SNOW SPARKLED IN THE EARLY MORNING light, and the scenery on the drive up to Dirk's house looked like the cover of a Christmas card. I had spent so many days under the fluorescent lights of the hospital that the sunrise through Parley's Canyon seemed magical and surreal. Kreg pulled into the driveway at Dirk's house and put the car in park. He squeezed my hand, gave me a soft kiss, and led me inside to meet our three anxious daughters, ready to open presents.

The girls giggled with delight as they ripped off the pretty paper to discover their Christmas gifts. We had really gone light on presents for financial and practical reasons, but our family and friends had provided the girls with a pile of presents that would keep them occupied for hours on end while Cody lingered on in the hospital. As the girls opened present after present I just kept thinking that God had already given me the best gift I could have asked for. Cody had a promise of recovery, our girls were healthy and happy, and I was married to the most kind and patient man in the world. The only thing left to ask for was to be able to go home and be a family again.

After presents were unwrapped and the girls had settled down a bit, we got them dressed and ready and drove back down to the hospital to be with Cody. Despite the enjoyable morning, I was still a little nervous to be away from him for too long. We packed the girls in the car and I loaded two big presents in the back.

"What are those Mom?" the girls asked.

"It looks like Santa brought some presents for Cody too!" I said. The boxes contained a motorcycle helmet and boots I bought at Action

Motorsports just before Cody had his hemorrhage. It seemed a little ridiculous now, giving a helmet and boots to a boy in a coma, but the therapists told us to treat him like everything was normal, and that might trigger some reaction or restoration of brain functionality.

When we arrived at the hospital the girls placed the boxes on Cody's lap and unwrapped them for him, exclaiming with surprise when they pulled out the shiny red helmet and boots. I watched Cody for a second to see if there was anything, even a twitch or a blink, but he just lay still and lifeless, his eyes half open as always, staring off into the distance. I put the helmet and boots on his bed at his side. Maybe they would yet spark some memory for him.

After a few hours of sitting with us in Cody's room the girls were getting bored, so my parents took them back up to Dirk's to play with their toys and gifts. It was nice to have them there, but the hospital really was no place for three active daughters. I tried my best over the next few days to follow Kreg's advice and make sure to give the girls just as much attention as I was giving Cody, though my mind always drifted back to Cody's care.

The girls seemed to understand that during this short period of time, until life got back to normal, I had to give extra attention to Cody. I could tell that they were concerned about Cody too, and his situation was weighing on them. One day, they came up to me and announced a plan.

"Mom, we made these for Cody." Each of the girls held out a handful of tiny colored bead bracelets. Margaret had bought the string and beads to give the girls something to do, and they had been hard at work making dozens of bracelets. "We want everyone to wear one for Cody, until he gets better." My heart melted.

These poor girls had been stuck in the dreary hospital for their entire Christmas break, with nearly all their parents' attention focused on their brother, and they felt powerless to do anything to help. And yet they spent their time making bracelets to show a united family effort to remember Cody and not give up until he was better.

"I think that's an excellent idea," I said. I grabbed one of the bracelets and tied it around my hand. Then I grabbed another and tied it around Cody's. Each of the girls fastened one to their wrists, and we left a big pile of bracelets on the table by his bed, handing them out to every family member as they came to visit. We promised not to take them off until Cody was well again.

Christmas break soon ended and the girls had to leave for Idaho Falls to go back to school. I was sad to see them go and grateful for their companionship and support, but knew that Carrie and Vicki would be able to take much better care of them, at least until Cody was awake and in recovery.

Despite my resolve to stay positive, I was starting to get frustrated with the slow pace of progress. It had been almost a month since Elder Zwick promised us that Cody would walk and talk again, but there was still no improvement. No blinking, no hand squeezes, no reaction of any kind. I would stare at him for hours on end, waiting for some sign, but there was nothing. He lay in bed motionless, his eyes staring off into the unknown, and his strong teenage body slowly giving way to a pale and feeble frame.

Whenever I got really discouraged, I pulled out the little yellow slip of paper Cody had written on, "Please untie me," and tried to remember that no matter what it looked like from the outside, he was in there, deep inside, and that my son would eventually come back to me. I replayed the words of the blessing over and over again in my mind, and clutched the little yellow paper tightly in my hands. Why wasn't there progress? What were we missing?

Would I simply wake up in my cot one day and see Cody chatting with a nurse? Would it be a miraculous and instant switch, like we saw after the car accident? Or would this go on for several more weeks, months even. Could it be years? No, I dashed the thought from my mind. No, Cody would be well soon, and that's all there was to that. I tucked the yellow paper back in my pocket, put a smile on my face, and refused to let the negative thoughts drag me down.

Unfortunately, the hospital staff didn't share my optimism. On New Year's Eve we were told we needed to meet with one of the hospital's social workers. We went down to her office and she informed us that because Cody was still in a coma and not improving, he was no longer a candidate for rehab. Her sudden pronouncement surprised us.

"What do you mean? What are we supposed to do then?" I asked.

"Most patients are moved to a nursing home at this point for long-term comatose care. Do you have a nursing home that you would prefer?"

Kreg looked at me with concern in his eyes, "I don't think so."

"Alright, I can look into that for you. Your insurance will cover some of the costs, but some of the nicer nursing homes would probably require some out-of-pocket spending. We could look at applying for government assistance as well." There was no way we could afford a fancy nursing home, even if it was subsidized. We were barely making ends meet as it was.

"No, I won't put him in a nursing home, he needs more care than that," I said, knowing that Cody would never receive the kind of rehabilitative care he needed if we went to a bargain-basement facility. They would stick him in a room and give him the minimum treatment possible. Besides, a nursing home was somewhere you sent a person to die, and my son was not going to die, he was going to recover, just as promised.

The social worker rubbed her forehead as she thought. "Well, he can't stay here, and if you don't want to put him in a nursing home, the only other option then is to take him home and do the caretaking yourselves, but you really don't want to do that."

I had an instant flashback of Cody's hospital bed in our living room during his first recovery. That was an ordeal, but at least Cody was in his own home. It was much better than a nursing home at least. I looked at Kreg and could tell he was thinking the same thing.

"Yeah, we'll take him home. Just tell us what we need to do," I said.

"No, I meant that taking your son home would be an absolute last resort. It's really not something you should be considering at this point. I'll make some calls to the nursing homes in your area and…"

I cut her off, "No, Cody is not going into a nursing home. If he can't stay here, we're going to take him home with us." I wasn't trying to be rude, but there was no way I was letting her put my son in a nursing home. I wanted the best for Cody, and if they wouldn't give it to him, I would.

"Okay then," the social worker raised her hands to signal her surrender, "I'll talk with the insurance company and let them know your plans. The funding for hospital care runs out on January 14th, so we have a lot to do before then to get ready. Tomorrow I'll send down a marriage counselor to talk with you. There are going to be a lot of life changes, especially with roles around the home and in your relationship together.

They'll help you sort some of that stuff out."

"A counselor?" Kreg asked. "I don't think that's necessary." It did seem like a silly idea, our primary concern was Cody, we didn't need marriage advice.

The social worker sighed. "Mr. Parmer, I don't think you fully appreciate how difficult it is to care for a child in your son's condition. The statistics show that ninety-nine percent of couples in your situation will be divorced within just a couple years. Ninety-nine percent. Now, everyone says it's not going to be them, but this takes a huge toll on families and marriages. We're required to have a counselor come talk to you, and I'd really recommend that you take advantage of what advice they have to offer."

I looked at Kreg and he stared back at me. There was no doubt that we would make it through this. We started our marriage with nothing, had raised four children together, and had already endured six months of Cody's health problems since the accident. It was terribly difficult, of course, but I knew that our marriage and temple sealing meant more to each of us than any health or financial burden that could possibly come our way. I could tell that Kreg felt the same way. No matter how bad it got, we would be there for each other.

She continued, "We'll also need to set you up with some specially trained nurses who can teach you how to take care of Cody at home. There's a lot to learn and not much time to do it in, so we'll need to hurry. Are you sure this is what you want to do?" The social worker gave us one last chance to change our minds.

"Yeah, set up the appointments," Kreg said. "Let's get started."

We went back to our room and sat down next to Cody. I had let the doctors and nurses take care of him for so long, but soon I would have to do everything they were doing, and it suddenly seemed daunting, but it was the best thing for Cody so we would make it work.

A nurse came in to check on Cody and she asked how we were holding up. We told her about the meeting that we had just had and our plans for taking Cody home.

"You need to call that counselor back and rethink what you're doing. That is never going to work. You can't take care of him on your own. It's impossible." The nurse shook her head and continued checking machines and vitals.

"Well, that's what we've decided to do, so we're going to make it work," I said resolutely. There was no one who was going to tell me that I couldn't take care of my son. If I had been worried before, all that hesitation melted away as I stood my ground. I could do this.

"You don't understand. It takes a whole team of nurses, seven or eight of us, and several doctors and CNAs and a bunch of folks just to keep your son alive. I'm telling you, this is a mistake."

Kreg knew I was about to let her have it, so he put his hand on my knee and cut in, "We appreciate your concern. Thank you." The nurse shook her head and walked out.

I was tired, I was emotionally worn out, and I was worried about all the unknowns ahead of us. But more than any of that, I wanted to prove that nurse wrong. After more than a month of sitting around waiting for things to get better, I finally had a chance to do something, to make a difference. I was scared, but I was ready.

The work began the very next morning. Our days were immediately filled with lessons and scenarios and health care training. Once one nurse left, another would arrive to teach us some new procedure.

We had to learn how to attach and clean Cody's feeding tube, breathing tube, and catheter. The doctors had inserted an IV-type tube called a PICC line in Cody's shoulder that needed to be cleaned and monitored, and we had to sanitize and change the plastic cannula that held the breathing hole open from Cody's tracheotomy. The nurses made sure I knew exactly how to open the sanitary plastic packages holding the medical equipment, put the gloves on just right, and touch everything in the right order so I didn't get anything contaminated and cause an infection.

Kreg and I worked side by side all day long learning and practicing. It was incredibly difficult for me. I had been a bystander to his care for more than a month, leaving the room whenever anything bloody or gross had to happen, but now I was thrown into the middle of it. The smells and fluids and dirty bandages made me sick to my stomach, but I pushed on.

"You know, Cody does qualify for government assistance. You can put him in a nursing home, that's what most people do," one of the doctors told me as we were practicing a particularly disgusting procedure.

"No. I'll die trying to care for him before I put Cody in a nursing home," I responded.

He stopped and looked me in the eye, "That's exactly what I'm afraid of."

I shook my head. "Let's keep going."

After we had most of Cody's immediate health needs down, it was time to learn how to move Cody from a bed to a wheelchair. It was no big deal for Kreg, but impossible for me. Cody at 16 years old was already taller and heavier than I was, and even though he had lost a lot of muscle in the hospital, moving him was like lifting a sack of potatoes. With so many lines and tubes hooked up, one bad move could cause serious damage. Kreg did most of the moving, but there were going to be times when I had to move Cody while Kreg was gone, and I was going to have to find a solution eventually.

One day I approached a kind little physical therapist in the rehab unit and asked for her help. She was maybe five-foot-tall and a hundred pounds at most, smaller than I was, and yet I saw her moving adult patients in and out of beds and around the physical therapy mats all day long.

"Can you teach me how to do that?" I asked. "You can move these big people around and I can barely even roll my son over in bed."

"Yeah, sure. There are a few tricks that help, but you have to do it just right. Hop up on this bed here and I'll show you." She had me lie down on a hospital bed and she hooked her arms under mine and lifted just right. In one fluid motion she had moved me to a wheelchair.

"Now you try," she said as we swapped positions. I tried to do it just like she had, but failed miserably. "No, no, no, you've got to keep your elbows in and your back straight, like that. And put your legs like this." She adjusted my arms and my stance. I tried again and failed. It was much harder than it looked. After about a dozen tries I finally got it working, but it wasn't easy and I was still too scared to try it on Cody. She came in and showed me the technique a few more times, then helped me as I tried to move him. Finally I tried it without her help. It wasn't pretty, but I was able to get Cody from the bed to the wheelchair and back without any damage.

I thanked the physical therapist for her help. She smiled and patted me on the back. "You'll be fine. I can tell you have a lot of fight in you."

Moving Cody was difficult, but even more difficult was learning was how to suction out Cody's lungs. Because he was not able to cough on his own and he was lying on his back all the time, his lungs would fill with fluid and mucus. Every so often a tube would have to be inserted down his throat and into his lungs and the mucus would be sucked out.

One of my favorite nurses, a young man named Kyle, taught me how to insert the tube at just the right angle and then turn on the suction. Every time, without fail, Cody would begin gagging and convulsing as the tube sucked the fluid from his lungs. Kyle made sure I continued and didn't stop until the job was done, but it was more than I could handle. Once Kyle left I had to lay down on the cot at Cody's bedside for fear of throwing up. It was a terrible thing to see your son in pain from an accident outside of your control, but a whole different thing entirely to induce gagging and convulsions from your child. It took me several hours before I could sit up again and start training once more.

After one week, and with only one week to go, the nurses pretty much left us on our own. They had taught us everything they knew, now it was time to put it into practice. We did everything we were trained to do, we cleaned bandages, checked IVs and feeding tube and medication levels, monitored his breathing and bathed and cleaned him, exercised his muscles and moved him from the bed to the wheelchair and back again.

On one of our first nights alone, I could hear Cody start to breathe heavier, and I knew that was the sign for suctioning out his lungs. Kreg was off running errands, and I didn't have anyone to verify my assumption, so I started second guessing myself. I got the equipment ready, but kept monitoring Cody's breathing. Did he really need his lungs suctioned out, or was I just imagining it? Should I wait a few hours? I didn't want to cause all that pain if Cody didn't need it, but I didn't want him to suffer without being able to breathe right either. I hit the nurse's call button. In a few minutes Kyle came in and asked what I needed.

"I kind of think Cody might need his lungs suctioned out, but I can't tell. Can you listen to him and tell me if he needs it or not?"

"Nope," he replied, his hands on his hips.

"What?" I asked curiously. We had a good friendship, and it was his job to take care of Cody, I couldn't understand why he wasn't helping.

"I'm not going to tell you. You can figure it out. Why do you think he needs it?"

"Well, his breathing sounds a little heavier, and the sound is a little wet. But I don't know if it's bad enough yet to do the suction."

"So what's your decision?" he said, prodding me along.

I thought a moment. "I think I need to suction his lungs."

"You think, or you are going to?"

"I'm going to," I replied more confidently.

"Okay then, you're right," Kyle said, affirming my decision. I started the procedure and Kyle stayed to watch. When I was finished and cleaning up, my stomach still turning from Cody's reaction, Kyle came up and patted me on the back.

"You'll do just fine," he told me. "You know, the first time I came in here and met you and Cody, I knew you were one tough lady." I scoffed at his compliment. I didn't feel very tough.

"I'm serious. You fight for Cody like nobody I've ever seen. I knew the first time I came in here that I was going to have to earn your trust, it wasn't going to come free, and that I needed to do everything perfectly or you'd probably run to my boss and have me thrown out."

"No way," I laughed.

"I'm serious!" he said, chuckling as well. "With your determination, and your dedication to Cody, you'll do just fine. You just have to trust yourself. Okay?"

"Okay," I smiled.

"Good, now get some rest. Have a good night!" Kyle turned and moved on to resume his duties and I was left there by myself.

He was right, I was determined, but I was also tired and exhausted. Taking care of Cody was so time consuming, how could I possibly balance that with homework and dinners and cleaning the house? Kreg was going to go back to work once we got things settled, and I would be by myself most of the day. I couldn't possibly imagine how I was going to be able to juggle being a full-time mom and full-time nurse, but I would have to find a way.

After a day or two it seemed like we had the routine down, but we were still calling nurses in constantly to teach us new things or give us advice, and they were pushing us to be more and more independent. One day, one of the doctors came in and handed us a prescription.

"Cody needs some of this medicine, why don't you get him into the wheelchair and take him down to the pharmacy and pick it up." Usually the doctors or nurses would just bring the medicine in for Cody, but it seemed like they were forcing us to do even the most simple things by ourselves. I looked at Kreg to see what his reaction was and he seemed fine with it.

"Okay," I said, and took the prescription. Cody was fine for a little while without his breathing machine, so we unhooked his breathing tube, feeding tube, PICC line, IVs, monitor lines, and catheter and moved him into the wheelchair. We buckled and strapped him in and after about ten minutes of work, we were ready to go.

The freedom felt good. We wheeled Cody down the hall and took the elevator to the first floor. The pharmacy was in the main lobby, and we cautiously wheeled Cody between the incoming and outgoing patients and doctors and families who were scurrying in every direction. I was proud of our independence, but as we slowly rolled along I noticed the look of shock on people's faces. We found our way into the pharmacy and took a number. As we sat down I looked around the room and saw that everyone was staring at Cody. They would avert their eyes when I looked back at them, but Cody was a spectacle, there was no hiding it.

I had been around him so much that I hadn't realized just how bad he still looked. His muscles were weak and he sat limp in his chair, held up by straps and buckles. The scar on his right side was still plainly visible and bright pink and the indentation from the missing skull piece sunk at least half an inch into his head. His breathing tube was detached, leaving a gaping plastic hole in his throat. His eyes were half open and wandered aimlessly, and his jaw hung loose. He didn't just look sick, he looked nearly dead.

In that moment I wanted to scream and chastise them all for judging my son with their looks of horror and fear. He wasn't a lost cause just waiting to die, he had hopes and dreams and a sense of humor and was kind and caring. He was more than his limitations, more than just his outward appearance. They couldn't see what was on the inside, and they didn't know what God had in store for Cody.

I paused a moment in my anger. Hadn't I done the same thing? Hadn't I judged others based on first impressions or just what I could see from my limited point of view? I had no idea what God had promised anyone else, and I didn't know their struggles and their trials. All I could see were the things that were visible from a passing glance, and I had done the exact same thing that all of the onlookers were doing. My anger faded away, but still, I had to protect my son.

"Kreg, I've got to take him back up to the room. I can't have him in here."

Kreg knew exactly what I was talking about. "No, you stay here, I'll take him up." Kreg wheeled Cody out of the room and I rested my face in my hand, shielding my eyes from the horrified stares of a dozen patients and customers.

The reality check hit me hard. Cody was not doing well. We knew that Cody's very survival was a miracle, but to others, Cody's condition was frightening. I tried to shake the doubt from my head, but frustration began to overwhelm me.

Why was it taking so long for him to get better? I wanted a recovery now, I didn't want to go through this whole process of moving Cody home and learning to take care of him. If he was going to walk and talk again, why not now?

I got the prescription and returned to the room and sat down next to Kreg, leaning into him. "How are we going to do this?" I lamented.

Kreg wrapped his arm around me. "We'll be okay. Don't worry." I knew that tone of voice, the one where he had to say something positive but didn't have anything to back it up with. I just let it stand. We had no other option, we had to take each day and each challenge as it came, no matter the consequences. What else was there to do?

In the final days of our stay in Salt Lake we started to see the first hints of progress. Kreg began noticing times when Cody seemed more awake, and times when he looked like he was fully asleep. When he was awake his eyes were a little wider, and his breath was more controlled. When he was asleep, his eyelids were mostly closed, and his breathing was softer. It was barely perceivable, but Kreg was right, Cody was changing.

The nurses were a little skeptical of our observations, but we spent the last few days working extra hard to try to coax some response out of Cody. Instead of focusing on stretching the muscles so much, we started talking to Cody and asking him to blink, make sounds, squeeze our hands, anything to signal that he could hear us. Nothing happened.

Just a few days before we were scheduled to go home we were working with an occupational therapist who was trying to get Cody to lift his thumb. As the therapist gave instructions to make a thumbs-up sign, I would move his fingers into position, hopefully reminding Cody's body how to use those muscles and what it felt like to make that sign. Again and again we practiced lifting the thumb and pulling the fingers into a fist, then I would flatten his hand out and start over again. At the end of the session the therapist gave the instruction again and told me to let Cody try on his own.

His hand was laying limp on his stomach and I watched his fingers for any sign of movement.

"Cody, let's make a thumbs-up sign. Pull your fingers in and lift your thumb." She kept repeating the instruction over and over. Then the thumb twitched. The first knuckle straightened out, ever so slightly.

"Kreg, look!" I shouted. Kreg jumped out of his chair and I pointed to the thumb. "Look, he's lifting it!"

"Good job Cody, let's keep going, straighten out the thumb and pull your fingers in to make the thumbs-up sign." But the thumb went limp again and rested on his stomach. The therapist kept trying for several more minutes, but there was no reaction. The session was over, and it was time for her to move on.

"Does this mean he's awake, that we can stay here and continue therapy?" I asked as the therapist gathered her things to leave.

"Unfortunately no, I don't think so. It may have been muscle memory from our exercises, or it may simply be a chance event. We don't really have a consistent pattern of response, and unless there's rapid improvement in the next few days, I don't think we'll be able to justify keeping him here. A physical therapist at home will be able to continue these exercises, and if there's a rapid improvement there, then you can give us a call and we'll talk about options at that point." The therapist then left our room and continued on to her next appointment.

"Are you sure you saw it move?" Kreg asked.

"Yeah, his thumb lifted up off the blanket. It was just a little bit, but it moved. I'm sure of it."

Kreg sat silent for a moment, taking it all in and weighing the possibilities. We watched Cody and tried talking to him, asking him to move his thumb again. Soon Cody's eyes grew lazy and we knew he was asleep. It would have to wait.

The last few days ticked off so quickly, and with each therapy session I noticed the tiniest improvement in the flex of the thumb muscle. I tried to convince other doctors to let us stay and continue therapy there, but they wouldn't sign off on it. The response was just too minor, it wasn't enough. But it was enough for me. I knew Cody was in there, working hard, trying to get better. I had known it for a long time, but now I had proof, even if the doctors didn't believe it.

TWENTY

J ANUARY 14TH CAME ALL TOO SOON. IT FELT LIKE WE WERE GETTING
kicked out, forced to leave long before Cody was all better, but we had
no say in the matter. We had worked hard to make sure all the necessary
things were in place for our return home, but I was still worried we had
forgotten something.

Insurance had paid for the necessary medical equipment to be delivered to our house and friends at home had set up the monitors and a
specialized bed in Cody's room. We got the motorhome cleaned up and
ready and we set up a portable breathing machine and his necessary monitors in the back by the bed.

It had been 45 days since we had arrived at LDS hospital and it had
become like a second home to us. Dr. Pike and Richardson both came to
say goodbye, as well as more than a dozen nurses and staff that we had
grown close to. It was difficult to adequately thank all those who had
spent so much time caring for Cody. They had been my lifeline and had
helped me through some tough times. Now that lifeline was being cut off,
and we would be on our own.

In some ways I was anxious to go home and sleep in my own bed
and have control over my surroundings, but I was also terrified as well. At
home there was no emergency button to push when I needed advice or
help. It would just be Kreg and I, and much of the time it was just going
to be me, alone, with my comatose son. There would be no hospital staff
to clean and cook and change bedsheets and do laundry. I would have to
take care of the home, be a mom, and play nurse and therapist at the same
time. But at least I would be home.

As we pulled out of the parking lot I was overcome with a flood of emotions. Fear, anxiety, excitement, sadness, anticipation, they all took turns spinning my mind around and around. In the end reality set in—it was going to be hard, really hard.

After a long slow drive from Utah we pulled up to our house and found a small army of family members, ward members, friends and neighbors ready to help, standing outside in the frigid January air. With the help of several men we got Cody out of the motorhome and quickly moved into the house.

We changed some of the bedrooms around and moved Cody upstairs to the room right next to the kitchen. We connected all the equipment as best as we knew how and Cody's room soon resembled his hospital room, except for all the Dallas Cowboys gear and motocross posters on the walls.

Kind ward members had stocked our fridge and freezer with meals and family members promised to come help watch Cody, clean the house, take care of the girls, or do whatever was necessary. That first day we were surrounded by a flood of helpers, but when night came, it was just our little family. We said our prayers, tucked the girls in and kissed them goodnight, and then collapsed on our bed.

"Oh it feels good to be home," Kreg said as he sunk into the covers and pillows. I couldn't relax.

"Do we need to suction his lungs?" I asked.

"No, it shouldn't be for a few more hours," Kreg said.

I sat silently and listened down the hall for a minute. "Honey, I can't hear Cody."

"Do you want me to set an alarm? What time?" Kreg asked as he reached for our bedside clock.

"No, honey, I need to hear him. In case he starts choking or some-thing. I can't hear him from in here." I rubbed my eyes. I was so tired, but I was terrified of going to sleep and having Cody in trouble. Our bed was only about 20 feet away from his door, but if I was too far away to hear him choking, there was no way I was going to get any rest.

I stood up and grabbed the blanket and pillow. "I've got to go sleep down there," I told him. I dragged the bedding to Cody's open door and looked around. There was no space to lay down in Cody's room with all the equipment around him. I was too tired to move furniture to make a place to lay down, so I dropped my stuff in the hallway and set up my pillow and blanket in front of Cody's open door. Kreg slowly walked out of our bedroom, pillow in hand, and threw it down beside me.

"Scoot over, I'm coming in. I've spent the last couple months sleeping under terrible conditions. What's another night, huh?" It was a tight fit in the hallway, but for the first time in a long time, I cuddled up to my husband and fell asleep.

After a day or two Kreg returned to work and I was by myself for the day while the girls were at school. It was terrifying. I tried to run through all the contingency plans in my head. What to do if his feeding tube got plugged, how to clean out the trache, what to do in case of infection, how to suction his lungs, the list went on and on. I would start to vacuum or make lunch, then run upstairs to check on Cody, just in case I had missed something while I was away. When all the chores were done, I spent all my time sitting next to Cody. Sitting and talking, sitting and reading, sitting and thinking.

In the hospital I had learned to be strong and tough, but in the comfort of my home, with nobody around, the tears flowed freely and often. The questions I had tried to push back and ignore for so long boiled over. Why us? Why Cody? Why hadn't the operations gone smoother, why hadn't God stepped in to fix things? Why did it have to be so hard? Why did it have to take so long? I cried and prayed and cried some more, until the tears just stopped coming.

In the quiet that followed my tears, I opened my scriptures and began to look for answers. I read as Alma and Amulek watched women and children being cast into the fire for believing in God, but they were restrained from stopping it. I read the same Alma's counsel to his son Shiblon, where he told him that if he was faithful, God would deliver him out of his trials after this life, but possibly not before. I also studied the accounts of many of the prophets and missionaries of the Book of Mormon who suffered terrible conditions, but God allowed it so that some greater good could happen.

I wasn't getting the answers I wanted. It didn't seem fair that suffering should be part of the plan of salvation, or that God should allow terrible things to happen to innocent people, even if there was some greater good.

I wanted some formula to escape my trials and have them removed, not promises of eternal rewards if I endured them well.

The more I studied, the more I came to understand that there was no promise to remove all our pain, except for after this life. In fact, the miracles performed by Christ and the prophets seemed so amazing because they were so rare. God had never revealed any secret formula to remove all our physical pain or eliminate our trials. On some occasions he stepped in to bless those who were suffering and he removed the trial, but those situations were few and far between. Instead, the scriptures promised help and assistance through our trials, but not their removal.

I then realized just how blessed we were to have had our own miracle, to have Cody's promise of recovery from a general authority of the Church. God didn't owe us anything, and there were so many others in the hospital who were good people as well who would not have outcomes as miraculous as ours. I began to feel embarrassed for asking for so much. I resolved to be strong like Alma and Amulek, to keep my faith and my

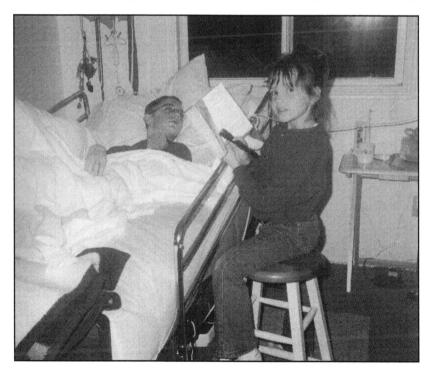

Krissa reading Cody a story at bedtime

determination even as I was forced to watch a good person like Cody go through a terrible tragedy. I would take the blessings as they came, thank God for his tender mercies along the way, and await the day when God would finally remove all our pain and sorrow. It wasn't going to be easy, but I would do my best to be strong. Even if it would take a lifetime.

I stood up, took a breath, and continued on with my duties. Check Cody's temperature, replace the feeding bag, suction his lungs, check his oxygen levels, stretch his legs and arms and massage his muscles. After that, apply more vaseline to his lips, clean out the trache, sanitize the hole for his feeding tube, roll him over to remove the sheets and wash the bedding, replace the catheter bag, give Cody his medication, and make sure to talk to him all the while to stimulate his brain and encourage him to try to wake up and listen to our voices. I was trying to be strong, but after just a couple hours, I was starting to question my resolve.

By the time Kreg got home, I was spent. I warmed up a dinner from the Relief Society and helped the girls with their homework. After putting them all to bed, we started setting things up to give Cody a bath. Because there was no room in our tiny bathroom for Cody and two adults to wash him, we set up a blow-up bathtub in the hallway just outside the bathroom and put a cot in it for Cody to lay on while we bathed him. We'd have to use a bucket to fill the tub with water from the bathroom, then drain it out again by bucket. It seemed daunting and I wasn't looking forward to it. Then the doorbell rang. I ran downstairs and found my brother Kip with a big bright smile on his face.

"Hey! Is it bath night?" he asked. I wasn't sure what he meant.

"Um, well, the girls took baths already, they're in bed now. Do you want to come in?"

"No, I meant for Cody. He needs a bath tonight, right?" Kip smiled.

"Well, yeah, we were just getting things set up. How did you know?"

Kip just shrugged his shoulders as he came in the door. "Go lay down and read a book or something, Kreg and I will take care of it." I had no idea how he knew we needed help, but it was so difficult for me to move Cody, and quite uncomfortable to be bathing my teenage son, so I was utterly grateful for the help. I gladly took Kip's advice to sit this one out, so I plopped down on the couch and closed my eyes while they gave Cody a bath. For the next several months, either Kip or Corey showed up every other night, right on schedule for bath time, allowing me a short but needed break from taking care of Cody.

The next day the therapists started coming: occupational therapists, speech therapists, and physical therapists. I told them all about the thumb movement, so we started working on hand signals. Almost immediately the little gestures that were barely recognizable became more obvious. He was trying, even though the results weren't consistent.

We started out with little things, opening the hand, making a fist, thumbs up, wiggling toes, blinking. By the end of the first week he could manage each of those tasks, but just barely, and only after hours of coaching. We still couldn't get him to answer questions though, so we worked on a couple hand signals. One finger meant yes, two fingers meant no. By the end of the second week, Cody could make the signs, but his responses rarely made sense. It was like he was living under a blanket of fog and understood just bits and pieces of the world around him.

The progress was slow, but it felt really good. Day by day, Cody was reminding us that he was still alive, still fighting to get better. I started a little calendar and wrote down each day's accomplishments. On January 22nd he moved his lips when we asked him to smile. On January 24th he was able to wrap his fingers around a ball. On January 28th he followed me around the room with his eyes. They were baby steps, but they were miracles to us.

On Saturday morning, January 29th, Kreg woke me up early in the morning, complaining about the cold. That was nothing new. The doctors had told me to keep the house cool because the heat increased the pressure in his head and they were worried about fevers and seizures, so I did. Everyone soon learned to bring a sweater or a jacket when they came over to visit. Kreg still didn't like it though.

"I've got three blankets on me, and I'm freezing. Cody has got to be frozen like a popsicle," Kreg said as he wiggled out of our pile of blankets and pillows in the hallway and squeezed through Cody's door. He grabbed one of the blankets and walked over to Cody, feeling his skin.

"I'm putting another blanket on him," Kreg said.

"Don't you dare, he's fine," I said, forcing myself to get up. I checked his equipment and put my hand on his forehead. He was cool, but not too bad. He seemed to have woken up from all the commotion, his eyes were wide open and he looked attentive. I pulled the extra blanket off. Kreg shook his head at me.

"Cody, tell your mom she's a loser," Kreg said, chuckling. He turned around and headed out the door.

"Kreg!" I shouted, "Look!" Kreg turned back and we both stared at Cody's hand as he raised it from the bed. He had stuck his index finger out straight, and his thumb out to the side, making an L shape. He was raising his arm to bring the L to his forehead and got about a foot off the bed before he couldn't lift it any higher.

I shouted with excitement, "Loser! Oh, good job Cody! Loser! That's right, your mom is a loser!" I could almost cry I was so happy. That was some of the most complex movement he had made, and we hadn't coached him at all. Despite being called a loser by my teenage son, it was one of the best days I'd had in a long time.

Progress seemed to come more quickly after that. The next week we worked on moving legs, squeezing hands, and by the end of the week he was able to use our one-finger two-finger method for answering questions. One of the first questions Kreg asked him was if he was cold. The answer was yes. I relented and let Kreg turn up the thermostat after that, but just a few degrees.

Having Cody able to answer simple questions was so nice. I could ask if he was comfortable, if he wanted to get in his wheelchair and go for a walk, or if he needed another blanket. It felt like the Cody we knew was coming back to us. Every day there was something Cody could do a little better, something to surprise us. Whether it was wiggling his toes or squeezing a hand, we loved the progress, but wished it was going faster.

By Valentine's Day, the 14th of February, we had been at home for exactly a month. It had been 77 days since Cody had fallen into the coma, and we started to realize that Cody was awake quite often. He couldn't speak and he tired easily, but he could understand basic concepts and was working hard at getting better. Kreg had finally convinced me to stop sleeping in the hallway and return to our bedroom, and I was much less frightened that something terrible was going to happen.

That morning one of the therapists came by with several pets. One after another she placed a puppy, a cat, and a rabbit on Cody's lap, had him answer yes or no questions about the animals, and helped him to pet them. Cody didn't seem too amused with the puppy or the cat, but the rabbit really got him excited. He lifted his hand up over and over again, softly petting the rabbit's back. It was some of the most sustained physical motion that Cody had been able to do on his own.

The therapist seemed so impressed, she made us an offer, "You know what, Cody's responding so well to the rabbit, you can keep him if you'd like. We have several more, and I think it might really help get his muscles moving." I thought it was a great idea, so she left the rabbit in his cage right next to Cody's bed where he could watch it waddle around and eat vegetable scraps.

The weather outside was turning stormy, so the therapist gathered her things and hurried on her way. I watched out the window as she drove off, glad to be safe inside as the storm hit our neighborhood. The wind was blowing hard and the trees were shaking violently and anything not nailed down seemed to be blowing down our street. A trampoline from a neighbor's yard was picked up and thrown on someone else's roof. I was getting a little worried, so I walked back upstairs to check on Cody, right as the power went out.

I felt my way through the dark hallway into his room and opened the blinds, but there wasn't much light outside to let in. It was eerie in Cody's room with the wind beating at the window in the dim light and without the sound of the various machines and monitors humming and beeping.

Once the blinds were all the way open and a hint of light came in, I realized Cody's bed had deflated. It was a special air mattress that inflated and deflated sections to prevent bed sores, but without power the air had completely escaped and Cody was lying on the hard metal frame. I also worried about his feeding tube getting clogged without the machine being on, but there wasn't anything I could do. I sat by his side for a while, hoping the power would come back on in just a moment, but it didn't come.

I tried to unhook Cody from his monitors and tubes so I could move him off the bed, but it was difficult to see and I wasn't sure I was doing it right. I found a flashlight, but of course, the batteries were dead. I stepped into the garage and grabbed the 72-hour-kit my grandpa had made years ago. No flashlight there, but there were some homemade candles made of sawdust and wax, and they smelled of diesel fuel. I grabbed a lighter, a couple of candles, and got a plate from the kitchen.

I set a candle on a plate in the living room and lit it with the lighter. Almost immediately the flames grew out of control and dark smoke began billowing from the candle. Flames shot up more than three feet, and the more I blew on it, the bigger they got. I ran to the kitchen and grabbed a pot lid. It didn't really fit over the candle and flames shot out from around the lid, but eventually I smothered it. Then there was pounding on the door. I coughed and wheezed through the smoky room and opened the door. There was my brother Kip again, coming to save the day.

"What in the world? Is there a fire?" Kip looked surprised.

"Not anymore, it's out, I tried lighting grandpa's old candles but it almost burnt the house down."

"Yeah, I can tell," he said, waving the smoke and diesel fumes away from his eyes. "Hey, I figured Cody wasn't going to do so well without power. I've got a generator in the truck, I should have your power up and running in about five minutes."

"Oh, thank you Kip!" I sighed. In just a few minutes we had power to all of Cody's equipment and his bed was re-inflating. He told me it would last several hours with the fuel in the tank, and he'd come back after work to check on it again.

Kreg came home just after the girls got out of school and just shook his head as I explained the whole ordeal to him. Apparently the storm had generated some tornadoes in our area, which was quite rare, and there was some serious damage in other parts of town. I was glad we weren't hit, and Kreg was glad I hadn't burned the house down.

As we walked up to Cody's room, the girls following close behind, he pointed to the cage on the dresser. "What's this?" he said with a surprised look. I had almost forgotten about the rabbit. I explained Cody's progress with petting the bunny, and that the therapist had given it to us to keep.

"Well, I know exactly what to call him," Kreg said, his hands on his hips.

"But Dad, we wanted to name him!" The girls begged.

"Nope. I'm naming him. His name is Stew, because that's exactly what he'll be if he doesn't stay in line!" Kreg smiled and the girls gasped in horror, but the name stuck. Luckily for Stew, he earned his keep by letting Cody pet him every day, and thankfully avoided the butcher block.

That night in bed, I made a proposal. "Honey, I think we can say that Cody's not in a coma anymore, right?"

Kreg thought it over before responding. "Yeah, he's not talking or anything, and he's not really aware of everything that's going on around him, but I wouldn't say he's in a coma anymore. I mean, he can answer yes and no, tell us if he wants another pillow or if he wants to sit up. That's pretty good considering where he was."

"Yeah, I think so too. So why don't we have a family party on Sunday and invite everyone over and cut off the bracelets? You know, to show that Cody's out of the coma, and that he's getting better."

Kreg rubbed the beaded bracelet on his wrist as he thought about it. It had been about two months since our whole family had put them on, promising not to remove them until Cody was well. "Yeah, I guess it's as good a time as any. He sure is better than when we put the bracelets on."

I thought back to our time in the hospital and shuddered. It had been so painful, so heartbreaking, so monotonously slow. I knew we had a long way to go, but I was grateful for the progress that had been made, grateful for the support of good friends and family, grateful for good doctors and therapists, grateful for Elder Zwick and his message of hope, and grateful for a Heavenly Father who had promised us yet another miracle.

"Okay," I said. "I'll call everyone."

On the next Sunday evening we packed everyone into our tiny house to have our bracelet cutting party. We put Cody in his wheelchair and brought him out to the kitchen to be with everyone else. Everyone cheered and clapped as Kreg and I cut Cody's bracelet off. I'm not sure Cody understood what was going on, but his eyes were wide and he seemed to know something important was happening. We passed the scissors around and let all the cousins, aunts and uncles, and grandparents remove their bracelets. When I cut mine off I felt relief, but wondered about the future. Cutting off the bracelets was a milestone, a sign that we had made it out of the coma, but there were many more miles, and milestones, left to go.

Later that week I called the trauma unit in Salt Lake to let Dr. Richardson know about the progress. He sounded amazed when I told him about all the things Cody could do. After a few questions about Cody's health, he suggested that we return to Salt Lake for eight weeks of rehabilitation. I shuddered at the thought of two more months of living in a hospital room, but I was grateful for the opportunity and excited for the progress Cody was going to make.

As the hospital worked to schedule us a slot for rehab, we picked up the pace on our exercises at home. We kept introducing new tasks and challenges, and Cody kept up with the added work. By the first week in March, Cody started shaking his head for yes or no, waving goodbye, and was able to lift his hand high enough to scratch his head. It was like living with a toddler, each day was a new adventure and another small step forward.

That weekend my brother Dirk came up to Idaho Falls to help out. We let him watch Cody while Kreg and I went back to church for the first time in several months. It was so good to be back with my friends and thank all the dear sisters who had helped us, but a little overwhelming at the same time. When sacrament meeting was over and we had shared handshakes and hugs with almost everyone in the ward, we headed home to make sure Cody and Dirk were alright.

"Brenda, you won't believe it," Dirk said as we walked in the door, "He talked!"

"What? What did he say?" I asked as I rushed to Cody's side.

"He said 'Mom!' It was a little hard to hear, but I'm sure of it." Dirk tried to coax him into speaking again, but nothing came. Talking was something we had been working on for a long time, but we hadn't even come close. To have him say a word was a great step forward.

We tried to get him to talk the next day, but nothing came. The speech therapists had suggested that we talk to him like normal and ask him regular questions throughout the day, so I tried to have conversations with him while I was in his room, even though they were always one sided.

A few days later I was finishing up Cody's morning routine and talking to him about my plans, "Okay Cody, everything is set up here and you're good to go. I'm going to go do my exercises, alright?" I double checked everything and picked up the portable phone I carried around the house with me. I looked at the phone and gave it a second thought. "You know what buddy, I'm just going to leave the phone here with you. If anyone calls, make sure to pick it up, okay?" I smiled and set the phone by his bed. Of course it was a ridiculous suggestion, but sometimes being silly in our conversations was the only way to stay sane when talking with someone who couldn't respond.

I started walking out the door but I stopped and turned back, giving it one more try. "Hey Cody, if someone called, what would you say?" Cody's eyes were staring at the ceiling, and he was breathing deeply. My son was inside there, somewhere, and it was exciting and excruciating at the same time, knowing that he was so close, yet so far. I turned to leave and was halfway through the doorway when I heard it.

"Hello." The sound was labored and barely resembled a word, but I could tell what he was trying to do.

"What did you say?" I tried to coax it out of him once more as I ran to his side.

"Hello." The same sounds, the same word, a little bit clearer than before. I could barely contain myself, Cody was speaking! I picked up the phone and quickly dialed Kreg's number at work.

"Kreg! Kreg! You've got to hear this!" I held the phone up to Cody's mouth. "Tell Dad what you told me."

"Hello, hello." Cody was getting excited about his newly-found ability and his voice was getting stronger each time he spoke. Kreg was crying on the other end of the line, trying unsuccessfully to maintain his composure. I told him what had happened and we shared a few happy words, then I let him get back to work. Cody and I worked on speech for the rest of the day. Most words just wouldn't come, but names, those came pretty quickly: Dad, Mom, all three girls. The words weren't pretty, it was still pretty rough, but you could absolutely tell that he knew what he was saying and he was giving it his best shot. After months of silence, I was in heaven.

By the next Sunday Cody had improved so much. He was able to shake hands, give hugs, play tic tac toe, and even say a word or two if you helped him through it. His school buddies had been checking in on him occasionally, but as he became more capable they started coming by more often. That Sunday evening we had a big group of boys over, just sitting around and talking about school and girls and sports. The boys probably couldn't see it, but I knew Cody was loving the company.

The phone rang and Kreg got up to answer it. I assumed it was just another one of Cody's friends, seeing if they could come over and join the party, but Kreg sounded surprised, then gave directions to our house. After he hung up, he turned to me, "That was Elder Zwick. He's passing through town and wanted to see us. He'll be here in five minutes."

"Five minutes?" I asked in amazement. Kreg nodded. I jumped up and started tidying up. I threw the dirty dishes in the sink, wiped down the counter, put the throw pillows back on the couch, and cleaned up the girls' toys. Everything was in its place, but we still had a dozen boys filling our living room. What do we do with the boys? The doorbell rang. The boys would have to stay.

"Hi Sister Parmer, and Brother Parmer, good to see you both!" I had forgotten how infectious Elder Zwick's happiness and optimism were. We welcomed him in and brought him over to see Cody. The boys parted to make way for the man in the dark suit, but Elder Zwick spent a moment talking to them and introduced himself.

I was a little worried about mixing the company. Not all of the boys were active church members, and some were a little on the wild side. Cody had always been a friend to everyone, and that meant he attracted a wide range of friends, but I wasn't sure how they would react when a general authority from the Church was right there with them. As it turned out, I was pleasantly surprised.

The boys were very respectful and let us tell Elder Zwick all about Cody's progress. Elder Zwick held out his hand and Cody shook it. The only time he had ever seen Cody was the day we were planning his funeral in the hospital, and the progress he made since then was incredible. After we had spent several minutes talking about Cody, Elder Zwick turned his attention to the boys. He talked to each one, learning a little bit about what they liked to do, how school was going, and what their goals were. He was kind and patient, and listened to each boy as they told him their plans.

"You sound like terrific friends. Cody will be very grateful for your support, I'm sure of it. And the Lord appreciates your service as well. You know, you'll be able to continue this kind of service as you serve missions. The same good feelings that come from serving Cody in his time of need will come as you serve Heavenly Father's children all over the world. There are millions, even billions of people out there, suffering from their own struggles. Maybe they haven't had accidents like Cody, maybe their suffering just comes from a broken heart, or loneliness, or fear, but they're suffering all the same. And the gospel of Jesus Christ can heal that. It can do it for you, it can do it for Cody, and you'll help others find the happiness that only comes from Jesus Christ. I believe in you. You're the future of the Church."

The boys were mesmerized, and so were we. Elder Zwick shook each of the boys' hands, then announced that he had to be on his way. Everyone stood up and we followed him to the door. Before he left he turned, put his arm around one of the boys and hugged him. "You're going to make such a good missionary!" He said with a smile. He then shook our hands and left.

The boys broke into a chuckle as the door closed. Of all the boys there, the one that Elder Zwick put his arm around was one of the most wild of the bunch. He was inactive and certainly not headed toward a mission, and everyone knew that. They laughed at the time, but soon enough that boy came around and got his life in order. Elder Zwick's statement was indeed prophetic; the boy turned out to be a great missionary.

After Elder Zwick left the boys returned to their normal conversations, and Kreg and I sat by ourselves and talked. Why were we so blessed to have Elder Zwick look after us? Was that a sign of our weakness, because we weren't able to do it on our own? We seemed so undeserving of such great blessings, but they were blessings we had needed so desperately. We had done our best to be faithful and strong, of course, but we still felt so weak and helpless. Surely there were thousands of people just like us who could use the help and comfort and support from a general authority. Why us? That question had come full circle, first out of grief and pain, and now out of gratitude and reverence.

Sitting there on the couch with my husband, hand in hand, it felt like our problems were almost behind us. Cody was almost talking, almost able to follow a conversation, almost able to move his arms and legs on his own. Pretty soon, we figured, everything would be back to normal. We were almost right.

TWENTY-ONE

M ARCH 27TH MARKED OUR RETURN TO LDS HOSPITAL. IT HAD BEEN two weeks since Elder Zwick had visited us in our home and Cody's progress had been huge. He was now able to pick up items all by himself, and even throw a ball to someone sitting a few feet away. His cognitive ability had improved so much that he could play a game of Uno, and he seemed to follow our conversations a lot better. Best of all, he had learned how to talk again.

Once Cody figured out how to speak, we couldn't get him to stay quiet. His voice was muffled and weak, but we learned to understand him fairly quickly. He asked a million questions and told us everything he was thinking. His memory was still suffering from the head trauma and our conversations were quite simple, but his personality was there and it felt like I finally got my son back.

Our plan was to stay at LDS Hospital for eight weeks. Our goals were ambitious: try to get Cody eating regular foods, using the bathroom by himself, improve his speech so he could have full conversations, and get him walking on his own. In short, I wanted him back to normal. It was a tall order, but we were determined. Kreg wasn't able to take the eight weeks off from work, but his boss let him leave early on Friday and show up late on Monday so he could spend the weekends with us, and my sister was taking care of the girls while I was gone.

Our therapy schedule in Salt Lake seemed to move at an incredible pace. The morning after we arrived Cody went in for an eating test to make sure he could swallow without the food going into his lungs. They gave Cody a pudding cup and he was in love. It was the first food he had eaten in months. With every bite, the doctors watched through an x-ray while the pudding moved down his throat and into his stomach. They decided he wasn't ready for solids, but yogurt and pudding were fine. The next day Cody ate three cups of pudding and almost two cups of yogurt. With every bite he let out a little sigh of happiness. He probably would have eaten pudding all day long if we had let him.

Then the therapists came. One after another, they showed up to work with Cody on a variety of exercises and tasks. Within the first week Cody learned how to move himself forward in a wheelchair, stand up with a walker, and roll over in bed by himself. It was amazing progress, but the therapists started to notice something we had worried about for a while. No matter how hard he practiced, his left hand and left leg were never as strong as his right side. Most of the time, his left hand either lay limp at his side, or curled up in a fist on his chest. The doctors told us that the limitations on his left side were likely the result of the injury to his right brain, but that the brain may be able to restore those functions with enough practice. So the practice went on.

That first Friday afternoon when Kreg arrived he was amazed at how much progress we had made in just one week, and Cody gave him a high five and a big smile. Just a few hours after Kreg showed up, we had a surprise visit from Elder Zwick.

"Hi folks! I hope it's alright I stopped in," Elder Zwick said as he stood in the doorway to Cody's room.

"Oh hello! Sure, of course, come on in! It's good to see you," Kreg said, waving him in.

"And how's Cody doing today? Making lots of progress I bet." Elder Zwick gave Cody his characteristic grin, and Cody answered back with a wide smile. We filled him in on all the progress and also the things Cody was still struggling with. Elder Zwick listened attentively and nodded as we explained our concerns about his left hand and leg.

"If anyone can pull through it, Cody can," Elder Zwick said, which got another big smile out of Cody. "Well, I didn't mean to take too much of your time today, I know they keep you on a busy schedule, but I came to ask if I could bring a visitor by."

Kreg and I looked at each other, there was no reason why he shouldn't be able to. "Of course, Cody loves visitors," I replied.

"Excellent. On Tuesday evening I have an appointment with Elder Scott of the Quorum of the Twelve Apostles. I'd like to bring him to see Cody, if you'll be available that evening." An apostle was going to visit us? We already felt so blessed to be watched over by Elder Zwick, but we were absolutely undeserving of the attention of an apostle. There had to be hundreds of sick LDS people in this hospital alone, and he was going to come to a rehab unit to see my son? Surely he had more important things to do than visit us.

"Oh wow, are you sure? He's not too busy?" Kreg asked.

"No, I've got to meet with him anyway. It will work out just fine," Elder Zwick said. So that was it. An apostle was coming to our hospital room.

Elder Zwick left and we tried to explain to Cody what was going to happen and who was going to be visiting him. Cody smiled. I'm not sure he understood fully, but he could tell we were excited, so he was happy too.

Tuesday evening came and sure enough, in walked Elder Zwick, accompanied by Elder Richard G. Scott. I was in awe as I shook their hands. I had always thought of Elder Scott as a calm and loving leader, but the feeling of warmth and compassion that came from his visit was beyond description. They visited with us for a while and we talked about everything that Cody had been through. It had been a long day of ther-apy, so Cody was pretty exhausted already, but he did his best to shake hands and say a few words.

Elder Scott then asked if we would like them to give Cody a blessing. What a silly question, I thought, who in the world would turn down a blessing from an apostle? Elder Zwick anointed, then Elder Scott gave the blessing. The feeling of peace and love was so incredible, I'll never forget it.

Elder Scott blessed Cody to pay close attention to the reasons his life was preserved, and commanded him to share his story with others. He instructed Cody to teach others where his blessings had come from and to stand as a witness for Christ at all times. He blessed his body that it would be whole, and that his spirit would be able to regain control over the physical body. He blessed us as parents, through Cody, and called on the rights of the apostleship on Cody's behalf. As he closed in the name of Jesus Christ, my testimony of the power of apostles and prophets grew ten-fold. There was no denying the divine authority of that blessing.

The experience not only renewed my faith, but also strengthened my resolve. After they left, Kreg had to rush back to Idaho Falls to be to work the next day, which left me alone again with Cody. After a weekend with my husband and a visit from two great examples of Christian service, I was pumped up and ready to take on the world, but I still wished progress would come faster.

Our second week was full of more tests, more therapy, and more little steps toward making Cody whole. They tried the eating test again and gave Cody the green light for solid foods. Cody's first request: a grilled cheese sandwich. Cody's weight had fallen to 110 lbs. since the hemorrhage, but the weight quickly came back after a steady diet of pudding and grilled cheese sandwiches.

Every day it was more training, more exercises, more tasks to master. It took Cody several hours to put on his socks the first time. They kept

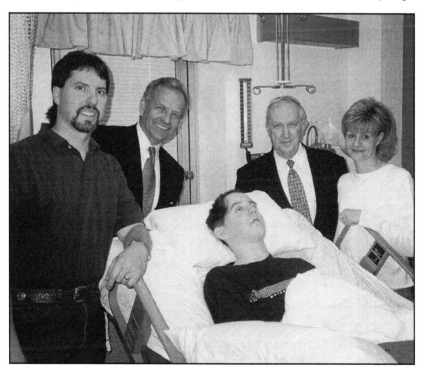

Kreg, Elder Zwick, Elder Scott, Brenda, and Cody

getting stuck between his toes, but the therapist told me not to help, to make him learn how to do it himself, so I did. Cody got pretty mad at me and he couldn't understand why I wouldn't just help him, but he never gave up. It took more than an hour to figure out how to not get the sock stuck between his toes, then pulling the sock up his foot was a whole new adventure. The whole process was painfully long for both of us, but after another week or so, putting on socks only took a few minutes instead of a few hours.

On the weekends when Kreg arrived with the girls, they became the makeshift therapists. They would play catch with Cody, or play a game of checkers with oversized pieces that were easier for Cody to pick up. The therapist brought in a puppy for the kids to play with, which the girls probably enjoyed even more than Cody. Having the girls push Cody to do better seemed to have a real effect. Cody had been their hero for so many years, and he was trying to be strong for them now.

After a month we had made tremendous progress, but Cody still was having problems with his left leg, so they gave him a brace that locked the leg straight while he tried to walk. With his brace, he was able to walk short distances between the parallel bars, an incredible improvement over where he had been just a month earlier. The doctors finally decided that five weeks was enough and that he could function at home with minimal assistance and continue therapy there. I tried to argue that we should stay until he was walking on his own, but they wouldn't budge. Getting kicked out of hospitals before we felt ready to go was becoming a habit.

All things considered though, things were much better. Cody was talking more easily, eating normally, able to walk with assistance, and capable of taking care of himself in a lot of ways. His speech was still slow and we had a long way to go, but we had come so far, I had no doubt we would be fine.

We got home and Cody told us he wanted to go to church, so we dressed him up in his shirt and tie, got him in the wheelchair, and headed to church as a family for the first time in almost six months. Many of the ward members had kept track of his progress through the reports of friends and family, but the reception they gave him as we wheeled him into the chapel was amazing. Cody felt like a superstar, shaking everyone's hands and smiling ear to ear.

That first Sunday back was also Fast and Testimony Meeting, and when it came time for testimonies, Cody signaled to Kreg that he wanted to speak. I was a little nervous that this might happen, and his speech was still slow and difficult to understand, but he could probably do it; I just wasn't sure what he'd say. Kreg wheeled him up to the front and the bishop lowered the pulpit. Cody spoke as clearly as he could into the microphone, and the chapel was perfectly silent.

"I'd like to bear my testimony. I love Heavenly Father. I love the gospel. I love my family, and my mom and dad. My mom especially, she has helped me so much. Thank you for the visitors. Thank you for the meals. Thank you for everybody's help. I know that Heavenly Father saved my life. In the name of Jesus Christ, amen." As Cody finished and Kreg wheeled him down the ramp, the sobbing in the audience grew louder and louder. I thought it was just me at first, but as I wiped my eyes and looked around, there wasn't a dry eye in the chapel.

Everyone had been so emotionally invested in Cody's recovery, there were thousands of hours of service and prayers on our behalf, and our whole ward had been pulling for him. To see him commit to bearing his testimony when it took so much energy was a wonderful feeling, and it felt like the culmination of a long road that our ward had traveled together. Even though there was a long way to go, everyone seemed to take a collective sigh of relief as they realized Cody was going to make it.

Back at home however, the struggle was as real as ever. Cody wanted help with everything, but he needed to learn how to do things on his own. This resulted in a lot of frustration and a lot of hard days. I learned to be tough when Cody got mad and begged for help, and Cody learned that I wasn't going to give in.

There were lots of good days as well. I tried to give Cody something new to do every day, like peeling vegetables, folding clothes, setting the table, or measuring out ingredients for dinner. Each new job was difficult for him to master, but after some really concentrated effort he could figure it out.

Cody had limited mobility, but he wanted to be involved in everything so badly. Brooke was in track and was training for the 800-meter race, so Cody took it upon himself to be her coach. At dinner he told her she needed to eat more spaghetti, through the afternoon he would have her sprint around the house, and in the evenings Cody would roll out onto the porch and give her pointers as she raced up and down the street. When Brooke placed second in the state track meet, Cody took full credit for her victory. The girls were so kind to Cody and helped him feel important and appreciated, but things were different, and I just hoped they would get back to normal soon.

Unfortunately, progress seemed to slow through the summer. There were still minor successes, but it was taking a long time for Cody to learn to balance and walk on his own, and his left hand simply stopped improving. Cody had a minor surgery that stretched some of the muscles in his left arm and hand so it wouldn't be curled up against his chest all the time, but it didn't do much to improve his use of it. The doctors were becoming less and less optimistic about Cody regaining use of his left hand.

July came and the doctors determined it was finally time to patch up the hole in Cody's skull. We had grown used to the indentation on the side of his head but others seemed quite startled by it, so we were glad for an operation that would help Cody feel more accepted and normal.

We returned to LDS hospital the last week in July. Dr. Richardson was scheduled to perform the surgery and I was glad that someone who knew our story was taking care of Cody. The nurses got Cody into a hospital gown and put him on a gurney to wait for the operation. After a few minutes Dr. Richardson came in to talk to us.

"Hi Cody, I'm Dr. Richardson, I worked with you last year when you had your accident and then again during the holidays. How are you?" Dr. Richardson said as he reached out to shake Cody's hand.

Cody raised his hand from the bed and gave the best handshake he could. "You fixed my brain," Cody said with his slow and simple words.

"That's right, I did perform the surgery when you came in, what, eight months ago, nine? You've done really well, I can tell you're working hard."

"I am. Mom won't help me anymore so I have to do everything myself," Cody said slowly, smiling. I rolled my eyes and Dr. Richardson chuckled.

"Your mom is probably right, the more you do on your own, the better you'll get." Dr. Richardson patted Cody on the arm and gave me and Kreg an understanding smile. "Alright, do you know what we're going to do today?"

"Fix my head," Cody replied.

"That's right, we're going to put a metal plate onto the bone to cover that hole. You'll still have to be careful, but it will be a lot safer for you to do normal activities. We're going to put you to sleep, put the plate in, then when you wake up we'll be all done. Alright?"

"Yep," Cody said. He had become pretty used to hospitals and surgeries and was more brave than I would have been. He had to know it would hurt after the surgery was over, but he didn't show it.

"Okay, then let's get started." Dr. Richardson called in a few nurses and they wheeled Cody out. I gave him one last kiss and Kreg told him to be tough, and then he was gone.

The surgery took several hours and when they brought him back with his head wrapped in gauze, I flashed back to the surgeries in December when they were racing to save Cody's life. We had come so far, but I still worried about how much farther we had to go before Cody was back to normal.

It had already been eight months since the hemorrhage, I had no idea it would take this long and we still seemed pretty far from where we wanted to be. Would it be another eight months? Eighteen months? We had a promise that Cody would be healed, but what did healed mean? Did healed mean absolutely perfect? Surely we were blessed just to have Cody alive and talking, but it seemed like his left side might never be as strong as his right. How much were we entitled to expect? Thinking about it worried me, so I tried to focus on other things.

A few hours later they took Cody off the anesthesia and he slowly woke up. He seemed a little confused, which was normal, but he was generally in good spirits. The doctors wanted us to stay for a few days to watch for infection, so when Cody started having terrible headaches, the doctors became concerned, and I became terrified.

After dozens of tests, the doctors concluded there was spinal fluid leaking into Cody's skull, and sealing it up with the metal plate had plugged the hole that was relieving the pressure. With the skull sealed off, the pressure continued to build and started causing Cody's headaches. All the worry from a year earlier came rushing back. Would there be more hemorrhages? How serious was the pressure? Was there ever going to be an end to this problem?

"Why didn't it work Mom? Why can't they fix it? What are they going to do?" Cody asked over and over. It used to be me asking those questions, but now that Cody was awake and talking, I had to be strong and tell him everything was going to be okay. However, in private moments with Kreg I asked him the same questions, and I was constantly asking God the same thing. Why couldn't we just be done with this? Why did we have to suffer so many complications? I just wanted to curl up and cry, hide from the world, and try to forget all the terrible struggles we had been through. Fortunately, God knew just what I needed.

I have learned that while God wants us to experience all that life has in store for us, he is also willing to go to great lengths to bless his children. For us, that blessing came once again in the form of a visit from Elder Craig Zwick, who I know was sent by God at exactly the right time, just when we needed him. I felt bad that our private issues would consume so much of the time and energy of someone whose responsibility it was to care for hundreds of thousands of people, but it taught me that God doesn't just love us as a group, he loves us individually. Each person is so important to him that he will use the best resources possible to bless them, whether that person is a loving home teacher or a member of the Seventy. For our family, Elder Zwick was just what we needed to calm our nerves, regain our strength, and commit to carry on.

Right before the doctors were scheduled to perform an operation to relieve the pressure, Elder Zwick arrived and offered to give Cody a blessing. With Kreg's help, he blessed Cody that everything would turn out alright, that a solution would be found and that Cody would overcome this.

After the blessing was over, he offered to bring Elder Scott back in a few days for another blessing, if we would like. I wasn't sure what to say. I didn't know if it was appropriate to ask for another visit, or if we had already given Cody too many blessings. So I decided to ask.

"Elder Zwick, how do we know when we've given Cody enough blessings? He's had so many, and the blessings say he'll get better, but then we give him more and more blessings. Does that mean that we don't have faith in the first blessings? Are we giving blessings too often? I just don't know, what are we supposed to do?"

He thought about it for a moment. "That's an excellent question. I believe that Heavenly Father wants his children to be healthy and happy, but pain and sickness are a natural consequence of mortality. The Lord has provided us with the power to give blessings for the sick and afflicted to remove a certain problem, if we are faithful and if it is the Lord's will. However, because we're mortal, we may become sick again, or other complications may arise. Any time a new problem or sickness or complication arises, it's appropriate to give another blessing."

That made a lot of sense and gave me a good basis for determining when to ask for priesthood blessings. I decided that Cody's new surgery was surely a cause for concern, and told Elder Zwick that we would be honored to have Elder Scott come by again, if he wasn't too busy. Elder Zwick smiled and told us he would do his best to make it happen.

The next day the surgeons made a couple large incisions and inserted a tube that led from his brain all the way into his stomach. Any excess fluid would be relieved through the tube. Once the doctors determined that the spinal cord was no longer leaking fluid into the skull, they would pinch off the tube and simply leave it in place. The surgery went well and the pressure problem was solved.

True to his word, Elder Zwick arrived a few days later with not one, but two companions. "Cody, this is Elder Scott, you met him a month or two ago," Cody shook his hand with enthusiasm, "and this is Brother Dale Murphy, he played professional baseball for many years and just returned from serving as a mission president in Boston."

"The Braves!" Cody said, excitedly.

"That's right, I played for the Atlanta Braves. Very good! I hear you're a baseball player too," Dale said, smiling.

"I was a pitcher," Cody replied, his speech was slow but the words were delivered as fast as he could get them out.

"I'll bet you're a great pitcher! Elder Zwick tells me you're just about the toughest kid he knows, and that you've been working really hard to get better, so I'm glad I got to come and meet you. I brought you a little something too, I hope it's okay," Dale said, reaching into his bag. He pulled out an autographed baseball and handed it to Cody. If Cody could have jumped out of bed from the excitement he would have. I could tell he was just dying to show his friends an autographed baseball from Dale Murphy.

Elder Zwick, Elder Scott, and Dale Murphy stayed and talked with Cody and us for some time, then offered to give Cody a blessing to help him heal from his most recent surgery. Of course we agreed, so Kreg joined in and the four of them stood around Cody's bed, placed their hands on his head, and offered a sweet and touching blessing of health and continued healing.

I just couldn't believe how blessed our family was. Cody's life had been preserved, he had overcome so many of the doctors' predictions, he had been the focus of prayers and blessings and well-wishes from hundreds if not thousands of people, and now he was surrounded by an all-star base-ball player, a sweet and attentive general authority, a loving apostle of the Lord, and the best father a kid could ask for, all calling upon the powers of heaven to bless him. We had already been blessed in so many ways, there was only one thing left to ask for: I wanted Cody back to normal.

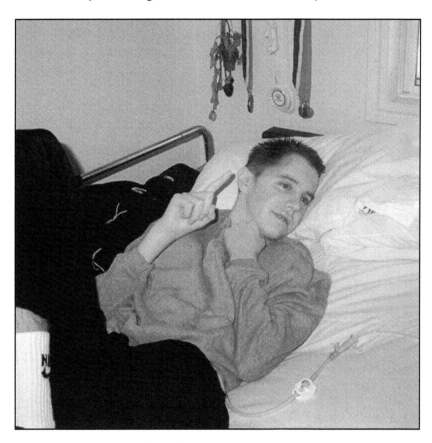

TWENTY-TWO

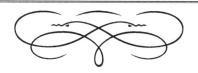

NORMAL, AS IT TURNS OUT, IS A SUBJECTIVE WORD. I WAS LOOKING forward to the normal life we once had, but as summer lingered on, we were faced with accepting a new normal. Cody's speech, mental capacity, and strength were improving, but very slowly. Instead of reaching new milestones every day, we marked progress by the week, then the month.

Despite our best efforts, Cody was still unable to walk on his own and needed to be in a wheelchair almost all the time. His left leg just wasn't able to carry any weight without buckling. His left arm was still mostly useless, and the vision had never returned in his left eye. Yes, he was alive and relatively well, but life was very difficult.

As we realized that Cody wasn't going to be back to his old self by the time school started again in the fall, we began working with the school to find a solution. Cody wanted to go back to school so badly, it was all he talked about some days. He wanted to be with friends and socialize and go on dates, but he still hadn't reached his full mental capacity, and he had never finished his junior year.

We took Cody to the school several times that summer to test his memory, his ability to reason and solve problems, and his reading and comprehension levels. After they reviewed the results, the school district decided to put him on an alternate learning schedule. They waived several of the requirements for his junior classes and had us do homework with him throughout the summer.

For whatever reason, Cody didn't want his junior-year government class waived, he wanted to say he had passed it. The school decided he could complete that requirement by reading the textbook, cover to cover. Cody's reading speed was so slow he'd never finish, so they decided I could read it to him out loud. I had just spent several months inside a hospital with nothing to do, but reading that government book to Cody was probably the most boring thing I had ever done. I read that book, out loud, page by tedious page, and Cody passed his government class and completed his junior year.

Cody was registered to begin school in September but he still wasn't walking, and we were a little concerned about his ability to take care of himself. Cody needed someone who could push his wheelchair and help him with his books during class. We looked around for someone who was available and decided to hire a young man named Jordan who just recently returned from his mission. Kreg drove Cody to school in the morning and wheeled him in to his first class where Jordan would meet him. It was a huge help having Jordan with Cody all day, but Kreg soon became concerned after seeing the kids' reaction to Cody.

For the first few days many of his classmates were really kind and encouraging to Cody, after all, Cody had been a friend to nearly everyone. People said hello and welcomed him back and Cody wanted to stop and chat with everyone, but there was no time to talk so Kreg just kept on heading to the classroom. Then, after a few days, Kreg noticed that some of the kids would intentionally avoid Cody or turn their backs as he came through.

One day, Kreg watched a boy duck into the bathroom after seeing Cody come down the hall. Kreg dropped Cody off and started back the same way he came. The boy was back out of the bathroom and talking to his friends as Kreg returned. The boy was telling his friends how he hated seeing Cody because he never knew what to say and Cody always wanted to talk to him, so he avoided him as much as he could. The boy's back was turned so he didn't see Kreg until he passed. He quickly realized Kreg heard the whole thing and looked really ashamed, but the damage was done. More and more often we started to notice kids avoiding Cody at school and around town. Most of the kids were really kind to Cody, especially Cody's long-time friends, but the number who avoided him was growing.

Around this time, we also started noticing things about Cody's behavior that puzzled us. Kreg was driving down the street one day with

Cody in the passenger seat. When they came to a stoplight, Cody rolled down the window.

"Hey, where are you going?" Cody asked the people in the car next to him.

"Uh, to the store," came the stranger's cautious reply, obviously caught off guard.

"Oh, what are you going to buy?" Cody asked.

Kreg broke in, "Cody! What are you doing?"

"I was asking him where he was going."

"Do you know him?" Kreg asked.

"No," came Cody's reply, then he turned out the window again, "Hey, what's your name?" There was no answer, the stranger just rolled his window up.

The light turned green and they started forward as Kreg rolled Cody's window up from the driver's side controls and locked the windows. "Why were you asking him that?"

"I just wanted to know where he was going," Cody replied. Kreg just shook his head. As they came to the next light, Cody tried rolling down his window again, but realized it was locked. So he opened the door.

"Hey, what are you guys doing today? Do you want to come over to my house?" Cody asked a new set of strangers while hanging halfway out the door. They looked startled and laughed nervously at Cody.

"Cody! Get back in here! Close the door!" Kreg shouted.

Cody did as he was told.

"What are you doing?" Kreg asked again.

"Just talking to people," Cody said, his feelings hurt.

"You know that's not normal, right?" Cody didn't reply. "You don't see anyone else just talking to people at the stop lights, do you?"

"No. I guess not." Cody hung his head, a little ashamed.

"Okay, well, no more talking to people at stop lights, you're going to scare someone, okay?"

"Sorry, I won't do it again," Cody said, embarrassed of his mistake. Kreg told him it would be alright, but it happened again a few days later. Cody rolled down the window and asked a panhandler at the intersection what he was doing. The panhandler came over to the window and held out his hand as Cody tried to make conversation. Kreg quickly dug in his pocket and reached across Cody to hand the man a dollar, then rolled up the window and locked them again. They had another conversation about not talking to strangers from the car window, but it happened again and again, until we learned to just keep the doors and windows locked.

Other strange things started happening too. One evening Cody was in the kitchen in his wheelchair and started shouting to Kreg in the other room. "Dad! I need to go to bed! You've got to take me to bed right now, I've got to go to sleep!"

"It's only 7:00 buddy, are you sure?" Kreg asked as he walked into the kitchen.

"Yes! I have to go to bed right now! Hurry!" Cody announced. Kreg pushed his wheelchair down the hall and into his room. Kreg wrapped his arms around Cody's chest and lifted him out of the chair into bed. As soon as Cody was upright, a dozen ice cream sandwiches slid out of his pant legs and onto the floor.

"What in the world?" Kreg said, setting Cody down on the side of the bed while he picked up the frozen treats. Cody sighed in relief now that the freezing ice cream sandwiches were not concealed in his sweatpants.

"Cody, why did you have ice cream sandwiches in your sweatpants?" Kreg asked.

"I wanted to eat them," Cody stammered, realizing he was caught.

"A dozen of them?"

Cody didn't answer. Kreg handed Cody a single ice cream sandwich and took the rest back to the freezer.

It was quickly becoming apparent that there were some problems with Cody's decision-making skills. He was able to follow along in school and could hold a conversation on almost any topic, but when Cody wanted something, he seemed to have no control.

Food quickly became a serious issue. Once Cody's reflexes were better, you had to watch your plate at dinner time. One evening we had finished dinner and I had given everyone a slice of banana cream pie. Cody had finished his slice before anyone else and asked Kreg to go get him another piece.

As soon as Kreg was up out of his chair and turned around, Cody reached over and grabbed Kreg's slice of pie with his bare hand and started shoving it in his mouth as quickly as he could, even though Kreg had just gotten up to cut Cody another slice. He just had no control over impulses.

If his impulses were just limited to sneaking food from around the house, we could have found a solution for that, but as we restricted his access to food he found more cunning ways to get what he wanted. One time a girl from school showed up on the porch with a dozen maple donuts.

"Here you go," she said as she handed over the box.

"Oh, what are these for?" I asked.

"Cody called and said you needed a dozen maple bars," she answered, as if I should have already known. I thanked her for her kindness and scrambled to find some money to pay her back, but she refused my cash and just gave a big smile as she walked away.

Cody had no idea that asking people to bring over food was inappropriate, at least not in the moment. We'd explain it to him, and he would feel sorry, but it would happen again. People showed up at the door bringing cookies, rice krispy treats, candy, pretty much anything Cody could think of. We tried hiding the phone where he couldn't reach it, but he would simply trick his sisters into bringing it to him. Kreg finally had to put a sign up on the door, "Don't Feed Cody!" Eventually Cody's friends learned what was going on and politely declined to bring Cody snacks.

The other major problem we faced was with girls. Cody had loved going on dates before the accident and many of his best friends had paired up with girlfriends since Cody's accident. Cody wanted a girlfriend of his own, but none of the girls he knew were really interested in dating someone with the physical and mental limitations he had. So he broadened his horizons, way too far.

Cody had a loose piece of binder paper that he'd keep in his pocket along with a pen. Whenever he met someone he'd ask for their phone number. Cody seemed harmless enough, and there were dozens of phone numbers scribbled randomly on the page, so they added theirs out of kindness. Then Cody started making calls.

We didn't realize what was happening until we started getting calls from angry parents. "We met your son in the grocery store the other day and now he's calling my daughter all the time asking if she wants to go out on a date. She's 12. This needs to stop."

Then we started getting calls from husbands. "Excuse me, your son called my wife and asked if she'd like to go out on a date, can you please make sure this doesn't happen again?" Any girl was fair game for Cody, from 12 to 65, married or not.

We sat down with Cody and had the same conversation a hundred times. "Cody, you understand that you can't just call people up and ask for dates out of the blue," Kreg and I would tell him.

"But that's what my friends do, they call someone up and ask for a date," Cody would reply, unassumingly.

"But they know those girls, they have a relationship with them. Besides buddy, you're calling married women and girls that are too young to date. That's inappropriate. No more calling girls without our permission, okay?" Cody would agree, but the next time he got a phone in his hands, the calls started right back up again.

We did our best to try to steer Cody's mind and activities in the right direction, but his limitations meant that he just couldn't participate in activities that he used to enjoy. Cody couldn't go ride dirt bikes, play football, or go fishing with his friends. Girls didn't really want to go on dates with Cody, so he missed out on the dating scene too. We understood perfectly why that was happening, but Cody didn't. To him, he was still the same fun-loving Casanova he had always been, and being left out of things hurt his feelings, a lot.

As parents, it was hard to watch. We wanted Cody to be accepted and to have friends and be successful, but we knew it wouldn't improve until Cody was better and could function normally. We used every situation as a teaching moment, trying to train Cody to remember what was appropriate or inappropriate, but progress was slow. At first Cody couldn't understand why his actions were different than anyone else's. Then he began to understand, but still couldn't change.

Once he understood that his actions were wrong, that brought on a whole new set of problems. Cody still had no ability to control his impulses in the moment, but afterward he would get mad at himself for doing something wrong. Depression set in, which would usually lead to more food, and without the ability to exercise much in his wheelchair the pounds started adding up. Cody had been thin and active before the accident, but the weight started to show around his belly and his neck and face. We tried to limit food and snacks, but Cody always found a way. It was tough for everyone. We didn't want to police Cody night and day, and he didn't understand why we had to.

Despite our difficulties, senior year had its bright spots. Cody loved being back in school, and even though some social situations were difficult for him, the majority of the kids treated him very kindly. The class elected Cody as Homecoming King, which gave him a huge boost of confidence. His friends were so kind to him and cheered him on as Kreg wheeled him onto the football field at halftime during the homecoming game. When it came time for Cody to stand up and be crowned with the Homecoming Queen, Kreg lifted him out of the chair, locked his leg brace so he could stand with just a cane, and stepped back. The crowd cheered, and Cody was the happiest kid on earth.

At the dance that evening his date sat on his lap as Cody wheeled around the dance floor. It was one of the best days of his life. Cody had everything he wanted: a girl who would pay attention to him, friends all around him, and respect from his classmates.

School continued on with hiccups here and there, which we gradually got used to. Some teacher or administrator would call about every week to report something that Cody had done or said that was inappropriate or that had made someone feel uncomfortable. We explained Cody's inability to control impulsive thoughts and behavior and suggested some ways they could resolve it. They, in turn, suggested we put Cody in special education courses.

We didn't want to segregate Cody, but we also knew that Cody's issues made it difficult for other kids to learn. Eventually we took their advice and brought Cody to meet the special education teachers. The classroom was full of individuals with severe learning disabilities, health problems, or attention issues. Cody was very upset when he realized what was going on.

"I'm not disabled," Cody told us, "all those people have bad problems, and I'm not like that. I'm normal, I'm just in a wheelchair, don't put me in that class!" He really didn't have any sense that anything was wrong with his behavior and despised the thought of being put in special ed. The truth was, he was mentally able to follow along in normal classes just fine, he would just speak out of turn or say things that were socially unacceptable. After considering all our options, we decided to keep him in regular classes and we got a couple counselors to stand behind us and defend our position when others questioned us.

We did our best to help Cody with his classwork when it was physically difficult for him to read or write, but we didn't do the work for him, he had to learn the material just like everyone else. The schoolwork challenged Cody, even on his modified curriculum, but he did his part, learned the material, and by the spring Cody was on track to graduate.

Then Cody came to us with an announcement. He wanted to walk across the stage all by himself to accept his diploma. That was a huge hurdle, way beyond what he was capable of. He had made very little progress with walking over the previous few months, despite lots of exercise and therapy. He could walk a few hundred steps with a cane, but he was pretty much helpless without it. Of course we wanted Cody to reach his goal, especially one he had set himself, but we tried to lower his expectations, knowing that it was going to be really, really tough to reach.

Cody didn't back down, he was determined, and he put in extra effort at every therapy session. After the therapist would leave, he would ask one of us to go out and walk with him up and down the sidewalk. He made some progress, but with just a month to go until graduation he was only able to take a few unassisted steps. His left leg just wouldn't cooperate and he usually ended up tripping or falling when he tried putting weight on it.

Graduation day came and he was still not ready, according to me at least, but he wanted to try it anyway. I tried to convince him to just use the cane, it would be a lot safer. As obedient as Cody usually was, I knew he wasn't going to listen to me. The moment came for the graduates to line up at the bottom of the stage. Kreg wheeled Cody to his place in line with his cane in his lap. When they got to the bottom of the stage Kreg helped Cody out of the chair and locked his leg brace so it wouldn't buckle at the knee. Cody used the cane and the handrail to slowly climb the few steps to the stage, while Kreg was standing right behind him in case he fell backward.

Once he got to the top of the stairs he stood and waited for his name to be called. "Cody Parmer!" the announcer said enthusiastically into the microphone. People clapped and cheered. Cody let go of the cane and it fell to the ground and bounced on the stage. I held my breath. He lifted his right leg and quickly found its placement about a foot ahead. The crowd went wild. He dragged his left leg up next to his right, then repeated the procedure. The audience realized what was happening and got to its feet. The clapping got louder and louder. Some of the kids started chanting "Cody! Cody!" I still couldn't breathe. Two steps, three steps, four steps. I prayed that his left foot wouldn't catch on anything.

Cody reached the announcer and accepted the diploma to the cheers of the crowd, but he was only halfway there. He still had to reach the other side of the stage. He smiled for a picture, then started shuffling again. Right foot, left foot, right foot, left foot. There was nobody to catch him if he fell, and he was already much farther than he had ever walked before. Kreg grabbed the cane off the stage, then ran over to the exit and stood at the base of the stairs, ready to receive Cody if he made it, or run to pick him up if he collapsed on stage.

Twenty feet. Fifteen. Ten. Just a few more left, he was almost to the

Cody receiving his high school diploma

stair railing. My chest was tight and I braced myself for the worst. Five feet, two feet, and done! He made it! The crowd was still on its feet, clapping and cheering, and I finally exhaled. Happiest of all was Cody himself.

"I did it! Dad, I did it! I walked, I did it!" Cody shouted as he reached the end of the stage, hardly able to contain his emotions. Kreg handed Cody the cane and helped him down the stairs, giving him a big hug when he reached the bottom. It was one of the greatest achievements Cody had made since the accident, and it gave Cody a lot of confidence in himself. That was a great memory for Cody to hold on to, because the next few years were going to be terribly difficult for him, and for us.

TWENTY-THREE

THE NIGHT KREG AND I GRADUATED HIGH SCHOOL, IT FELT LIKE A floodgate of opportunity was opened to us. We were now free to go to college, get real jobs, fall in love and get married, go on missions, move out on our own, and do almost anything we wanted to do. The world was ours for the taking. But for Cody, the end of high school didn't open doors, it closed them.

High school had been a closely monitored environment where Cody was led through the appropriate steps and kept on track by teachers, administrators, and his helper Jordan. It was a safe place where he could interact with others and where people knew his limitations and made adjustments for them. It was accommodating to him in ways that the real world just couldn't be.

After graduation, Cody's friends scattered in every direction. Some got full time jobs, others went to college, several began preparing for missions, and a few quickly fell in love and got engaged. As everyone else was continuing on with their lives, Cody was stuck at home. He didn't realize what was going to happen until it had already taken effect, and he didn't know how to deal with it. Cody would call his old friends that summer and see if they wanted to come over and watch sports, but most had found full time jobs or had moved away for work or school. Some would stop by after work to check on Cody every now and then, but it became obvious that they were moving on with their lives, and Cody wasn't.

Kreg and I knew that Cody's recovery was slower than we had anticipated, but we still hoped for the best. By the time Cody graduated we had expected him to be walking and able to take care of himself. We expected him to be able to go to college and then leave for a mission when he turned 19, but all of those things came into question when graduation came and Cody hadn't hit the milestones we expected him to hit. Cody was making a little progress though, his walking was getting better and he was able to take care of himself for the most part, so we tried to push forward with our plans.

Cody had an appointment with a neuropsychologist that summer who was supposed to help us figure out where Cody stood with his mental and social capabilities and how to help him improve. He ran Cody through a battery of tests and came back with pretty bleak results. Cody's mental capacity was below normal, it had been set back and stunted by the brain damage. The results of his social skills tests were all over the place, in some areas he was close to normal, and in others he was like a little kid.

"I'd recommend continuing therapy for the time being. There are some nice work programs for young adults that he might enjoy where he can socialize with other people on his own level and make a little money doing simple tasks under careful supervision. It would be good for him to get out and continue socializing to develop those skills," the doctor told us.

That was not the advice we wanted to hear. The doctor's analysis seemed to limit Cody to a life of activities designed for people with physical and mental disabilities. Of course, Cody had both at the time, but we didn't want to stop there, we wanted to push him toward a full recovery.

"We were thinking," Kreg responded cautiously, "that we wanted to start him in college classes in the fall."

The doctor thought about it for a moment, flipping through the pages of test results on his desk. "Some of the community colleges hold classes for people with disabilities, though it still might be a stretch with his social limitations."

"No, I mean, we already have him enrolled at BYU-Idaho in the fall. The classes are pretty easy, introductory stuff, but we wanted to get him started while we continued with the therapy, so he doesn't get too far behind his friends. We have an apartment rented and we would only be half an hour away if he needed something."

"Mr. and Mrs. Parmer," the doctor leaned forward in his chair and shook his head, "Cody is nowhere near ready for that kind of independence. He won't be able to associate with his peers on the same level, he'll need full-time assistance, and the test numbers suggest that he just couldn't keep up with even introductory level courses. I'm sorry, it's just not going to work."

We decided to make it work anyway. In the fall we drove Cody up to school and got him settled in an apartment he shared with four other boys. Cody had been working hard on his strength training that summer and was able to walk most places with just a cane. He knew how to take care of himself for the most part, and he knew he could call us whenever he needed help and we'd be just a half hour away. Cody insisted that he would be fine.

We met Cody's roommates as we were moving his stuff into the apartment, and we explained his situation to them. They all seemed very kind and agreed to help Cody however they could. Then we took Cody around to see where his classes would be and showed him how to use his meal card at the cafeteria and helped him set up a study and homework schedule. Then we left. It was a moment of truth, leaving Cody there to fend for himself, but we hoped it would help accelerate his growth and independence. We were wrong.

Four weeks later we got a call from the school informing us that they just weren't set up to accommodate someone with Cody's limitations, and he would no longer be allowed to go to school there or stay in student housing. I had been driving up and visiting him almost every day and called several times throughout the day just to make sure everything was going alright. We suspected that Cody wasn't keeping up with the homework, but we didn't expect them to kick him out, at least not so soon.

Kreg and I drove the truck up and packed up his things. His roommates looked weary and exhausted, Cody's excitement about life had been overwhelming. Every little thing warranted a conversation and a million questions. He just didn't understand how to respect the personal space or privacy of others. In our home, we could deal with those issues and establish boundaries; with roommates, it was too much.

When Cody realized we were going home for good, he got angry. He had just started a new life and had made a hundred new friends. There were always new people to talk to and places to go and things to do and now we were robbing him of all that. We tried to explain to him that what he was doing bothered other people and he promised to do better, but we knew that no matter how good his intentions were, he just didn't have the capability to follow through. For all of Cody's pleas and protests, driving him home hurt me more than it hurt him. We had hoped for the best, but it was time to face the reality of the situation: Cody was different.

After that day I spent many nights and mornings on my knees asking for guidance and direction. I wanted my old Cody back so badly. We had come so far and we had gotten so close, but it just didn't seem like we could make it over those last social hurdles. I was okay if his left hand never regained full functionality, if his left eye never worked again, or even if he couldn't walk unassisted. I just wanted his brain to work normally so he could hold down a job, get married, and find the happiness and independence that he so desperately wanted.

I cried and begged for an answer from God, "Why isn't he getting better? After all we've been through, why can't we fix these last few things? You've been so good to us, and blessed us with so many miracles, is one more too much? Isn't asking for Cody to be able to go on a mission and get married a good thing to ask for? Then why can't we get there? Why save his life and then leave him impaired and unable to take care of himself? Is there something we're not doing right? Aren't we doing all we can do?" There were more questions than could be spoken, and more grief than could be explained.

It had been more than a year and a half since Cody had come out of the coma and he had made so little progress with his social problems. I had always assumed he'd get better, overcome those obstacles, move on, but I was coming to the realization that it might not be possible. As much as I prayed otherwise, I was starting to think that Cody's social issues might not be resolved in the near future, if ever. That was a terribly hard thing to accept, and it really tore at my soul.

I tried not to show it, but the pain of my realization made me feel so overwhelmed and added a shade of sadness to everything I did. The depression wasn't debilitating, but it was constant. I felt so overwhelmed with the prospects of caring for Cody for the rest of our lives in this condition. If he couldn't overcome his impulsiveness, he would likely never be able to marry, have children, hold down a job, live on his own, or any of the normal things we wished for our children. Kreg and I would have to care for Cody until we were too old to care for ourselves, and then what? What would Cody do after we were gone? Who would care for him? These thoughts played through my mind on repeat for a long time, but I kept praying for guidance, hoping that God would send some kind of answer or comfort our way.

After I had cried all I could cry, and worried all I could worry, the peace came. I finally came to the conclusion that I just had to enjoy the blessings I had. I couldn't wait any longer to be happy. If God decided that Cody was going to have these limitations for the rest of his life, we needed to make the best of it and God would help us through it. I couldn't spend every moment wishing things were different or trying to force Cody to be something he wasn't. I made the resolution to be happy and enjoy the miracles we had been given, and not focus on what could have been.

There was a magnet on my fridge from a Relief Society lesson that stated plainly, "Put your shoes on and get back to work!" In the background it showed a picture of President Hinckley waving his cane to an onlooking crowd. That magnet inspired me every day. I tried to forget all the ways that Cody's troubles limited us, instead I would put my shoes on and get to work. Of course I still hoped for better days ahead for Cody, and I still got upset plenty of times when things were really tough, but I tried every day to find joy in the blessings we had already received. It was hard, and some days were better than others, but giving control of the situation to God and trusting in his wisdom brought me real peace.

Though I had struggled through the frustration and depression and had finally come out the other side, it seemed that Kreg was still having a hard time. He didn't show his feelings like I did, but I could see it in the way he talked and acted when Cody was around. Cody was his only son, and they had a special relationship that just couldn't be replaced.

We had three beautiful daughters, but Kreg always loved that he had a son to raise and carry on the family name. He longed for the day when Cody would come home and tell him he had found the one, and they could sit and talk about marriage and how to be a good husband. Kreg wanted to pass all the things he learned on to his own son and teach him how to preside in the home and bless and care for his wife and children.

He wanted to be at Cody's side when Cody taught his children how to fish, or play baseball, or ride a dirt bike. There were a million father-and-son dreams that Kreg had for the two of them, and Kreg couldn't accept that all those dreams were vanishing.

Kreg kept pushing Cody to try harder and get stronger, make better decisions and learn from his mistakes. He was tough on Cody, trying to force him to improve. After lots of talks, Cody began to recognize on his own when he had done something wrong, but that realization only came after the fact. Cody still had no ability to control his impulses in the moment.

That brought on new problems, because once Cody recognized he was doing something wrong, and was powerless to fix it, he started beating himself up over it. Until that point of self-realization, Cody had no idea that he was any different than anyone else. He couldn't understand why people avoided him, or why girls didn't want to date him, or why he had to come home from college.

"Why do I do bad things, Mom?" Cody would ask me, his heart wrenched in pain. I explained over and over that it was just a result of the accident, but my justification didn't make anything better. Time after time, Cody acted on some impulsive thought, then began to feel bad about it. Kreg and I hoped that maybe his self-awareness would help him overcome the problems, but it didn't.

Despite all the problems he faced, Kreg and I knew that if we just kept Cody at home all day, he was never going to overcome his depression. He needed to have some purpose to his life, even if it was something small. We decided to help him find a job that would accommodate his limitations. We hoped that with a routine, some regular outside exposure, and the opportunity for Cody to excel at something, he might find some happiness and purpose in life again.

Kreg got a recommendation from our bishop and took Cody down to Deseret Industries where they hired him to clean shoes. We drove Cody to work in the morning and picked him up in the afternoon, and for several hours a day he was his own man. Cody did really well, for about five minutes, then he would get bored. He would leave his shoe-cleaning station in the back room and go stand at the front door to be a greeter. He gave a big smile and a welcome to everyone who came to the store, then asked for phone numbers from every girl. Once his boss would find him, they would usher Cody back to the shoe cleaning station where he would do another three or four pairs, then wander off again. After about a year and a half of this routine, the managers at D.I. decided it was time for Cody to move on.

After D.I., Cody started job hopping every few months. He worked the cash register at a gas station my dad owned, then he worked in the parts department at a friend's motorsports dealership, then he picked up a janitorial job. Each time the problem was the same, Cody talked to the customers too much and started driving away business. Our family and friends were so good to him and tried to provide him with plenty of job opportunities, but we just couldn't stand to see their businesses suffer because of Cody's interactions with the customers.

Finally we found him a job cutting shrink tubing into three-inch sections so it could be used in manufacturing fishing line. It wasn't that technical, but without the use of Cody's left hand it was a challenge to measure, hold, and cut the shrink tubing. A friend of ours made a little contraption that he could use to hold and measure the tubing and cut it at precisely the right spot, designed just for Cody so he could do everything with just his right hand. That worked great for quite a while, as long as we could keep Cody focused, but eventually the company got a machine to do the job and Cody was out of work again.

Again and again we would find Cody a job, and then he would have to move on. Cody made very little mental progress in the years after graduation, though he did finally regain the ability to walk without a cane. His left leg had only a small amount of control or strength, but it was enough for him to get around. We were a little nervous to let Cody wander around town on his own, but the freedom did wonders for his spirits. When Cody wasn't cutting tubing or watching TV, he was out walking around, usually picking up applications for other jobs. As long as Cody felt like there was hope and purpose, we did fine.

Meanwhile, life moved on around Cody, and our girls were growing up. Kira maintained excellent grades through all of high school and became the head cheerleader her senior year. She graduated and went to BYU-Idaho, majoring in Psychology. Brooke, just a year behind Kira in school, excelled in gymnastics. She placed first at the state gymnastics meet on the bars, and her coach became quite upset at us when we said we weren't interested in pursuing an Olympic career for her. As Brooke grew older she moved from gymnastics to cheerleading, and she also became the head cheerleader her senior year. After graduation she went to school and became a dental assistant. Once Kira and Brooke left, it was just Kreg, myself, Cody, and Krissa at home.

Krissa was five years younger than Brooke and she cried and cried when her older sisters left for college, but she and I grew really close when we were the only two girls left in the house. She became my little shadow, helping me with chores and spending time with Cody when he needed a little extra attention. Krissa had been so young when Cody got hurt that she didn't really remember what our family was like before the accident. For her, life with Cody's limitations was just normal, and her acceptance of the situation helped me to not worry so much.

As Krissa grew older she decided she had been to enough cheerleading events to last a lifetime and wanted nothing to do with it, so she signed up for volleyball. Cody and I went to all her games and cheered her on. As Krissa began to be more and more involved in practices and activities that kept her away from home most of the day, I began to get a glimpse of what life would be like when it was just Cody and I at home all day.

The start of Krissa's senior year in the fall of 2009 marked almost ten years since Cody's hemorrhage. Cody had made some tiny steps in his ability to control his impulses, but not much, and the doctors had decided that it was time to start controlling some of his conditions through medication. They installed a medication pump that released a muscle relaxer between his shoulder blades and loosened up the muscles in his left arm, letting his hand hang limp instead of curling up to his chest. They placed him on anti-depression and anti-seizure medication, and gave him a shot once a week to lower his testosterone to help with his confrontations with girls.

Because Cody's inhibitions were almost non-existent, he had no ability to decide when it was appropriate to eat and his weight continued to climb. We tried to get Cody on a diet, but he had almost no ability to stick to it. The doctors became really concerned about his weight and decided to put him on pre-diabetic medication. They told us we needed to find a way to get Cody some more exercise, but what were we supposed to do?

Cody couldn't walk fast enough to work up a sweat, and he only had the use of one arm and one leg, which really limited our options.

Then I saw an ad in the paper one morning for a sprint triathlon in Rigby, just north of Idaho Falls. Half a mile of swimming, 12 miles of biking, and 3 miles of running. Cody wouldn't be able to swim, and he couldn't run, but maybe he could do the bike portion.

We contacted the race organizers and asked if Cody could ride on an adult tricycle, and if they would let me do the run and Kreg do the swim. They agreed to our situation and let us sign up. When I told Cody about the triathlon he was so excited and asked if we could start training immediately. When I told Kreg about it, he shot me a look like I was crazy, but he agreed. Kreg went to the gym the next day and called me after his first swim workout.

"What the heck did you get me into?" he panted.

"How did it go?" I asked with a chuckle.

"Well, I had no idea that you could sweat and swim at the same time, but it's possible. I thought I'd just take my time and do the full half-mile, but I didn't even get close."

"Oh honey, I'm sorry!"

"This is going to take a while to get ready for, but maybe it will be a good thing for this old fat guy to do some real exercise," Kreg said. I just laughed.

Kreg put in the work to get ready for the swim, I started training for the run, and Kira volunteered to bike along with Cody for the race, but it was up to me to train with him and get him ready. We bought Cody a tricycle and began training, but it wasn't easy. Cody would push with his right leg, then let the momentum bring the pedal back to the top where he would push again. His left foot sat on the pedal, but it was no help. Steering was a bit of a challenge too, with only one hand. Cody had put on a lot of weight, and when the tricycle got going in the wrong direction, his momentum was hard to change. I quickly realized that this triathlon was going to push all of us to our limits.

Cody and I barely made it one mile on the tricycle when we started, but we kept at it. All through the fall we would train once or twice a week, slowly working up our distance each time. It took us a long time to get to three miles, then our goal was six miles. Then the winter came and our ability to train outside came to a halt. We started working out on a stationary bike indoors, and when the snow melted in the early spring we bundled up and got back on the tricycle.

The race was the last Saturday in May, and with only a couple months to go Cody was still only able to make it six miles. I was pretty sure that Kreg and I would be able to complete our portions, but if Cody couldn't finish his part, it would devastate him. We picked up the training schedule and started biking every other day. As our training progressed, the furthest we ever made it was eight miles.

We knew that 12 miles would be a stretch, but we decided to go for it anyway. Cody was losing a lot of weight, which was great, but he needed a milestone in his life, a success to point to when times got tough. He needed a moment like he had at graduation, where he pushed himself beyond anything he had done previously and walked across the stage unassisted. I just prayed he'd have the same kind of resolve when it came to those last few miles.

The morning of the race came and the weather was terrible: just over 40 degrees with a steady cold breeze and light drizzle. It was an awful day for a triathlon, but we got bundled up and drove up to Rigby. The swim segment was first, and I ached for Kreg as he tiptoed into the frigid water in Rigby Lake with about a hundred other swimmers. When the gun went off, Kreg dove forward and began the loop.

Cody and Kira got ready for the bike ride and made sure that he had everything in place. We knew Cody was going to be slower than normal, so the race organizers let me start the run early so I could catch up with Cody later. I checked Cody's jacket and made sure he would stay dry, then left him and Kira to start the race by themselves. While Kreg was swimming and I was running, Kira and Cody pushed off and started on their 12-mile journey.

Cody started with a blast of enthusiasm, pushing his right foot down, letting it come back up, then pushing down again. His body rocked forward with each push to give him added momentum, then straightened out again as he waited for his right foot to reach the top.

For the first mile or so Cody was pushing hard, then he slowed to a more steady pace and found his rhythm. Kira let Cody ride ahead of her, encouraging Cody when he started to slow. As they got further out of town the course changed from city streets to rough country roads, bordered on each side by a little gravel and a ditch. After a few miles Kira could tell that Cody was starting to struggle. Cody shifted his weight to lean on the right pedal more, but that started pulling him closer to the edge of the road. Cody was able to use his one good arm to keep the tricycle straight, but he was losing strength. Then Kira saw Cody's right rear tire slip off the road into the gravel.

The added resistance of the loose rock pulled him quickly to the right, and his one working arm wasn't enough to stop the change in momentum. Kira yelled out to Cody but it was too late. His front tire had turned into the gravel as well, and his right tire slipped down the steep bank. The tricycle overturned and Cody was thrown down into the weed-filled ditch. His reaction time was too slow and he couldn't catch himself, hitting the ground hard with his shoulder and head.

Kira jumped off her bike and slid down the bank of the ditch to Cody's side. "Are you okay?" she asked, as Cody tried to gain his bearings. He looked a little stunned but nothing seemed broken. The race organizers had appointed a chase vehicle to follow Cody so they could keep an eye on him, and as soon as Cody went into the ditch they jumped out of the vehicle to help. Half a dozen bicyclists from the race had also seen what happened and were quickly at Cody's side. Even with all the help, Cody's weight made it difficult for them to get him up.

"Come on Cody," Kira said, "let's get you into the car and we'll take you back to the medical station."

"No," Cody said, "I'm not quitting." Cody lifted himself to his feet and crawled up the edge of the ditch. The support crew pulled his tricycle up and set it on the road.

"Cody, you don't have to do this, we can go get you checked out," Kira tried to convince him. The support crew in the chase vehicle tried to get Cody to walk back to their car, but Cody was determined.

"No, let's go. I'm going to finish. I'm not quitting." Cody didn't wait for a discussion, he just hopped on his tricycle and began pedaling again, with dirt, mud, and weeds still stuck to his clothes and helmet.

Kreg and I arrived in our own vehicle just a short time after the fall. Once we caught up the support crew hopped out of their car to come tell us what had happened. "So, we lost your son a few miles back," one of the support crew told us in a slow Idaho drawl.

I began to panic for a second, but the man explained what had happened and how Cody had decided to push on. I had always been worried about what would happen to Cody if he got hurt when I wasn't around, now I knew. Cody was strong, he was a fighter, and he wasn't going to give up easily. As much as I wanted him to stop and make sure he wasn't hurt, I was proud of his determination to push forward.

Cody pedaled on without much to say as he and Kira passed four miles, then six, then eight. Trailing slowly behind him in our car, we cheered him on and watched him pedal forward mile after mile. We hadn't ever made it further than eight miles before, and I expected his legs to give out at any moment, but he just kept pedaling. As the town of Rigby came back into view, Cody started picking up the pace. Push with

Kira and Cody on the bicycling leg of the Triathlon at Rigby Lake in 2010

the right foot, wait, push with the right foot, wait. Before we knew it, the finish line was in sight. Our family and friends were there cheering, and a couple reporters realized something was going on and came over to watch. With only a quarter mile to go, we raced forward to be at the finish line when he arrived.

We took our places among friends and started chanting "Cody! Cody! Cody!" as he drew nearer. Cody could hear our chant and started pedaling with all his might for the last hundred yards. He pushed and pushed until he crossed the line, then his legs gave out as he coasted to a stop. We all ran to his side and gave him hugs and praise as he struggled to catch his breath.

Cody was in heaven, but he had just endured the most difficult physical challenge since his accident. He got off his tricycle and took a few steps with a shaky and weak leg, then doubled over and threw up. We cleaned him up and found a place for him to sit down and rest. Through the sweat and shaky legs and terrible weather, I caught a glimpse of the old Cody, the one who believed he could do anything and would stop at nothing to achieve his goals.

Between heavy breathing and bouts of nausea, I could tell that Cody had learned something about himself as well: the old Cody and the new Cody were one and the same. There was a drive and determination that couldn't be quelled by physical or even mental limitations. It was part of who he was, it was part of his soul. Though it had cost him every ounce of strength he had, the triathlon was a victory for Cody that would last a lifetime.

TWENTY-FOUR

ODY COULDN'T STOP TALKING ABOUT THE TRIATHLON, HE TOLD EV-
eryone he met about his training, the fall into the ditch, and his glo-
rious ride across the finish line. When the newspaper story came out about
the event and featured his picture, Cody felt like a superstar. The event had
lifted his spirits and had given him something to look forward to. It took
his mind off his problems and helped him build muscle and lose quite a bit
of weight. Despite the difficulties, we considered it a success.

The event changed my understanding of what Cody was and was not
capable of. We hadn't been pushing him as much for the past few years
as the girls went through high school, but maybe we should have been.
We had just come to accept our limited expectations, but maybe we were
wrong.

Cody also felt the renewed sense of accomplishment, and a desire
for progress. Unfortunately, his goals weren't always realistic. He saw his
friends getting married and having families, and he wanted that too, even
though he didn't necessarily understand why it wasn't possible. Still, he
wanted more than the stay-at-home life we were providing.

"Mom, Dad," Cody said one evening, "I want my own house." It
was something he'd brought up many times before, so we knew to just go
along with it.

"That sure would be nice, wouldn't it Cody?" I replied.

"I'm serious. I don't want to live here anymore. None of my friends
live with their parents. None of my friends' parents tell them what to do.
I should be living in my own house, making my own decisions," Cody
said forcefully.

"I know, but that's different."

"No it's not. I'm 27 years old. I'm too old to be living here. When can I buy my own house?"

I could tell he was very serious, and I felt bad for him. He really didn't understand why he needed someone to watch over him. He could do most things himself, but he needed someone to tell him to take his medication, help him stay on schedule, and take care of things around the house. I wished he could be on his own, and he was so close to being able to, but it just wouldn't work. Then again, maybe we hadn't expected enough from him. Maybe there was some way to give Cody more freedom and personal responsibility. Maybe he would rise to the occasion.

Kreg stepped in, "Cody, what about an assisted living home." Kreg must have sensed what I was thinking. We had talked about it before, but Cody didn't see himself as disabled, and he didn't want to live in a place where people treated him like he was.

"No, I want to live on my own." Cody was adamant.

"Well, what if we could find you a place with some roommates and someone who could just help out sometimes when you needed it?" Kreg was on to something, it was all about how we framed it. I could see Cody was mulling it over.

"Where would I live?"

"I don't know, we could find someplace close, so you could still see your friends and come visit whenever you'd like."

Cody was sold. "Mom, can we look on the internet for places to live?"

"Woah, woah. Just hold on. Your mom and I will talk about it, but we'll have to find just the right place. It might take some time, okay?" Kreg had planted a seed and there was no way to stop Cody's mind from running wild.

"Okay. Can we start looking now?" Cody asked.

"No."

"Can we start looking tomorrow?"

"Maybe, we'll see. It's going to take some time."

"Can I get on the computer and look for it myself?"

"No," Kreg said coldly. Kreg and I looked at each other and just shook our heads. We weren't going to hear the end of it until Cody was all moved out. There was no turning back now.

After several weeks of looking, Kreg and I found a group home where Cody could have quite a bit of independence, but still have someone on staff at all times in case he needed anything. Cody wasn't too excited about living with "disabled" people, but it was his one ticket out of the house, so he took it. The house was just a short distance from our home, too far to walk, but close enough that we could get there in a few minutes if he needed us.

The first few weeks were difficult. The staff at the house had to call us to help resolve disputes between Cody and the other residents, and Cody didn't like following their rules. Gradually Cody got used to it though, and the calls from staff became less frequent.

The calls from Cody, on the other hand, only increased over time. Cody called every morning right as he woke up, then a dozen or more times throughout the day, just to see what we were doing. If we didn't answer, he'd try again two minutes later until we finally picked up the phone. Cody was getting bored fast, and he wanted someone to entertain him. It turns out independence wasn't as exciting as Cody thought it might be.

Though our responsibility for Cody and the constant phone calls meant that we were never really free, it felt like Kreg and I had finally passed a milestone. Kira and Brooke were both married, Krissa was off to college, and Cody was living on his own. We were officially empty nesters. Though Cody's group home cost quite a bit, it allowed us to finally breathe.

Soon, our youngest daughter Krissa came home with big news: she was engaged. It was difficult to believe my youngest child was going to be married, but we were so happy that she had found a good guy and would be able to be sealed in the temple. As we started planning the wedding, Krissa brought up a question we were not expecting.

"Dad, do you think Cody would be ready to go through the temple, so he could come to my sealing?" Krissa asked.

When our oldest daughter Kira was engaged, Cody wanted so badly to go through the temple with her and watch the sacred sealing ceremony, but we pushed back. We knew that in order for Cody to participate, he would need to receive his own endowments, and we weren't sure he was ready to make those sacred and spiritual promises to God. A couple years later when Brooke got engaged, we fought the same battle again but came to the same conclusion. But now the request was coming from the other side—it was Krissa, not Cody, asking if it was time.

"Well honey, I don't know. I just don't think he's able to right now," Kreg replied.

"Why not?"

"You have to make promises to God as part of the endowment, promises to follow God in all that you do, and to keep his commandments at all times, and I don't know if Cody has the ability to keep those promises yet."

"When do you think he'll be ready?" Krissa asked.

Kreg thought about it for a minute. "I don't know."

That short conversation led to several long talks between Kreg and I. Would Cody ever be able to go through the temple? Was it appropriate to have him go through, even if he wasn't fully capable of understanding the obligations he was making? Kreg and I went back and forth, not wanting to hold Cody back if there wasn't a good reason, but not wanting to make him accountable on a spiritual level for promises that he couldn't keep. We decided to make a phone call to our old friend Elder Zwick.

"Kreg and Brenda, so good to hear from you! How is your family?" came the enthusiastic voice from the other end of the phone. We had kept in touch with Elder Zwick over the years, sending Christmas cards and making quick visits occasionally, but we hadn't had a reason to call him in quite some time. After catching up, we presented our question.

"Elder Zwick, we're just not sure what to do with Cody. His sister has asked about having him go through the temple so he can be there for her sealing, but we're not sure if he's ready. He still has some limitations, he really can't control his impulses, and we just don't want him to be held accountable for things he might not understand."

"That's a hard decision. We went through the same thing with our son Scotty. He's in a very similar situation to Cody, but he was born with his disabilities, as you know. We weren't sure if he was really capable of understanding everything either. After a lot of prayer we came to the conclusion that it would be better to give him the opportunity to accept and keep those commitments, rather than to hold him back.

"I've spent some time with Cody over the years and I can tell you that I know he has a testimony of the gospel, and he wants to do the right thing. That's the most important part. None of us really understand everything God has to teach us, and a lot of times we fall short, but the temple can help us to aim higher, to strive for better.

"Scotty received his own endowments several years ago now, and we haven't regretted it one bit. He loves going and serving there, he goes almost every week in fact, and it helps him to focus on the right things. I think Cody would benefit just as much as Scotty does.

"Kreg, Brenda, the Lord knows your son, and he understands that Cody is doing the best he can. That's really what matters." Elder Zwick always knew the right thing to say. I immediately felt at ease with the decision. We had underestimated Cody's ability to succeed so many times over the past few years, it was time to take another leap of faith. We thanked Elder Zwick for his advice and immediately called our bishop to set up an appointment.

There was a lot to do and not much time to do it in. Not only did we have to plan and prepare a whole wedding and reception, but we had to teach Cody about temple covenants as well. We got Cody set up in a temple preparation class and spent every Family Home Evening talking about the temple and how important it was to take it seriously and be ready to commit your life wholeheartedly to Christ. Cody studied up on the scriptures he was assigned in class and made a lot of progress in understanding the purpose of the temple and the endowment.

Shortly before Krissa's wedding, we took Cody through the temple to receive his endowments. Cody couldn't stop talking on the ride to the temple or in the dressing room as Kreg helped him get into his white pants, white shirt, and white tie, but when they walked into the endowment room, Cody was silent. Cody's attention was focused and he sat quietly through the two-hour endowment and paid reverent attention to the lessons and promises. I had been crossing my fingers the whole time, hoping Cody would be good, and once again Cody exceeded our expectations.

A couple weeks later we all gathered together to watch Krissa and her husband be sealed for eternity in the Salt Lake City Temple. I had been running ragged trying to make sure the arrangements for flowers and decorations were all in place, the out-of-town guests and family were all taken care of, and Cody wasn't getting into trouble. I barely had time to think about the sacred and beautiful ceremony until Kreg and I were standing outside the temple, waiting for everyone to arrive. I closed my eyes, took a deep breath, and tried to clear my thoughts.

"This is a good day," I told myself. "Be happy, be calm, enjoy it." I took another deep breath, exhaled, then we stepped inside.

After the beautiful ceremony in the temple I stood together with Kreg, Kira, Brooke, Krissa, our three sons-in-law, and Cody, and the tears began to flow. How wonderful it was to be all together in the temple, but I couldn't help but look forward to that day after this life when our family would be gathered together in the presence of God. There, all our pain and sorrow would be taken away, and Cody would be freed from all his limitations. Thanks to the blessings of the atonement and the resurrection, Cody would have a perfect mind and a perfect body. Everything that had been taken from him, every ability and every opportunity, would be restored. I could even imagine him walking up to us to introduce his newly found eternal companion. I'm not sure who will be happier in that day: Cody, for the blessing of a perfect physical body, or Kreg and I, for the blessing of seeing our son made whole again.

As I stood in awe of the miracles yet to come, tears of joy and gratitude fell freely and I thanked God for the promise of eternal families, and the promise of a perfect resurrection.

TWENTY-FIVE

D ESPITE HIS RECENT PROGRESS, THINGS STARTED GOING DOWNHILL
for Cody soon after the wedding. The medications that Cody was
on seemed to be losing their effectiveness, and Cody was getting in trouble for little things I thought we had overcome. Cody was acting more
impulsively, calling random strangers again, and getting upset with his
roommates. The phone calls from the staff at his group home were becoming more frequent, but we had no answers for them.

We tried taking Cody out with us more often, changing things in
his environment, and finding new activities for him during the day, but
nothing improved his situation. We talked to the doctors and they adjusted the dosages on his medication, but that didn't help either. The
doctors said they had no more options, no more answers, and nothing
more to suggest. Things were not looking good and I was beginning to
lose my mind.

I got so frustrated one day after Cody got in trouble that I sat down
at my computer and searched the internet for "traumatic brain injury
medication." It had been almost 15 years since the accident, surely there
must have been some advancement in brain science since then.

I found some forums that discussed experimental treatments, medications, and therapies that were showing positive results for individuals
who had long-term effects from a brain injury. For a few weeks I studied up on every possible option, praying we would find something that
would work for Cody.

At night I would tell Kreg of my findings and we would talk about
what life would be like if we found some kind of solution for Cody's con-

dition. So many people online were reporting great success with various methods, it seemed like we would be crazy not to try them. We finally decided to take the next step. I called three offices that specialized in traumatic brain injuries, one in Phoenix, one in Denver, and one on the East Coast. I told them about Cody and what we were facing. All three said they might be able to help, but the office in Phoenix seemed more kind and helpful than the others, so I chose to work with them.

I made an appointment for a phone interview with Dr. Allbee, their lead doctor, who asked me lots of questions about Cody's accident and surgeries, his condition, his current mental state and his limitations. He sounded optimistic, so we called LDS Hospital and had them send all the records of Cody's surgeries for him to look over. After reviewing all the information we provided, Dr. Allbee told us Cody sounded like an excellent candidate for one of his treatments, but he couldn't be sure until he had done an in-person consultation and had run a new MRI, because somehow Cody's old MRI had not been sent with the records. The consultation itself would cost a fortune, but it was worth it if it was going to mean an improvement for Cody.

We bought our tickets and flew to Phoenix in April of 2013. Cody understood the importance of what was happening. He knew that we were going down to try out some new treatment, and that it might help with his social problems. He was excited and started dreaming big about all the things he would do when he was better. He wanted to move out of the group home and open up a ski and fly fishing shop, hopefully get married, and have a bunch of kids. We tried to limit his expectations, but of course we were excited about the prospects as well, so we let him dream.

We arrived in Phoenix and met at the doctor's office for a day full of consultations. We met Dr. Allbee who asked lots of new questions, did a few basic tests, then sent us to wait for an MRI. A nurse told us to take a seat in the waiting room and she would call us when we were ready. We sat down and talked a little, then picked up some magazines as the time wore on. Suddenly Cody stood up, walked across the room, and took a seat right next to rough looking man covered in tattoos and facial piercings.

"Hi, how are you?" Cody asked. Kreg and I winced, not knowing what Cody was going to say. His blunt manner could upset people sometimes, and this guy wasn't the kind of guy we wanted to make mad.

The man put down his magazine and turned to Cody, "I'm doing fine," he said coldly.

"Where did you get those tattoos?" Cody asked. My heart sank. This was not going to go well.

"Prison."

"Really? Why were you in prison?" That was enough, I put my magazine down and got up to intervene.

"Selling drugs."

"Really? Have you heard of the Church of Jesus Christ of Latter-day Saints?"

"I've heard of a lot of religions," the man replied, making it clear that he wasn't a fan of any of them.

"Well, you know, if you would just read the Book of Mormon, your life would be so much better and you would be so much happier." I walked up to Cody and put my hand on his shoulder. "Mom, do you have a pen, I need to get this guy's address so we can send him a Book of Mormon."

The man didn't seem to be protesting much, so I handed Cody a pen, though it went against every inhibition I had. Cody pulled out a wrinkled piece of paper from his pocket and wrote down the man's address. I was terribly embarrassed, but at the same time I was proud of my son. He understood that the gospel of Jesus Christ was the greatest force for good in this world, and he saw a person who could benefit from it and he wasn't scared to tell them about it. Cody was always doing things like that, sharing the gospel in the strangest of places, but people didn't seem to be offended when it came from someone as harmless as Cody. I just wished I had as much courage as he did.

We returned to our seats and the nurse called Cody in a short time later to prepare for his MRI. After the MRI, Cody visited with an occupational therapist, physical therapist, and speech therapist to go over all the aspects of his condition and his possible treatment. At the end of the day they sent us back to the hotel and told us to return the next morning when the whole team would go over the results with us.

It was difficult to sleep that night. The doctors and therapists had all been so kind and positive, I just couldn't wait for what they had to say. This office was touted as one of the best in the country, they had helped lots of soldiers who had come home from Iraq and Afghanistan with severe wounds and brain injuries, and had assisted in some miraculous recoveries. I was sure that Cody's little accident was nothing compared to the wounds of war. Still, I had to tell myself to just wait and see.

The next morning we drove in for our meeting and were shown into Dr. Allbee's office. We expected the other members of the team to be there, but it was just the doctor.

"Hello, good to see you again, have a seat." The doctor pointed to three chairs in front of his desk. "I'd like to start off by talking about the results of the MRI. Have you seen one of his MRIs before?" Dr. Allbee slipped the large piece of translucent plastic out of a sleeve and placed it on the desk in front of us.

"Yeah, Brenda and I have seen it, Cody hasn't," Kreg said.

"Alright, then I will explain what you're seeing here for Cody's benefit. Each of these images represents a small slice of Cody's brain, starting at the top of the skull and going all the way down to about the base of the nose." He pointed with a pen to each of the twenty or so cross sections.

"That's what my brain looks like?" Cody asked. I placed my hand on his arm to signal to him that it was time to be quiet.

"Yes, Cody, this is your brain. This gray portion here is the brain matter, and this white portion here is the area where the brain matter has died. Almost half of the brain matter is damaged or missing." Cody was silent. It was one thing to know that your brain had suffered an injury, but actually seeing the damage seemed to have a terrifying effect on him.

The doctor continued, "Mr. and Mrs. Parmer, I have to be honest, I would call you liars if you had sent me this MRI and told me it belonged to your son. If I hadn't taken it myself, I would tell you that there is no way that this is an MRI from the same person who is sitting right here." Dr. Allbee adjusted himself in the seat and leaned forward.

"I don't mean to be rude, but this MRI should belong to someone who is sitting in a wheelchair drooling on themselves. From my experience, this MRI tells me that this person cannot walk, cannot talk, cannot think, cannot function in any normal way. There is no way that this MRI should belong to Cody." He leaned back in his chair again and waited a moment for that to sink in. We sat in silent disbelief, waiting for his next words.

"Unfortunately, none of our treatments will work on someone with this amount of brain damage. If your previous hospital had sent me this

MRI, I would have told you to not even bother coming down, because there is no way to restore any functionality at all, but here he is, sitting right here, able to walk and talk and think with an amazing amount of capabilities. I'm frankly stunned by what I'm seeing, and I don't say that very often."

"Are there any experimental options or treatments to try?" I asked, hoping he might have something up his sleeve.

"I'm sorry, but no. All of the treatments, medications, therapies we have could not possibly work on a brain like this. My advice to you, Mr. and Mrs. Parmer, is to go home and enjoy what you have. Your son is a living, breathing miracle." Dr. Allbee stood up from his chair and held his hand out to Cody. "Cody, it was sincerely a pleasure to meet you. I wish you the best." Cody reached up and shook his hand, but was still too stunned to say anything.

We walked out to the car and Cody got into the back seat while Kreg and I climbed in up front. Kreg started the car and put his hands on the steering wheel, but just sat there looking out the window without saying anything. I couldn't tell what he was thinking, but I knew it was best to just wait. We all sat in silence for a minute. I hoped Kreg wasn't upset. The meeting had cost a lot of money, and it was really our last hope at finding a major breakthrough for Cody.

Finally Kreg turned to me and spoke. "Maybe I've been too hard on him," he said with sadness in his voice.

I shook my head. "Oh Kreg, you're a great dad. You're so good to him." I reached out and softly rubbed his shoulder.

"No, I've always expected him to be more than he is. I've pushed him too hard, I get mad when he messes up. I need to be more patient." Kreg rubbed his chin and sighed. "I guess," he paused, "I guess I always hoped that if I pushed him, he would learn, he would get back to normal. I think I just need to learn to be happy with where we are." I just nodded.

It was a realization I had come to long before but had lost sight of as I started to look for a new miracle cure. Kreg had never been satisfied with accepting that Cody might not get any better than he already was, but now it looked like we were both on the same page. Cody was indeed a living, breathing miracle. It was time to stop worrying about what might or might not happen, and learn to find joy in the journey.

Twenty-Six

I WOKE UP EARLY AND GOT READY FOR THE DAY. IT WAS A BEAUTIFUL summer morning and I didn't want to miss any of it. Kreg ran off to work at the crack of dawn and I got my chores done as quick as I could. I dusted, then vacuumed, in that order of course, then grabbed my scriptures and headed out to the back patio. The house we moved to a few years earlier was on the edge of town and backed up against fields that alternated between grain and potatoes. It was a grain year, and the flowing green waves seemed to go on forever.

I read a few chapters from the Book of Mormon then closed my scriptures, rested them on my lap, and just sat there taking in the beauty of the morning. The flowers I had planted last year were coming in nicely, and I loved the smell they carried through the breeze.

The ringing of the phone broke my serenity, but I just closed my eyes and took in one last breath of fresh summer air. I knew who it was even before our automated caller ID system announced it.

"Call from...Cody Parmer."

I picked up the phone and answered, "Hey Cody! How are you?"

"Good. Hey mom, guess what?"

"What buddy?"

"I'm going to put in an application at a car wash today." Cody was always looking for a new job and spent most of his day walking around searching for help wanted signs. I think he got more enjoyment out of dreaming about jobs than actually working them.

"Really, what are you going to do there?"

"They have a cash register, and I think I can run it. I don't think I want to wash the cars though. But maybe if they asked me to do it some-times, I could probably do it if I needed to. But just sometimes. I really just want to work the cash register."

"Well, that sounds exciting, you'll have to let me know how it goes." He was going to let me know how it went either way, so I might as well make the best of it, right?

"Okay, gotta go Mom. Love you!"

"Love you too Cody, be safe."

"I will, bye."

I hung up the phone and returned to my chair on the back porch. It had been a day much like this, 16 years ago, that Cody had rushed off to go fishing and our lives had changed forever. I never could have imagined that this would be our life, but we've tried hard to make the best of it.

Cody still lives in a group home where someone is available 24/7 to remind him to take his medication and to help him out when he needs it, but he enjoys his freedom. At least once a week I take him to a doctor's appointment to refill his medication pump or perform some other rou-tine procedure. Then Kreg and I pick him up once a week and take him to the temple where he is able to sit and focus on God's love. Besides that, he spends most of his time walking around town, meeting new people, and picking up job applications.

The people of Idaho Falls and our church community have been so good to Cody. Several times a month some businessman or farmer or church leader will pick him up and take him out for lunch. Cody will ask a million questions about how their business runs or what products they sell, and the men will politely answer all his questions. Cody's even been invited to tag along on private flights to Texas or California for the day, which he has really enjoyed. The generosity and kindness of the people who meet Cody never ceases to amaze me. Even 16 years after his acci-dent, people are caring, concerned, and helpful.

Cody still dreams big and he surprises us all the time with his de-termination to get what he wants. Cody is always planning some new business venture, but recently he has decided that he needs to use his experience to teach others how to overcome trials and make the best out of life. Reading and memorizing are very difficult for him, but he's prepared a short motivational speech that he gives at local organizations and businesses. He stands up at the podium and tells people about his accident, his miraculous recovery, and how he gains the strength to overcome his trials.

Cody teaches people to look on the bright side and work hard to achieve their goals, and he's a living example of those principles. When the crowd gives a hearty applause at the end, Cody's face lights up and he's on top of the world. Back at home, life isn't so simple. Cody's limitations affect every aspect of his life, but he is always trying to use the principles he teaches in order to overcome his challenges.

Despite our best efforts to work with Cody and help him progress, life can be really hard, and there are still times when I just want my old Cody back. I imagine him running into the house after a long day of school in his white t-shirt and Dallas Cowboys hat, rummaging through the pantry for something to eat and coming up with some adventure for the evening. I miss that Cody.

Sometimes I close my eyes and imagine what it would be like if he had never been in that accident, if he had married and started the construction business he dreamed of and had a house full of little kids. Who would he have married? What would he name his children? What kind of man would he become? What would he have accomplished?

When I was younger and I imagined this time in my life, I thought Kreg and I would be enjoying long European vacations and traveling to visit our children and grandchildren whenever we wanted. I never imagined I'd be driving my adult son to doctor's appointments and motivational speeches. My heart aches when I think about it, but then I stop, take a breath, open my eyes, and realize the Lord has blessed me with so much, just in different ways. Our lives will never be "normal," but like I always tell Cody, normal is just a setting on the dryer.

After many years we've discovered that striving for "normal" or trying to fit into some preconceived notion of what life should be like really limits our perspective. We spent so long just waiting for things to get better that sometimes we didn't fully appreciate the little blessings along the way—the visits from apostles, our relationship with Elder Zwick, the service and companionship from family and friends and ward members, and the pure miracle of Cody's survival. Too many times we overlooked what we had in the moment because we wanted something different, something we thought was better. We thought we'd find peace when life got back to the way it was, but I never imagined that peace would come once I stopped worrying about what was normal and what wasn't.

It took me a while to come to terms with the idea that Cody wouldn't completely recover, and maybe I still haven't accepted it fully, but my heart is more at ease than it ever was in the past. I finally realized that everyone has trials, and why should we be any different? We've met so many people who have endured much worse than we have, and who have handled it so much better. Some of those trials are very visible, like Cody's condition, and others, like the silent pain of depression, often go unnoticed.

We have friends and family who have lost wives and husbands, parents and children, all long before they should have. We've seen unemployment, poverty, divorce, accidents, birth defects, cancer, persecution, and mental health problems in people that we know and love. There seems to be no end to the variety and sharpness of trials that people endure, but no matter what the trial is, the solution is always the same: turn to God, trust in his love, and do your best. There's no other winning formula and there are no shortcuts, but he does send his tender mercies along the way.

Nearly every time I get frustrated or upset with our situation, the Lord will send me some beautiful experience that never would have happened otherwise. Sometimes I meet a wonderful person I never would have met. Other times he leads me to a scripture or talk or article that will calm my heart. In those moments I recognize God's hand, realize that he knows me, he loves me, and that he is watching over our family.

Through the trials and miracles God has sent us, I have learned more about myself that I ever wanted to know. I look back at the beginning of this journey of ours and shudder at the weakness of my faith. I knew that God was real, I trusted in him, and I tried to follow his commandments, but my faith was so shallow, it lacked the depth of experience and testing. It was only when I was pushed to my limit, when my faith and hope were almost gone, that I finally began to see what kind of a person God wanted me to become.

Kreg and I have learned so much and have grown so close over the years, and our faith in God is so much stronger than it ever was before.

Of course, Cody's accident has been a terrible thing in so many ways, but I'm proud of who we've become, amazed at the positive influence Cody has been for so many people, and I'm not sure we would be the people we are today without the trials we've endured. Kreg and I have a great marriage, stronger than it has ever been, and I've learned patience and faith to a degree I never thought possible. We've still got a long way to go, but I'm confident that God is at the helm of this ship, and he knows the best course to get us home.

Often times Kreg and I are asked, "Why do you think this happened to you?" It's a question that I can't answer, because I don't know the reason. Every time I try to think of some possible explanation, I can tell it falls so far short of God's plan for our family. Like the prophet Nephi, I am forced to reply, "I know that he loveth his children, nevertheless, I do not know the meaning of all things."

In reality, very few of us ever really learn why certain trials are given to us. We may speculate from time to time that they were meant to give us opportunities to serve or learn some lesson, but we'll never know the exact reasons, and maybe we're not supposed to. Life is a test, a place for us to learn about God and ourselves, a place to gain experience and see what we're made of. None of us should expect to pass through this life without experiencing trials that will test us to the very core. A life without trials would be like a test without questions; we wouldn't learn a thing.

What matters isn't the frequency or the variety of our trials, but rather how we handle them. We must develop a faith that is active, that grows and expands with every day and every moment. True faith isn't a passive thought or fleeting emotion, true faith is a choice, a decision we make. We decide to have faith much like we decide to say our prayers or read the scriptures. That is the only kind of faith that can sustain us when the trials seem insurmountable. Even then, God will likely take us to our very limits, so that we can learn just how strong we really are.

When we learn how to develop true faith, we face our trials head on. God never promised us a life that is free from pain or suffering or trials of faith. We're not even promised that God will solve all our problems when we ask him to. What we are promised, and what is more important than anything else, is that if we have faith, Christ will walk with us through our trials and support us every step of the way. True faith is the only thing that can provide true peace.

Our family has been through a lot. We've had some amazing and unforgettable memories, and some terrible and heart-wrenching experiences. The Lord has let us endure some very difficult trials, and he has also provided us with unbelievable miracles. Through it all, our faith has been tested and has grown. That growth didn't come because we experienced trials, and it didn't come because we witnessed miracles. Our faith grew because of how we decided to face the trials and how we chose to react to the miracles God provided. In the end, it isn't the trials or the miracles that define us, it's what we do through the trials and after the miracles that proves what we're made of.

Brenda, Kreg, and Cody Parmer

EPILOGUE

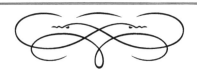

I WAS ON TOP OF THE WORLD IN 1999. I HAD A NEW TRUCK, A NEW DIRT bike, I was on the football team, I had a bunch of friends and loved going on dates with the girls from school. Then I went fishing one day and came home in a life flight helicopter, and everything changed. I went from being a good-looking athletic teenager to getting pushed around in a wheelchair and having only one hand that worked. Life was hard.

What made it even more difficult was the fact that I remembered my life before the accident perfectly. I could remember what it was like to run down the football field with the ball. I could remember what it was like to drive my truck through the mud. I could remember how it felt to like a girl and have her like me back. I remembered being popular, and athletic, and having the whole world in front of me, and then it was all gone.

I was glad to be alive, but I couldn't understand why I had a bad leg, a bad arm, and a massive brain injury, when my friend Jeff had a full recovery. Why would God let this happen to me? Why didn't he just make me better? I knew that God loved me, but why didn't he take away all my problems?

After my accident I started doing a lot of praying and thinking. After a lot of prayer, I think God helped me see the big picture. I realized that everyone on earth has a special purpose, but everyone would also have to be tested. We knew that this test of life would be tough before we even came here. God probably showed me a picture of what my life would be like, that things would be difficult for me, but that I could also help lots of people by telling my story and testifying of God's power. I would like to think that I stood up and told God, "I know it will be hard, but I'll do it."

I've had a lot of opportunities to tell people about what God has done for me and give people advice on how to get through tough times. Some people have been in accidents like mine, some were born with disabilities, and some have trials that no one will ever see. I wish I could just give everyone a big hug and tell them it will get better, but sometimes things will just continue to be hard for a long time. Sometimes it's not about getting rid of your trials, but rather learning to be happy even when life is hard.

When I get a chance to talk to people about how to deal with their problems, I tell them that it all comes down to two things: your family, and your faith in God.

Your family is the most important group of people in the whole world. When I was in the hospital, my mom and dad dropped everything to be there. They held my hand and took care of me when I couldn't even breathe on my own. Everyone in my family was so supportive and helpful and they kept praying for me, even when it looked like I wasn't going to make it.

If it wasn't for my family, I never would have recovered as well as I have. They believed in me and helped me pull through, they worked with me and pushed me to be stronger and to try harder. It would have been much easier to sit in bed and just give up, but my family loved me enough to push me, and I owe them everything for that.

I have to give the most credit to mothers. Everyone in your family is important, but mothers are extra special. My mom lived in the hospital with me, even when I was in a coma and couldn't see or hear or respond at all. She cried over me and prayed for me and refused to let me die. I know there were so many people praying for me, but I think Heavenly Father listens extra hard to a mother's prayers. For all her efforts, spiritually and physically, my mom is the reason I am still here.

Before the accident I don't think I really ever told my mom or my dad how much I loved them and how much they meant to me. Now I try to tell my family all the time that I love them and appreciate them. And it isn't just my parents. My sisters, my grandparents, all my aunts and uncles and cousins, they are all so important to me, and your family should be just as important to you.

If you're going through a tough time, turn to your family. They can care for you and love you like no one else can. Open up to them and tell them what you're feeling and why things are difficult for you. They may not be able to fix it, but it feels so good knowing that you're not alone and that someone else is praying for you and cares about what you're going through.

The second and most important thing I tell people is that they need to get closer to God. I always had a testimony of the gospel and I attended church and served in callings, but ever since my accident I look at God in a completely different way. He knows me on a first-name basis. I wake up every morning and say my prayers and just thank him for another day that I can be alive. The more I pray, the more thankful I am, the happier I am, and things just seem to go better.

If things are looking bad and you're not happy, work on your relationship with God and you'll find peace. Read your scriptures, go to church, pray as much as you can. It all sounds so simple, but when you do it, you realize that it actually works. You shouldn't need to have a brain hemorrhage to start turning to God. The whole plan is so simple and he asks so little of us, but he offers so many blessings in return.

Life really isn't that complicated. If you get those two things down, family and faith, then everything else will go so much better. It doesn't mean that every problem you have will be taken away, I'm a living example of that, but you will feel better and be happier.

I always tell people that I'm a walking, talking miracle. People may not recognize that when they first see me, but after they hear my story and understand what I've been through, they realize how amazing God is. He does perform miracles today. Sometimes they come through prayer, sometimes they come through family, sometimes they come through amazing disciples like Elder Zwick and Elder Scott, but they will come.

Even after telling people what I've been through and what I've seen, some people still have a hard time believing in God, but not me, I know he is real. I've seen too many miracles and had too many answered prayers to say otherwise. I feel God's love every day when I pray, when I read the scriptures, when I make good choices, and when I'm with my family. You may feel like God isn't real, or that he doesn't love you because you've had some hard times, but if you just give faith a try, I promise you'll be happier.

God knows each of us and he can work miracles in your life. Having a miracle doesn't mean that he'll take away every one of your problems, but it does mean that he will show you in a very personal way that he is real and that he loves you. After that, it's up to you to do your part. Just hang in there, take it a day at a time, and I promise you, with God you can make it through anything.

– *Cody Parmer*

Made in the USA
San Bernardino, CA
23 November 2016